LIVING THEURGY

Βούλευσαι ἐπιμελέστερον,

γνωθι σαυτόν,

ἀνάκρινον τὸ δαιμόνιον,

δίχα θεου μὴ ἐπιχειρήσης.

Take careful council,

Know thyself,

Consult the daimon,

Undertake nothing without God.

- Delphic Maxim

Joyful Hermes, hoary Djehuti,

God-like Michael, bless this work

with your wisdom and fill us with

a glory that none may shirk.

Published by Avalonia
BM Avalonia
London
WC1N 3XX
England, UK
www.avaloniabooks.co.uk

Living Theurgy: A Course in Iamblichus' Philosophy, Theology, and Theurgy

First Edition, May 2014
ISBN 978-1-905297-71-9

Design by *Satori*, for Avalonia.

British Library Cataloguing in Publication Data. A catalogue record for this book is available from the British Library.

LIVING THEURGY

A COURSE IN IAMBLICHUS' PHILOSOPHY, THEOLOGY, AND THEURGY

Jeffrey S. Kupperman

Published by Avalonia

www.avaloniabooks.co.uk

Acknowledgments

To my family: Gretel, Ilyana, and Evelyn. To the Gnostikoi who encouraged me to not stop writing: Bishop +Shaun McCann, Bishop +William Behun, Bishop +Martin Jacobs, Bishop +Laine Petersen, Monsignor Scott Rassbach, Rev. Tony Silvia, Rev. Donald Donato, Rev. John DiGilio, Rev. Michael Strojan, and especially Monsignor Jordan Straford, who graciously allowed me to steal the name of one of his books. To my other friends who have supported this work with their interest and encouragement: Shilo Orellana, Glenda Shephard, Damon Lycourinos, Christopher Plaisance, Dean Wilson, Paul Hardacre, Sibylle Leon, Alex Rivera, Perigrin Wildoak, Candice Bundy, Stephanie Austin, Al Billings, John Griogair Bell . . . and an angelic choir of others who simply won't all fit here.

Table of Contents

Introduction....11

A Brief Survey of Five Important Neoplatonists....18

A Living Philosophy....31

Virtue....40

On Evil....54

Political Philosophy....62

Beauty....69

Love....78

First Principles – The One....91

The Spiritual and Natural Realms....99

The Demiurge....108

The Greater Kinds, the Gods, and Theology....121

The Greater Kinds, Continued....136

The Human Soul....145

Cultus....155

On Theurgy....173

Medicine, Talismancy, and the Pneumatic Vehicle....184

Animated Statues and Divine Possession....205

The Invocation of the Personal Daimon....228

Appendix A: An Apophatic Theoria....255

Appendix B: Guide to Pronouncing Hieratic Names....258

Bibliography....267

Abbreviations

General Abbreviations

AJ: *Apocryphon of John*

CO: *Chaldean Oracles*

ETH: *The Emerald Tablet of Hermes*

Jn: *Gospel of John*

PGM: *Papyri Graecae Magicae* (Greek Magical Papyri)

Aristotle:

Nich: *Nichomachean Ethics*

Dionysius the Areopagite

CH: *Celestial Hierarchy*

DN: *Divine Names*

EH: *Ecclesiastical Hierarchy*

MT: *Mystical Theology*

Ficino, Marsilio

DAm: *De Amore*

DV: *De vita libri tres*

Iamblichus

DA: *De Anima*

DM: *De Mysteriis*

In Alc: *In Alcibiadem*

In Phaednm: *In Phaedonem*

In Phileb: *In Philebum*

In Tim: *In Timaeum*

In Soph: *In Sophistam*

L2: Letter Two – To Anatolius, *On Justice*

L3: Letter Three – To Arete, *On Self-Control*

L4: Letter Four – To Asphalius, *On Wisdom*

L5: Letter Five – To Dexippus, *On Dialectic*

L8: Letter Six – To Dyscolius, *On Ruling (?)*

L8: Letter Eight – To Macedonius, *On Fate*

L10: Letter Ten – To Olympius, *On Courage*

L12: Letter Twelve – To Sopater, *On Fate*

L16: Letter Sixteen – To Sopater, *On Virtue*

L19: Letter Nineteen – To an Unknown Recipient, *On Marriage*

Theo Arith: *On Ethical and Theological Arithmetic*

Plotinus

Enn: *The Enneads*

Plato

Crat: *Cratylus*

GHip: *Greater Hippias*

Gorg: *Gorgias*

Parm: *Parmenides*

Phaedr: *Phaedrus*

Phil: *Philebus*

Rep: *Republic*

Soph: *Sophist*

Symp: *Symposium*

Theat: *Theaetetus*

Tim: *Timaeus*

Porphyry

DAb: *De Abstinentia*

Proclus

ET: *Elements of Theology*

Sallustius

CGU: *Concerning the Gods and the Universe*

Chapter One

Introduction

This book is about a way of life. This way is founded on the principles of something called "Neoplatonism." The word describes a number of schools of Platonic thought, beginning with the Egyptian Platonist Plotinus. The word "Neoplatonism" is never used by the Platonists who develop the philosophies and theologies now described as such. Until the 18th century these philosophers are simply known as Platonists, which is how they think of themselves. The Neoplatonists, or late Platonists, do not see their interpretations of Plato and Aristotle as new. To them, Neoplatonism is simply Platonism, six centuries after Plato.

That Platonism changes during this time is not surprising and, given the mythology surrounding Socrates and Plato, neither are the ways in which it has done so. There are, of course, innovations. There is likely as much new thought in Neoplatonism as there are traditional Platonic ideas. This does not change the fact that through the Renaissance, a person reading Plotinus assumes he is simply a non-political, and possibly somewhat more accessible, version of Plato.

The Neoplatonists make good use of the Platonic corpus. They also draw on elements outside of Platonism. The first of these is the works of Aristotle. Typically, Aristotle is seen as an enemy of Platonism, stressing empiricism over pure reason. The Neoplatonists, beginning with Plotinus and exemplified by Iamblichus, see Aristotle differently. Yes, they criticize him when they believe he is wrong, but they also incorporate some of his ideas and terminology into their philosophies.[1] Beyond Aristotle, the so-called "later" Neoplatonists, from Iamblichus onwards, engage with Pythagoreanism, the *Chaldean Oracles*, and theurgy, the ritual practice of "god working." All the Neoplatonists also contend with Christianity to some degree, and one can occasionally discern a dialogue between the Neoplatonists and various Christian sects within the Neoplatonic corpus.[2]

---

[1] Dillon and Gerson, *Neoplatonic*, xvii-xix.

[2] For instance, Plotinus, in the *Enneads* II.9, "Against the Gnostics," is writing specifically about the Sethian Gnosticism of his time.

All this gives rise to heavily synthetic, mystical, religious, and esoteric forms of Platonism. The importance of theurgy in the lives of the late Platonists cannot be undervalued. Philosophy is purifying, religion illuminating, but theurgy is uplifting. Together these observances enable the practitioner to rise above their mortal life to participate in immortal life. For Iamblichus and Proclus and Ficino, it is inappropriate to consider them simply philosophers or simply theurgists. These two elements are so interwoven as to lose distinction. One element can no more be removed from the other while keeping either intact than a person can survive without their heart or a heart can survive without its person. This is living theurgy.

The theurgic practices of Neoplatonism are a kind of ritual mysticism not quite what we normally think about when we think about mysticism. It is not a series of "peak experiences" upon which we focus for the totality of our spirituality. It is not, as Professor E. R. Dodds once said of the famous theurgic text *De Mysteriis*, "a manifesto of irrationalism."[3] Instead, theurgy is a way of life fully complementary to philosophy and religion.

On Words and Ideas

There are a number of ideas basic to Platonic thought. Some of them are discussed in depth in the pages of this book. Some are not. Two such basic concepts are "discursive reasoning" and the "dialectic." Discursive reasoning, *dianoia*, is the primary way Platonists engage in non-intuitive thought. And not just Platonists, this is how humans think. Discursive reasoning engages in the comparison of things to better understand them and achieve knowledge. Such knowledge is as objective as possible, based on the faculties of reason and intellect, but is still, ultimately, subjective. This is because in discursive reasoning there is always a difference between the object of thought and the thinker. I do not ultimately know the subject of my enquiry; I only know what I think about it. Such a distinction is obliterated in intuitive knowledge, *noera gnosis*, which transcends the object/subject relationship.

The second basic concept, which informs much of the Philosophia section, is the dialectic, *dialektiki*. Dialectical discourse is carried out between two or more people. In the Platonic dialogues, Socrates almost always acts as the main interlocutor, challenging those with whom he speaks to justify, through reason, their beliefs. According to Iamblichus, the dialectical method is of divine origins, revealed by Hermes, whose symbol is that of two serpents looking at one another, and stemming from Kalliope,[4] the oldest of the muses and goddess of eloquence and poetry.

---

[3] Clarke et al., "Introduction," in *De mysteriis*, xxvi.

[4] L5.

Dialectic and discursive reasoning are the backbones of Platonic philosophical practice. They are wielded to disassemble irrational thought. This is not to find the truth, as that is fully accessible only through intuitive knowledge. Instead, it is to demonstrate what we do not know, what we think we know, and why. Beyond these two terms, Platonism makes use of a rich technical language. This language is used throughout *Living Theurgy*, both in Greek and in translation. A glossary of technical terms is provided at the end of the book. Each entry begins with the transliterated Greek term, accompanied by the Greek spelling, translation and a brief definition. Technical words in the body of the book, such as with discursive reasoning above, give only the Greek term in transliteration.

My Perspective – A Living Platonism

Living Theurgy is an amalgam of sorts. You will find it filled with scholarship. I am a professional scholar as well as a writer. However, unlike many scholarly treatises, I do not approach the subject as one filled with some kind of "anthropological atheism"[5] or "methodological agnosticism."[6] Nor, however, is it coming from a "method of compassion."[7] All of these represent the viewpoints of scholars standing outside of what they study, attempting to grasp foreign ideas without being grasped in return. The idea of this being at all possible is somewhat difficult. The Western academic system is a product of Platonism, and everyone within it engages with Plato in some manner, even if it is through rejection. Without Platonism there is no academy.

Although scholarly, *Living Theurgy* is written from the perspective that the Neoplatonists essentially know what they are talking about. Yes, there are variations, developments, and cultural and religious differences over late Platonism's 1000+ year lifespan. This apparent set of differences gives way to the fact that behind it all is a core ideology accepted by polytheistic and monotheistic Neoplatonists alike. I approach the subject from this basic understanding, I also hold that the contemplative and theurgical practices espoused by the Neoplatonists, from Plotinus through Ficino, effectively bring about changes in the practitioner, regardless as to the divine or psychological, or both, causes of those changes. As such, this book not only represents Neoplatonism as an historical tradition or traditions, but as a modern, living entity as seen through the experiences of a practitioner.

At first, this might appear unusual. Again, this is a scholarly text. A great deal of research has gone into this book to make sure that the facts reported are, in fact, facts. That means a poring over of primary texts, scholarly articles and books and many, many citations. Where in all this is there a place for the practitioner's

[5] Ewing, "Dreams," 571.
[6] Pike, "Emic," 29.
[7] Salomonsen, "Methods," 49-51.

voice? There is a great deal of space for such a voice. *Living Theurgy* is not just a book about Neoplatonism; it is a book *of* Neoplatonism. Neoplatonists are scholars, historically amongst the intellectual elite of their times. That they practice what they teach only makes sense. Philosophy and religion are, after all, living things. If they do not affect your life, if they are not something that can be lived by, then they are largely useless.

This is not, however, a "Neoplatonism 101" book. While I write about concepts basic to Platonism, those concepts are not necessarily simple to comprehend or engage with. That is to say, they are not particularly basic. Neither is this an introduction to ritual practice. Several rituals are explained, outlined, and visualizations and instructions to carry them out are provided. They are not, however broken into bite-sized morsels, nor are theories behind ritual itself explained. Both of these are simply beyond the scope of the book, and so research on your part may be necessary.

To be sure, this book may not be a *magnum opus* the likes of Iamblichus' *De Mysteriis* or Proclus' *Platonic Theology*. Nevertheless, it is a piece of living Neoplatonism and an addition, however humble, to the Corpus Neoplatonica. If it inspires you towards a life of simplicity, aesthetics, and movement towards union with the One, it has done all that I might ask of it. If it does more, well, that's probably within the realm of the Good, too.

Reconciling Pagan and Abrahamic Neoplatonism

Unlike Plato, born some 400 years before the beginning of the Common Era, Neoplatonists lived, and continue to do so, with the Abrahamic religions. This means one thing for Plotinus, who is active while Christianity is illegal within the Roman Empire, something else entirely for Proclus, active when Christianity is the official religion of the empire and paganism is outlawed, and something completely different for Pseudo-Dionysius and Marsilio Ficino, who are Christians.

As such, late Platonists have different reactions to Christianity, especially, in a way we don't always see with other religions. Plotinus and Porphyry, for instance, are in dialogue with the Sethian sect of Gnostic Christianity. Plotinus clearly disapproves of some of their theology, putting a fine point on it rather than simply being in disagreement with its totality. Equally clear is that he is influenced by it as well. Alternatively, Iamblichus, living under the pagan emperor Julian, seems largely neutral on the subject, having even learned Aristotle from a future Bishop. Proclus is quite against Christianity and his work stresses the polytheistic nature of Platonism in a way found unnecessary just a hundred years earlier.

This is just a sampling. Many pagan Neoplatonists teach whoever comes to them for instruction, regardless of religious background. That there were, and are, Christian, Jewish, and Muslim Neoplatonists as well as pagan Neoplatonists of all varieties is undeniable. That these Neoplatonists contribute important elements to the body of philosophy, theology, and theurgy is equally undeniable. All of which leaves us in an interesting position.

The goal of this book is to engage you, the reader, in a living Neoplatonism, regardless of your religious identity. This includes philosophical and theological elements. How can this be done in a way that makes both poly- and monotheists comfortable? Is it even possible?

The answer to that is "yes, under the right conditions." Neoplatonism is a hermeneutic and episteme, a lens through which we see and interpret the world. Anyone willing to see and experience life through that lens will find a place for themselves in this book.

Beyond this, however, there is a dependency upon what form of pagan Neoplatonism we're talking about; some being more easily reconcilable with monotheistic thought, and vice versa, than others. For instance, Plotinus does not focus a great deal on polytheistic theology, and much of his philosophy and contemplative methods can be easily employed, with little change, by monotheists. However, Plotinus is no theurgist, and is perhaps barely a theologian. Alternatively, the paganism of Proclus is distinctly polytheistic and often anti-Christian, possibly in response to the pressures of a dominant Christianity and an increasingly anti-pagan culture.[8]

Iamblichus, the most influential of the later Neoplatonists, rests as the mean, and *Living Theurgy* is largely a book of Iamblichean Neoplatonism. Certainly, Iamblichus' Neoplatonism is pagan. But whether or not it must be polytheistic is another question. Although Iamblichus is an expert on the gods of his native Syria, and demonstrates a similar knowledge of Greek, Egyptian, and Orphic deities, his approach to them is more panentheistic than polytheistic. Iamblichus views the gods as *monoeides*, "in the form of singularity," a term used by Plato to refer to the Good, or God.[9] Whereas Proclus' gods are individuals before being a whole, Iamblichus' have a single essence first.[10] In this, the gods seem to lose their polytheistic nature to become something more unitary and emanatory. Like the Gnostic Aeons, the Iamblichean gods are manifestations of their singular, divine source, functioning as horizontal extensions of the same power, and ultimately leading back to that unity.

The existence of a singular, divine source is common to all pagan Neoplatonism, and is explicit in monotheistic Neoplatonism. In Platonic and Neoplatonic writings, this source is variously called God, the One and the Good. The nature of the One varies between Neoplatonists. The One can be absolute negative reality, somewhat akin to the later Kabbalistic idea of Ain, nothing, as the ultimate "form" of God. This negative reality is also the source of Pseudo-

---

[8] Butler, "Offering," 10-11.
[9] Clark, "Gods," 56-7.
[10] Cf. DM, I.17, 65.

Dionysius' *apophatic* or "negative" theology. The One can be the positive source of all things that it, of itself, does not actually create but whose existence is necessary for there to be anything else. Or it can be the active source of all being from which all things emanate. Or, as in the case of Iamblichus, all three at once. The singular nature of the One as *one* is undeniable, and perhaps the most common point of connection between mono- and polytheistic Neoplatonisms.

Besides the question of polytheism vs. monotheism, there is the issue of Iamblichus' "greater kinds," the chain of spiritual beings connecting the One to humanity. The classical pagans understand that the world is filled with spiritual beings. Until recently, this was a common notion within the Abrahamic religions as well, and still exists in their more mystical forms. This includes the various forms and choirs of angels and demons, as well as nature spirits, elementals, and a host of other beings.

In this, I argue that the belief in such entities is neither "pagan" nor "Abrahamic" in nature. Instead, though such views are codified by religious thought, they are not confined by them. Nothing within the Abrahamic religions requires its adherents to deny the existence of such beings, let alone condemn them as evil. Instead, it is a product of Modernity, and its child Materialism, to see the world as un-ensouled. To view the world Platonically is to see it filled with life, both seen and invisible.

Organization – Hierarchy is Important

Platonists take their hierarchies seriously. This means we see the world as ordered, from the One to the many, from the universal to the particular, and this order is important and real. Other hierarchies are important as well. The theoretical, coming from the realm of the intellect, is superior to the practical, which functions in the realm of generation. Also, theurgy is the summation of Platonic practice, reigning over and unifying theology and philosophy. As philosophy is an engagement in discursive reasoning it is inferior to theology, which Iamblichus understands as knowledge of the gods, or God, originating with the gods, or God. This is distinct from modern theology which may be viewed as a form of philosophy.

Given the above, *Living Theurgy* is divided into three sections: Philosophia, Theologia, and Theourgia. The philosophy section introduces several basic areas of Platonic and Neoplatonic philosophical thought. This is by no means complete, nor is it meant to be so. Such an endeavour is impossible in a book this size. Instead, section one serves as an entry way to the theory of Platonic philosophy and its theoretical and practical engagement. Philosophy is not a thing to be discussed and then put away. The lover of wisdom, like the lover of a person, engages with the object of their love in every way possible.

Section two focuses on the natures and relationships of the One, the Demiurges and the various "greater kinds," from the gods to purified souls and then human souls. Again, this is both theoretical and practical. While it is important to understand the relationships between the various ontological levels of being, to do so without engaging in them is pointless. Neoplatonism, especially its later varieties, is a religious hermeneutic as well as a philosophical one. To this end, the Theologia section ends with a discussion of *cultus*, or religious practice.

Theourgia is the final topic. Although theurgy dominates this triad, it is pointless without a grounding in philosophy and theology. Theurgy finishes what philosophy begins: to make the practitioner as similar to God as possible. This section looks at the theories behind what makes theurgy possible and examines, and engages in, several kinds of theurgic practice.

And that's it. *Living Theurgy* culminates with the invocation of the personal daimon, a spiritual being, much like a holy guardian angel, designated to watch over your soul from the moment it is sewn into the orbit of its divine leader. Do not expect to read through the book once and be done with it as a master theurgist. Though hardly a beginner's book, *Living Theurgy* is still something of a Neoplatonic primer, and the theurgist who has only just encountered their daimon is still a neophyte. Neoplatonism is a living and lived thing, and a single achievement, even this one, is only a single step along its ever-winding road. No matter how far along this road you travel, you will always be accompanied by philosophy, theology, and theurgy.

Chapter Two

A Brief Survey of Five Important Neoplatonists

What follows is a series of brief biographies of the five Neoplatonists most influential on the writing of this book and, arguably, on Neoplatonism in general. The biographies are to help you understand the overall context of both Neoplatonism and this book.[11]

Plotinus, the Founder

Neoplatonism begins in first half of the third century CE with the Hellenized Egyptian philosopher Plotinus. The philosophy of Plotinus is, as is ancient Hellenic philosophy in general, a practical one. It is not, as we tend to think of philosophy, just about technicalities of logic and academic jargon, but about how to live our lives in an ethical and conscientious manner. It is a lived and living philosophy.

As a Platonic philosopher, Plotinus does not consider his work, nor his school, "Neo," new. He, like the Neoplatonists who follow, understands himself to be in a line of transmission from Plato and his original students. As mentioned in the introduction, the "Neo" appellation is a much later addition, put there by 18th century scholars as they divided Platonic thought into three periods: Platonic, including the Old and New Academies, Middle Platonic, and Neoplatonic. That Plotinus understands Plato's teachings differently from those before him is undoubtedly so. But the development of innovative lines of thought within Platonism is nothing new. Despite Plotinus' innovations, the core doctrines of his thought are in line with the core doctrines of Platonism in general.

Plotinus lives during an interesting time. Though Christianity is not legalized in the Roman Empire until 313, some 43 years after Plotinus' death, it has considerable influence on Roman and Greek culture during his lifetime. Both

---

[11] For a broader view of the personalities of late Antique Neoplatonism, see O'Meara, *Platonopolis*, chapter two.

then, and for the next few hundred years, Christians and pagan Neoplatonists struggle for the minds and souls of the people of the Roman Empire. As Brian Hines writes, the doctrines of one of these factions can be summarized as follows:

> *There is only one God, who is all love; every human being has an immortal soul, whose highest destiny is to be united with God; if we live virtuous lives, we will join our heavenly Father after death, but if we do not, justice will be done; we must humbly yield to the divine will, accepting with equanimity whatever life brings us; to be attracted to the sensual pleasures of this world is to be distanced from God, the Good we seek but never find in material pursuits.*[12]

This is Plotinus' philosophy in a nutshell. That it resembles Christian thought in many respects is no accident. Scholars now accept significant Platonic influences on early Christianity,[13] even as it is likely later Neoplatonists borrow concepts from Christianity. Further, both Plotinus and his student Porphyry are in dialogue, albeit a tense one, with the Sethian Gnostics, to whom the ninth chapter of the second of Plotinus' *Enneads*, *"Against the Gnostics"*, is likely directed.[14] As exhibited by Porphyry's *Against the Christians*, Emperor Flavius Claudius Julianus Augustus's 4th century *Against the Galileans*, and Proclus' 5th century *Against the Christians*, the tension between Neoplatonism and Christianity exists for centuries. Be that as it may, Neoplatonic thought, though largely stripped of its paganism, is eventually embraced by some forms of Christianity. Eventually Platonic, and especially Neoplatonic, thought greatly influences all of the Abrahamic religions as well as pagan religiosity.

Plotinus is born in Egypt around 205 CE, over 550 years after Plato's death in 347 BCE. What we know of Plotinus' life comes from the writings of his student Porphyry of Tyre. Though it is sometimes difficult to distinguish between what Porphyry writes to describe Plotinus, and what he writes to promote himself on Plotinus' back, a general picture of Plotinus and his life is discernible.

Interestingly, the first thing we learn of Plotinus is his loathing for the physical world. The first sentence of *On the Life of Plotinus and the Arrangement of His Work* reads *"Plotinus, the philosopher our contemporary, seemed ashamed of being in the body."*[15] His apparent hatred for the physical form extends as far as not allowing anyone to paint his portrait, as he considers such a thing merely an image of an image. He even refuses to take medicine.[16] For Plotinus, the physical life is to be shunned for the philosophical, an attitude Plotinus, and Porphyry after him, acquire from Middle Platonist teachings and is found, to an extent, in the Platonic dialogues as

---

[12] Hines, *Return to the One*, xvi.
[13] C.f. Ward. *God*, 113.
[14] See Mazur, "Plotinus' Philosophical Opposition to Gnosticism," 95 and Majercik, "The Existence-Life-Intellect Triad," 475.
[15] Porphyry, *Life of Plotinus*, cii.
[16] Ibid.

well. This likely also stems from Plotinus' teacher Ammonius Saccas, as well as his ongoing conversation with Sethian Gnosticism.

Beyond this, however, Porphyry portrays Plotinus as a kind and gentle individual, one in whom the lives of children are entrusted.[17] He is a man who prefers discussion over dictation and encourages the independent thought of his students.[18] Students should not simply agree with Plotinus because he is Plotinus, they should agree with Plotinus only because they understand what he is saying and have come to agree with the reasoning behind his words. In his life, Plotinus writes, apparently with poor penmanship, a total of fifty-four brief philosophical treatises. Porphyry assembles them into six sections of nine treatises each, now known as the *Enneads*.

In Porphyry's biography of Plotinus, we learn Plotinus is possibly a practitioner of, or at least recognized the efficacy of, magic. The story says Olympius, a rival philosopher, attempts to harm Plotinus through recourse to sorcery. Plotinus' soul, however, proved too strong for Olympius' "star-ray" attack. Not only does Plotinus survive the attack, but Porphyry's story suggests Plotinus uses magic to turn the harmful sorcery back against Olympius, causing the sorcerer no small amount of distress.[19]

However, Plotinus is no theurgist. He appears hostile to theurgic ritual, a hostility continued through Porphyry's attack on the subject in his *Letter to Anebo*. As the above quotation from Hines shows, Plotinus believes a person could become one with God, *henosis*, but unlike the later Neoplatonists, he does not believe this is accomplished through ritual practice, something he considers material in nature, and therefore unable to connect the human soul to the immaterial divine.

If not theurgy, then what practice does Plotinus teach his fellow Platonists in order to achieve divine union? The answer is philosophy, the practice of the love of wisdom. In particular, however, Plotinian philosophy is contemplative in nature. In the *Enneads*, Plotinus makes several references to mystical contemplation, *theoria*, and seeing and experiencing the divine realm through the part of the soul he believes always remains with God.

For instance, in the sixth *Ennead*, *"On the Good, or the One"*, Plotinus writes:

> *Thus we have all the vision that may be of Him and of ourselves; but it is of a self-wrought to splendor, brimmed with the intellectual light, become that very light, pure, buoyant, unburdened, raised to Godhood or, better, knowing its Godhood, all aflame then – but crushed out once more if it should take up the discarded burden.*[20]

---

[17] Ibid., cix-cx.

[18] Ibid., civ.

[19] C.f. Merlan, "Plotinus and Magic," 341-3. Merlan's conclusion that this episode suggests Plotinus is schizophrenic can be safely ignored.

[20] *Ennead* VI 9.9.

This vision, and we must presume Plotinus experiences it himself, is not simply that of Godhead, but of the identification of the soul with the Godhead immanent to the soul. This is a vision and experience of *henosis* with God, a God that is simultaneously external to and within us.

At some point both Plotinus and Porphyry may have recommended the practice of theurgy to their students. From Porphyry's *Letter to Anebo*, a polemic against theurgy as a way to *henosis*, it is clear Porphyry is both familiar with the practice of theurgy and has come to repudiate its practice. However, if theurgic practices are recommended at some point in their philosophical careers, these practices are seen by Plotinus and Porphyry as purifying preliminaries to contemplation.

The focus on contemplation as the means to divine union changes by the third generation of Neoplatonists, when it becomes secondary to ritual practice. Whereas Plotinus criticizes theurgic ritual as too material to connect the soul to an immaterial God, the leader of the theurgic Neoplatonic movement, Iamblichus of Chalcis, criticizes contemplation as the means to divine union:

> *. . . for it is not pure thought that unites theurgists to the gods. Indeed, what, then would hinder those who are theoretical philosophers from enjoying a theurgic union with the gods?*[21]

For Iamblichus, *theoria* is incapable of achieving *henosis* because the level of mind is beneath that of God.

The Divine Iamblichus [22]

Born around 245 CE in Chalcis-ad-Belum, modern Qinnersin in northern Syria,[23] Iamblichus is possibly a descendant of Syrian royalty. What we know of Iamblichus' life is sketchy. The primary source is written in the style of a hagiography by a student of a student of a student of Iamblichus, a sophist named Eunapius. Still, there is enough in Eunapius and other sources to piece together a biography.

Eunapius says Iamblichus is introduced to Platonism by way of Anatolius, who ranks "second in command"[24] to Porphyry, which can mean he is either second in command in Porphyry's academy or second in general philosophical renown to Porphyry. Anatolius becomes Bishop of Laodicea sometime after 270 CE. Though possibly not significant to Iamblichus, that Anatolius is a Christian priest is important to us, and it is worth noting that of the four major pagan Neoplatonists covered here, Iamblichus is the only one not to write an invective against Christianity. During this time Iamblichus, possibly with wife and child,

---

[21] DM 96.12-97.1.

[22] A thorough account of Iamblichus' life is found in Dillon's *Platonic Commentaries.*

[23] Dillon, *Commentaries*, 3-4.

[24] Dillon and Polleichtner, *Letters*, xiii.

leaves Chalcis for Caesarea, where Iamblichus studies Aristotelian philosophy under Anatolius before studying with Porphyry himself.

At this time Porphyry is in Sicily, sent there by Plotinus, to return to Rome sometime in the 280s. Whether Iamblichus studies with Porphyry in Rome or in Sicily is unknown, but he does study at Porphyry's academy, at least for a short time. Iamblichus even dedicates at least one of his books to Porphyry.

Porphyry is born around 234 CE, only nine years Iamblichus' senior, which may explain their somewhat rocky relationship. At this point Iamblichus is in his mid-thirties, hardly a young disciple fawning over his wizened teacher. This tension is attested in Iamblichus' writings. For example, in the surviving fragments of his commentary on Plato's *Timaeus,* Porphyry is mentioned 32 times, 25 of which are critical of Porphyry's position and seven in agreement.[25]

Sometime in the 290s, about a decade before Porphyry's death, Iamblichus leaves Porphyry's academy and returns to Syria, Apamea rather than Chalcis, to open his own school. By this time his son is thought to have married one of Plotinus' younger students or admirers, a woman named Amphicleia.[26] Descriptions of Iamblichus' academy are somewhat reminiscent of Plotinus', replete with devout disciples and long philosophical discussions. He converses frequently with his students and is not demanding in his lifestyle. Eunapius describes the wisdom of Iamblichus' words as being as filling as nectar so that his disciples are always desirous of listening to him.

We know, at least generally, Iamblichus' curriculum, which includes both Plato and Aristotle. Though not unheard of, many Platonists of that time feel Aristotle's disagreements are incompatible with Plato. Iamblichus, however, views them as complimentary. In this view, Aristotle writes about the physical world, Plato focuses on the divine.

Iamblichus is a prolific writer. However, with the exception of some of his letters, his refutation of Porphyry's anti-theurgic *Letter to Anebo*, and four books on Pythagoreanism, only fragments of literary work remains. His works include a ten volume treatise on Pythagoras and Pythagoreanism, a tract on the nature of the soul, fragments of which survive as *De Anima*, or *Peri Psyche,* commentaries on six of Aristotle's books and twelve of Plato's, as well as books on Hellenic, Syrian and Chaldean theology. Fragments of his Platonic commentaries survive in the commentaries of Proclus, the Platonic Successor, amongst others.

As with Plotinus, Iamblichus believes philosophy is a way of life. But for Iamblichus philosophy is not the crown of life. That honour is not given to philosophical contemplation or religion either, but to theurgy. When exactly Iamblichus is introduced to theurgic practices, and the *Chaldean Oracles* supporting

---

[25] Dillon, *Commentaries*, 10.

[26] Dillon, *Commentaries*, 6-7.

them, is unknown. He possibly learns it from Porphyry before the latter's rejection of it, or he may be already involved with the hieratic arts before his involvement with Porphyry. What we know is that for Iamblichus, the gods, and the One above them, are not only beyond the physical realm, they transcend the realm of the mind.[27] As the divine Mind, *Nous*, is beneath God itself, how can a mere human mind, even one linked to the divine Mind, hope to connect itself to the gods above? Contemplation can only take the philosopher so far, the gap is filled by theurgy.

Through theurgic rituals practitioners purify themselves, attain to divine illumination, and perfect their souls. In doing so, theurgists engage in the work of the Demiurge, the divine intellect and Mind, as it governs the divine and physical worlds. Nothing less than theurgy is capable of this.

Proclus

Proclus Lycaeus, born in February of 412 CE, in Constantinople, is one of the last, great pagan Neoplatonists. Like Iamblichus, Proclus comes from a well-connected family, although not a royal one. Though successful as a lawyer, Proclus eventually comes to study Aristotle under the tutelage of Olympiodorus the Elder, and mathematics under a man named Heron. Proclus surpasses the level of philosophic education available to him by 431 CE and leaves for Athens, the centre of Platonic study. There he eventually becomes the head of the Academy until his death, when he is succeeded by his student Marinus of Neapolis. Marinus acts as Proclus' biographer, but unfortunately the biography sometimes reads more grandiosely and hagiographically than Iamblichus'.

In his own right, Proclus is very important in the history of Neoplatonism, and produces one of the most complete and systematic bodies of literature on the subject. However, as we are focusing on Iamblichean Neoplatonism, for our purposes Proclus' importance lays elsewhere. First, it is in his preservation of the works of Iamblichus, whom Proclus, along with many other later Neoplatonists, calls "divine." Second, it is through his demonstration that Iamblichus' addition of theurgy to the Neoplatonic corpus, and the metaphysics necessary to understand it within the Platonic tradition, continue after Iamblichus' death and are not simply an irrational and temporary flaw in the system. Finally, Procline ideas, along with those of Iamblichus and Plotinus, survive in the writings of Pseudo-Dionysius and Marsilio Ficino, both of whom are discussed below.

Though not always in agreement with Iamblichus, much of Proclus' work relies heavily on his predecessor's, and in many ways is a continuation of it. However, the differences between Proclus and Iamblichus, especially in the ways they view the natures of the gods, should not be ignored. Understanding these

[27] The ontological realms are discussed in chapter ten.

differences is important. They are due partly to the nearly two centuries that separate them, and the illegalization of paganism within the Roman Empire. When Iamblichus is active, paganism is still active, even if in decline. For Proclus, Christianity reigns and openly practicing pagan religions may lead to death. This leads to Proclus focusing a great deal more on the individual nature of the gods within a strongly polytheistic system of Neoplatonism.

Dionysius the Areopagite

Relatively little is known about the figure known as Pseudo-Dionysius, who writes at the end of the 5th or the beginning of the 6th century CE. The works of the man writing under the pseudonym of Dionysius must be separated from the historical Dionysius, a member of the Greek Areopagus, or ruling body, who is converted to Christianity by Saint Paul.[28] The identity of our Dionysius is unknown. He is possibly a member of the monophysite[29] circle of Severus of Antioch.[30] Alternatively, he may have been a pagan Neoplatonist of the Athenian Academy under Damascius.[31]

The actual identity of Dionysius is not particularly relevant to us. Instead, it is the body of Christian Neoplatonic texts he leaves that is significant, both for the importance of the texts themselves and because of who they influence. Dionysius' ideas, based at least in part on Plotinus, Iamblichus and Proclus, impact both the Eastern and Western Churches, and catch the imagination of such lights as Marsilio Ficino. Even Pope Benedict XVI recommends his writings, despite Dionysius' Neoplatonism rather than because of it, to be read by all Christians.[32]

Of all of Dionysius' contributions to religious and philosophical thought, perhaps three rank as the most important. The first is the development of what he calls "apophatic" or "negative" theology. Casting the idea of the transcendent, Platonic One onto the Abrahamic God, Dionysius examines the various ways scripture describes and names God. For Dionysius, these descriptions are divinely inspired, and so are related to, even if not identical with, the theurgic names the *Chaldean Oracles* warn us to never alter. However, beyond these names is a God that transcends all description. God cannot be known by what is revealed, because although God is manifest in creation, God is beyond creation. Apophatic theology

---

[28] *Acts 17:34.*

[29] Monophysitism is the belief that Christ has a single nature and not a dual nature, meaning Christ's essence is either only divine or simultaneously human and divine rather than the human and divine natures being distinct. Monophysite Christology is rejected at the Council of Chalcedon in 451 CE.

[30] Wear and Dillon, *Dionysius*, 2-3.

[31] Lankila, "Crypto-Pagan," 14-15.

[32] Benedict XVI, *Audience*, http://www.vatican.va/holy_father/benedict_xvi/audiences/2008/documents/hf_ben-xvi_aud_20080514_en.html.

allows us, through a contemplative approach, to access that part of God that is not evident in the world.

Dionysius' second lasting effect is his angelic hierarchy.[33] This now standard hierarchy of nine angelic choirs[34] is still in use today. We see it both within mainstream Christianity and numerous forms of Christian-esotericism. This hierarchy is connected to the priestly hierarchy, the highest member of which, the Hierarch, is associated with the lowest of the celestial counterparts, the angels.[35] The overlapping of ontological levels is again common to both Iamblichus and Proclus. There is also a connection, generally unrecognized, between Dionysius' angelic hierarchy and Iamblichus' hierarchy of gods and "greater beings." This is discussed in chapter twelve.

Connected to Dionysius' discussion of the celestial and ecclesiastic hierarchies is another triad related to the theurgic nature of both hierarchies and the sacraments overseen by the latter of the two. Dionysius' approach to theurgy, which some scholars gloss over or simply deny, is an element of his religious thought[36] that builds on his pagan predecessors.

While previous Neoplatonists recognize the importance of the traditional Greek myths,[37] their theurgic rites implement them obliquely, and the paraphernalia of those rites are based on natural objects; rocks, animals, plants and the like connected to those stories. Dionysius' understanding of the nature of scripture isn't significantly different from the pagan theurgists. However, he goes a step further. Instead of using natural objects for their divine harmony to connect with God, Dionysius uses the constructed symbols of the scriptures instead.[38] This form of material practice, given life in Dionysius' theurgic sacraments, continues in numerous esoteric practices, such as Freemasonry and its numerous scions, today.

Marsilio Ficino

Marsilio Ficino is the father of Renaissance Neoplatonism. Born in October of 1433, Ficino is the son of Figline and Alessandra Valdarno. Figline is a doctor working under the patronage of Cosimo de' Medici, one of the most powerful figures in Florentine history. Through his father's connections, Ficino becomes tutor to Lorenzo de' Medici, known as Lorenzo the Great, a man who rises to power as did his grandfather Cosimo.

---

[33] Dionysius also coined the word hierarchy.

[34] Seraphim, cherubim, thrones, dominions, powers, authorities, principalities, archangels and angels.

[35] CH, 292C-293B.

[36] Shaw, *Dionysius*, 573-577.

[37] See, for example, Sallustius, *On the Gods and the World*' chapters III and IV, http://hermetic.com/texts/on_the_gods-1.html.

[38] Shaw, *Dionysius*, 583.

Under the de' Medici aegis, Ficino translates the *Corpus Hermeticum* in the 1460s, publishing it in 1471, just six years before he is ordained as a Roman Catholic priest. The translation of the *Corpus* interrupts his work on the Platonic dialogues, because Lorenzo believes it is older than Plato, a popular but erroneous idea of the time. Beyond Plato, Ficino translates Plotinus, Porphyry, Iamblichus, Proclus, Dionysius, the *Orphic Hymns*, and others important texts from their native Greek into Latin. His two great treatises are *Theologia Platonica de immortalitate animae*, the *Platonic Theology or On the Immortality of the Soul*, and the *De vita libri tres*, *Three Books on Life*. Both are heavily dependent upon Neoplatonic interpretations of Plato, astrology, magic, and theurgy. Nearly his entire body of writings survives to influence generations of esotericists.[39]

Ficino's Platonist writings rely heavily on Plotinus, Iamblichus, and Proclus. His system of theurgy is based on *Ennead* 4.3, Proclus' *De sacrificio*, which Ficino translate into Latin, and Iamblichus' *De Mysteriis*.[40] Although pagan Neoplatonic theurgic practices are now lost to us, with only fragments preserved in Proclus and Iamblichus, Ficino gives us an insight into a more modern theurgy, one combining ancient theurgy with the esotericism of his own time. His writings, especially *De vita*, provide a robust framework for theurgic practice based on norms with which many magical practitioners may already be familiar. However, make no mistake, what Ficino writes of is not common magic, but the soul raising work of theurgy:

> *[T]his [the World-soul's spirit] is absorbed by man in particular through his own spirit which is by its own nature similar to it, especially if it is made more akin to it by art, that is, if it becomes in the highest degree celestial.*[41]

A Living Theurgy

What I present above is, as must be the case for a subject of this complexity, only a brief sampling of some of the major figures in the history of Neoplatonism. Each figure has easily filled volumes. The goal of this book is not to simply repeat or understand the past, though both are important. Instead, *Living Theurgy* represents exactly what the title suggests, a *living* practice; one grounded in history but existing in the present and, hopefully, growing into the future.

The following chapters describe Neoplatonic metaphysics, theology, ethics and more. While they rely on traditional texts, they are my interpretations of those texts. The philosophers we examined; Iamblichus, Dionysius, Ficino and others, write for particular audiences, pagans and Christians, ones now centuries dead. One of my goals for *Living Theurgy* is the bridging of the expanse between the Abrahamic and pagan Neoplatonists. This is not as difficult as it seems. Already

---

[39] See Kupperman, "Ficino," 151. This paper summarizes Ficino's importance to the development of Renaissance Neoplatonism and modern ceremonial magical practice.

[40] *Ibid*, 154-5.

[41] DV, 259. Emphasis added.

Dionysius has used Plato's *Timaeus* myth to place Christ in the role of the Demiurge, and the Kabbalists and Sufis have permeated their thought with Platonic philosophy and theurgy. Already has Plato given us a singular, transcendent, all loving deity. With these solid foundations under foot, let us move forward.

Philosophia

Chapter Three

A Living Philosophy

Fittingly, we begin a book on theurgy with philosophy, which falls third in Iamblichus' hierarchy of theurgy, theology and philosophy.[42] This is because *"[i]t is not thought that links the theurgists with the gods: otherwise what should hinder theoretical philosophers from enjoying theurgic union with them? The case is not so.'*[43] The rational mind alone cannot access the fully divine realms, and this is the primary mode of philosophy: dialectic. Only theurgy is capable of transcending the level of Nous to the gods, and God, above. But, in order to practice theurgy, the mind, and soul, must first be trained in philosophy.

Unfortunately, the last few generations of scholars have mimicked E.R. Dodds' misunderstanding of the differences between "irrational" and "arational." More significantly, this has led many scholars to simply dismiss later Neoplatonism, especially Iamblichus' school, as non-philosophical in nature. Nothing is further from the truth. The single remaining biography of Iamblichus, discussed in chapter two, demonstrates this. In the biography, Eunapius, despite his tendency towards mythologizing, shows that for quite some time Iamblichus only teaches philosophy in his academy in Apamea. Only later does he begin teaching theurgy as well. Dodds' view has led to a general ignorance of Iamblichus as a philosopher.

The overall Corpus Iamblichus[44] demonstrates the philosophical depth of Iamblichus' thought. Further, it is Iamblichus who sets the program of Platonic readings used by the Athenian Academy until its close in the sixth century CE.[45] These "greater mysteries," the teachings of Plato, are preceded by the study of Iamblichus' body of Pythagorean texts[46] and selected treatises from Aristotle. The fragments of several of Iamblichus' commentaries on the Platonic dialogues also survive. He is considered by his contemporaries and the Neoplatonists who follow to be one of the greatest of philosophers.

---

[42] DM, I.2, 9-11.
[43] DM, II.11, 115.
[44] This is described at length by Dillon, *Iamblichi*, 18-25.
[45] O'Meara, *Platonopolis*, 62-3.
[46] Dillon, *Iamblichi*, 14-15.

Philosophy and its Role in the School of Iamblichus

What is philosophy? Anyone who has taken an introductory college philosophy course knows the English word "philosophy" comes from the Greek word *philosophia*. This, in turn, is composed of the Greek words *philia* and *sophia*, love and wisdom. Philosophy is the love of wisdom, a philosopher is a lover of wisdom. Tradition says the word *philosophia* is first coined by philosopher-mystic Pythagoras, whom Iamblichus idolizes and about whom he writes several volumes. In Platonic terms, a lover of wisdom, a philosopher, is one who knows they know nothing. Unlike the sage, who is a master of wisdom, the philosopher is a seeker after the object of his or her love.[47] Such a quest is necessary because wisdom, embodied as the goddess Sophia, is otherworldly and transcendent, the highest of virtues, and nearly impossible to obtain by any mere mortal. Such a quest, as daunting as it is, is that with which the philosopher engages.

Anyone who has taken an introductory college philosophy course may not recognize what they learned about philosophy as what I describe. For many, philosophy is an intellectual activity, a trick of logic and reasoning, or as I used to put it when I was in college, little more than the rhetorical knocking down of other philosophers' sandcastles. This has certainly been lamented in the past,[48] and will invariably be lamented in the future. This shell of intellectual and linguistic acrobatics is not the philosophy of Pythagoras, Plato or Iamblichus. It is, instead, closer to the sophism Socrates so deplores in the *Sophist*.

Then what is philosophy? To the Hellenes,[49] philosophy is a living practice and a way of life. We see this in the biographies of Plotinus and Iamblichus. They do not simply hold lectures and then send everyone home to write papers. Students and teachers travel and sometimes live together. Iamblichus' *Vita Pythagoras* shows an even deeper commitment, with the development of an entire Pythagorean society. The *Vita*, or *On the Pythagorean Way of Life*, emphasizes that philosophy is lived, not just spoken. While the *Vita* is more ideal than actual, it demonstrates Iamblichus' view of how a philosophical society might look.

The philosophical way of life involves some of what goes on in college classrooms. The proper use of logic in the evaluation of any statement or theory is invaluable and, as Socrates shows, potentially devastating. This devastation is the point, but not necessarily in a "knocking down of other philosophers' sandcastles" way. Socrates' use of dialectic is only obliquely aimed at a given statement or the knowledge and truth it purports to represent. The destruction of Socrates'

---

[47] C.f. Hadot, *Philosophy*, 58, 90, 147.

[48] For example Needleman, *Heart*, 5.

[49] Classically, those living a Greek lifestyle and who have been heavily influenced by Greek thought, whether or not they are themselves from Greece.

opponents' thought structures leads to the far more important aim of leading the student to the knowledge of which they, much like Socrates, know nothing.[50]

The use of logic, however, is not enough to truly accomplish this. The classical philosophical schools also teach what Pierre Hadot calls "spiritual exercises."[51] Such exercises save philosophy from descending into sophistry. They bring together thought, imagination, ethics, and in short: *"raises [the philosopher] to the life of the objective Spirit . . . re-plac[ing] himself within the perspective of the Whole."*[52] Through spiritual exercises, the teachings and methods of the student's philosophical school are brought into their everyday life. Through these practices, the philosopher holds the core truths of the philosophical way of life so they are not merely memorized but integrated.[53]

For Iamblichus' school, spiritual exercises likely involve not only engaging in the Socratic method of philosophical dialogue, but the study of the *Golden Verses* of pseudo-Pythagoras, and the Pythagorean "symbols" or esoteric phrases. Iamblichus considers the later a uniquely Pythagorean mode of teaching, replete with symbolic or "initiated" meaning,[54] and an important mode of philosophical engagement within Pythagoreanism acting as a prelude to his Platonism.

The role of philosophy is cathartic, or purifying. Through the critical examination of our lives, the thoughts we think, the things we do, and the way we respond to the stimuli of the world around us, we are able to remove the dross layers of the world of generation so our souls may better bask in the light of divine Intellect. The cathartic nature of philosophy is seen especially in the study of virtue, which preoccupies Iamblichus[55] and is a major component of the Platonic dialogues.[56] Virtuous living is of the utmost importance, both for the individual and society as a whole. In his Pythagorean *Exhortation to Philosophy*, Iamblichus begins with fifteen statements concerning the importance of virtue and philosophy:

> *As we live through the soul, it must be said that by the virtue of this we live well; just as, since we see through the eyes, it is by virtue of these that we see well.*
>
> *It must not be thought that gold can be injured by rust, or virtue tainted by baseness.*
>
> *We should betake ourselves to virtue as to an inviolable temple, in order that we may not be exposed to any ignoble insolence of the irrational element of the soul.*
>
> *We should confide in virtue as in a chase wife, but trust Fortune as we would a fickle mistress.*

---

[50] Hadot, *Philosophy*, 89-90.
[51] See Hadot, *Philosophy*, ch 3.
[52] Ibid., 82.
[53] See Hadot, *Philosophy*, ch. 3, especially 89-93, "Learning to Dialogue."
[54] Iamblichus, *Exhortation*, 94. Iamblichus lists 39 Pythagorean "Symbols" and explains both their inner and outer meaning in his *Exhortation to Philosophy*, 95-111.
[55] See, for instance, O'Meara, *Platonopolis*, 50-68.
[56] Cf. Hadot, *Philosophy*, 89-95; Needleman, *Heart*, 23-4.

> *It is better that virtue should be received with poverty, than wealth with vice; and frugality with health, than abundance with disease.*
>
> *As much food is injurious to the body, so is much wealth pernicious to the soul evilly inclined or disposed.*
>
> *It is equally dangerous to give a sword to a madman, and power to a depraved man.*
>
> *Just as it is better for a purulent part of the body to be burned than to remain diseased, so it is also better for a depraved man to die than to live.*
>
> *The theorems of Philosophy are to be enjoyed as much as possible, as if they were ambrosia and nectar; for the pleasure arising from them is genuine, incorruptible and divine. Magnanimity they are also able to produce, and though they cannot make us eternal beings, yet they enable us to obtain a scientific knowledge of eternal natures.*
>
> *If vigour of the senses is desirable, much more should prudence be sought; for it is as it were the sensitive vigour of our practical intellect. And as by the former we are protected from deception in sensations, so through the latter we avoid false reasoning in practical affairs.*
>
> *We shall worship the Deity rightly if we render our intellect pure form all vice, as from some kind of stain or disgrace.*
>
> *We should adorn a temple with gifts, but the soul with disciplines.*
>
> *As prior to the greater mysteries the lesser are delivered, so a disciplinary training must precede the study and acquisition of Philosophy.*
>
> *The fruits of the earth are indeed annually imparted, but the fruits of Philosophy at every season of the year.*
>
> *Just as land must be specially cultivated by him who wishes to obtain from it the best fruit, so the soul should be most carefully and attentively cultivated, in order that it may produce fruit worth its nature.*[57]

This is why we study philosophy, to sufficiently purify ourselves, intellect and soul, in order that we may be properly prepared for theurgy. Just as philosophy descends into sophistry without spiritual exercises, theurgy descends into sorcery58 without philosophy. The contemplative exercises in this section are comprised primarily of 1) *lectio divina*, Latin for "divine reading," and 2) what is sometimes called "guided visualization."

Spiritual Exercises: Lectio Divina and Visualization

Lectio divina dates back to the Christian Platonist Origen Adamantius, who lives between the second and third centuries CE. *Lectio divina* consists of several phases, and we will employ a Platonically modified version of this practice. When starting a session of *lectio divina* settle into inner silence before beginning the

---

[57] Iamblichus, *Exhortation*, 22-3.

[58] C.f. *In Soph*, fr. 1, where the sub-lunar Demiurge, who according to Iamblichus is the subject of the *Sophist*, is called a sorcerer, *góes*.

reading. When ready, read the provided passage,[59] quietly but aloud. Do not rush through the text. Read it slowly and clearly. Allow each word to have its own weight and importance. Allow each word to sink into your mind as your read them.

Although this phase is called "*lectio*," reading, what you are really doing is listening. This is what Socrates does; he listens to the people talk, and attempts to fully understand them and their thoughts. What are you listening for? Much as Socrates, you are listening to understand, or at least realize you do not understand. Each time you engage in *lectio divina* you may hear something new, something different. By being quiet and listening to the words you will, with practice, come to intuitively know what it is you are listening for. Keep in mind this is not an ecstatic practice. Do not expect sudden, glorious visions of the One or the gods, or for deep knowledge about the divine nature of wisdom to flood your mind. Listen for the small voice rather than the great.

After you read the text, and you may read it more than once if you wish, contemplate upon what you have just read. If you can, memorize it and repeat each word to yourself, letting them sink further into your mind. Turn each word over in your thoughts. For now, do not look for specific meanings but let thoughts simply come to you. Do not worry about distractions. If you find yourself pulled away from your contemplation of the passage simply offer those thoughts to God, the One, the gods, your daimon or guardian angel, or whatever you might understand as a higher power, whether it be external to yourself or internal. Take as much time as you feel necessary for this step. Never rush any part of this, or any, contemplative practice.

When you feel you have gained all you can from your contemplation, it is time to respond. This is the time for discursive reasoning, with your inner thoughts acting as interlocutor. What do you think is the meaning of the passage? Why do you think this? Is your reasoning sound? Review your entire thought process, looking for every hole in your argumentation. Remove what cannot be supported and restate your conclusion, repeating until there is nothing left but what can be rationally supported.

Pause for a moment before beginning the next step. Take the opportunity to clear your mind and begin your second response to the reading. This response does not take the form of deeply thought out replies, but instead is a chance to externalize what you have gained from the first two steps. It is a chance to participate in the divine Intellect and speak not from the process of discursive reasoning, but from gnosis. Your response may be spoken aloud or in your mind, as you feel comfortable.

---

[59] Once you have become more familiar with the Platonic and Neoplatonic corpus, and the various texts that have influenced it, such as the *Chaldean Oracles,* the *Hermetica*, and numerous Pythagorean writings, you will be able to choose your own passages to contemplate.

Finally, it is time to rest. Let go of your thoughts and contemplations, release the words from the passage and simply let yourself be. Words are no longer necessary at this point. Words are active, rest in silence as a form of apophatic contemplation, allowing yourself to connect to that part of reality, so far as possible, that is beyond sound and action. Rest in this state for as long as you wish.

As the name suggests, guided visualization consists of imagining a series of pre-determined images. In practicing guided visualization, especially if you are working alone, I recommend either memorizing the given contemplation, or, if possible, making an audio recording of it. If you are working with others, you can take turns reading the description or, again, make an audio recording so that everyone may engage fully in the contemplation. When reading the contemplations, be sure to speak slowly and clearly. Also, it is important to provide enough time for you or others to both relax into the visualization and to create the mental imagery described, as well as to respond to those parts of the contemplation that are not pre-determined.

When beginning this, or any, contemplation, allow yourself some time to be still and silent. These kinds of spiritual practices should not be engaged in while your mind is loud and cluttered. By allowing yourself several moments to become still you greatly enhance the effectiveness of the exercise. When you are finished with the visualization, return to your stillness for several moments before ending the practice. This will help you re-attune yourself to your surroundings. You will find it necessary to keep a journal of your exercises, whatever thoughts or feeling may arise from them, and any dreams or other experiences you might have that you feel are related to them, or even simply may be related to your spiritual exercise.

The Iamblichean Curriculum

The curriculum of Iamblichus' school in Apamea is the model for later Neoplatonists, and is recorded in an *Anonymous Prolegomena to Platonic Philosophy.* Dominic J. O'Meara contributes a great deal to the understanding of Iamblichus' curriculum, and divides the Apamean school's program into "minor" and "greater" mysteries, an idea we will modify. The minor mysteries curriculum consists of non-Platonic material such as Iamblichus' *Corpus Pythagoras*, moral instruction, and commentaries on Aristotle.[60] Of the nine or ten volumes of the *Corpus Pythagoras*, four survive intact. These are the *Pythagorean Way of Life*, the *Exhortation to Philosophy*, *On the General Theory of Mathematics* and *On Nichomachus' Introduction to Arithmetic.*[61] Excerpts of books V-VIII survive in the writings of the

---

[60] The last of these had already been integrated into Platonism by Plotinus.

[61] Dillon, *Iamblichi*, 19-20.

Byzantine Christian Neoplatonist Michael Psellus.[62] Iamblichus is also thought to have written commentaries on Aristotle's *De Interpretatione*, *Prior Analytics*, *De Caelo*, *De Anima* and the *Metaphysics*.[63]

The greater mysteries focus on the more purely Platonic material, consisting of a study of particular dialogues and their commentaries. This course of study is divided into two sections, consisting of a series of ten dialogues and two dialogues, respectively. Each text teaches a particular subject. The first series consists of the *Alcibiades*, *Gorgias*, *Phaedo*, *Cratylus*, *Theaetetus*, *Sophist*, *Statesman*, *Phaedrus*, *Symposium* and *Philebus*. The *Alcibiades* teaches us, following the command of the oracle, to know ourselves. The next dialogues teach about the first five levels of virtue: natural (the *Sophist*), ethical (the *Cratylus* and the *Theaetetus*), social, (the *Gorgias*), purifying (the *Phaedo*), and theoretical (the *Symposium* and the *Phaedrus*).[64] The second series consists of the *Timaeus* and *Parmenides*, which teach of physics and theology.[65]

Of these, only fragments of Iamblichus' commentaries on the *Alcibiades*, *Phaedo*, *Sophist*, *Phaedrus*, *Philebus*, *Timaeus*, and *Parmenides* survive. Noticeably missing from the above list are the *Republic* and the *Laws*, both of which are referenced by Iamblichus in various places. This is likely because of the length of the texts[66] but also because Iamblichus considers the themes of the *Republic* to be Pythagorean in origin,[67] and possibly includes the study of elements of the *Republic* in the preliminary, Pythagorean-focused, section of study in his academy.

It is also likely there is a now missing third course of reading, focusing on theology and theurgy rather than philosophy. This may include texts such as the lost *Peri Theon*, or *On the Gods*, *Theologia Platonica*, and Iamblichus' systemization and Platonization of the *Chaldean Oracles*. Unfortunately, with the exception of a few fragments, this later material has been lost.

Our Course of Study

While I encourage you to read the Platonic dialogues, and the fragments of Iamblichus' commentaries on them, doing so is in no way required to gain value from the following chapters. However, it is impossible to be a Platonist while remaining unfamiliar with the dialogues. While we will not focus exclusively on the dialogues, we will explore important Platonic themes and how they are approached by the Neoplatonists. These, in turn, rely on their interpretations of the dialogues and related texts. Our study enables us to engage more fully as

62 These have been reconstructed in O'Meara's *Pythagoras* Revived.
63 Dillon, *Iamblichi*, 21-2.
64 Westernick, *Prolegomena*, 48.
65 *Ibid., 46*
66 *Ibid.*
67 O'Meara, "Republic," 195-199.

human beings, and human souls, in the physical world, but also serves as a jumping point to discussions about theology and theurgy.

We begin with the most basic theme, that of the virtues, and the idea of virtue ethics, which form the basis of Platonic ethical theory. Following this is a discussion of the nature of evil, which for the Platonists is as much a philosophical notion as it is theological, and is directly relevant to the preceding discussion on virtue. Iamblichus is largely silent on this subject, so we turn to Proclus and Pseudo-Dionysius for a deeper understanding of this important subject. The section on ethics concludes with an examination of Neoplatonic political theory, which is impossible to practice without having first incorporated the virtues into our lives. This chapter looks at the role of the *Republic* and the *Laws* in Iamblichus' school. The last two chapters examine the closely related concepts of aesthetics and love. Here we once again rely on Iamblichus, but also explore the thoughts of Marsilio Ficino.

As we've discussed, philosophy isn't simply something you read, it is something you do. To help facilitate this exercises are presented throughout the chapters. Is it necessary to practice these exercises? The short answer is "yes." Philosophy is the gateway to theology and theurgy. Without the purification brought about by a philosophical life, the practice of theurgy is not only problematic, but potentially dangerous. With proper practice and a philosophical way of life, theurgy leads the theurgist towards the divine life.

Exercise

For your first exploration of the philosophical life, you will explore what "philosophy" means to you. At this point it is okay to forget what I have said on the subject. Unless this truly reflects your thoughts, ignore the idea of philosophy as a way of life, for now, anyway. Instead, write a few sentences about your understanding of philosophy. Importantly, don't simply write down a definition of philosophy, but also explore *why* you think of philosophy in that way. The why is always as important as the what, sometimes more so. Remember, when Socrates wanders the markets of Athens questioning people, it is the why he attempts to deconstruct, not necessarily the what. With the edifice of why destroyed, what crumbles without resistance.

Return to this exercise as you work through this book and digest what it offers. This is a good way to keep track of your understanding of philosophy as time passes and your thinking process about the subject. Examining our thinking processes allows us, like Socrates, to deconstruct them. This leaves us free to pursue our love of wisdom, rather than presume it has already been attained.

A Final Note on Philosophy's Finality

Philosophy is extraordinarily important in our lives, and is itself a way of life. However, philosophy isn't really about life, or at least not only about life.

According to Socrates in the *Phaedo*, philosophy is about training for death. Only in death can we be with our superiors, the angels, gods, or God. According to the dialogue, the death of a non-philosopher does not lead to this. In pagan Platonic thought such a person simply reincarnates because of the impurities surrounding their soul. The philosopher, however, frees themselves from such corruption, and is able to bear witness to the divine realm.

This is not as morbid as it may appear. We are not talking about suicide, which Socrates forbids as impious.[68] Nor are we talking about unnecessarily risking our lives, which is little more than suicide. Instead we are simply talking about death and dying, and that the philosopher should not fear doing so. When the soul incarnates it partakes fully of the body's mortality. Upon the death of the body the soul is freed to its immortal life. For the philosopher, living is being dead and after death we, our soul, come to live.[69]

---

[68] *Phaedo*, 62a-c.

[69] *Gorg*. 492e-493a.

Chapter Four

Virtue

The ethical modes coming from ancient Greece, and running through late Antiquity, are somewhat different than those of Modernity. Modern theories, beginning only a few hundred years ago, focus on duty and what we ought to do, and consequences, to what we should aim. The virtue ethics of Antiquity focus on how we ought to be.

There are several well-known ethical theories. Two of the most well-known are perhaps Immanuel Kant's deontology[70] and John Stuart Mill's form of utilitarianism. Briefly, Kant's deontology uses the idea of the "categorical imperative." A categorical imperative is the foundation of a universal ethical law.[71] This means that ethical rules should follow absolutes that are always applicable to all people. These do not constitute what we would like to do, but what every reasonable person ought to do.

Mill's utilitarianism is based on the "greatest-happiness principle." In utilitarianism, what one ought to do is that which causes the greatest happiness for the greatest number of people. In this case, happiness is defined as pleasure and the absence of pain. In utilitarianism, motive is irrelevant. The only relevant things are results. If an action, regardless of the reasons for it performance, increases pleasure and removes pain, it is morally good. If an action increases pain and decreases pleasure, it is morally bad. Different kinds of pains and pleasures are seen as more significant than others.

As you can see, these are concerned with why we do the things we do, and their outcomes. In both cases, they are about doing. If your actions follow the categorical imperative or the greater-happiness principle, respectively, then you are a good person. To the Hellenes this is backwards. What you are determines how and why you act, not the other way around.

---

70 Literally "obligation" or "duty."

71 Kant, *Grounding*, 30.

The Four Cardinal Virtues

Plato's *Republic* presents the reader with an idealized and divinized community. In doing so, Plato presents four cardinal virtues: wisdom, bravery, temperance, and justice.[72] These virtues are carried into Christian tradition by St. Augustine, who is influenced by Platonism, and are named "cardinal virtues" by Augustine's approximate contemporary, St. Ambrose.[73]

According to Iamblichus' letter to his chief student Sopater, virtue is nothing less than the "perfection of the soul."[74] Consequently, virtuous acts are the best acts, and Iamblichus heaps praise after praise upon such "boniform" actions.[75] Attaining to virtue, especially its higher levels, is hardly a simple manner. One's intellect must be free from the influences from the realm of generation usually described as "passions". The passions are those things tying us to the physical world at the cost of the spiritual.

Though Plato divides the virtues into four, virtue itself is an indivisible Form or divine archetype. While many things may participate virtue, and the virtues, virtue remains undivided, simultaneously existing in everything that participates it. Coming from the divine realm, virtue has no beginning or end, and exists outside of time. Virtue is also unchanging. Although the ways beings participate it, and so express virtue in the world, may vary, virtue itself remains the same.[76] As such, virtue is gained not simply through practice, which exists on the level of generation, but through contemplation and, at its highest levels, theurgy.

In his treatise on the virtues, Plotinus describes the four cardinal virtues as follows:

> *The Prudence [wisdom] which belongs to the reasoning faculty; the Fortitude [bravery] which conducts the emotional and passionate nature; the Sophrosyny [temperance] which consists in a certain pact, in a concord between the passionate faculty and the reason; or Rectitude [justice] which is the due application of all the other virtues as each in turn should command or obey.*[77]

Beyond these four virtues are subsidiaries, including superior sense-perception, gracefulness, memory, quick wits, friendliness, a love of truth and knowledge and a hatred of falsehood, and distaste for wealth.[78] All of these, to varying degrees, are necessary for philosophical and spiritual progress. However, that does not mean having them in perfection but rather simply having them and not their corresponding vices or opposites.

---

[72] *Rep.* 427e.
[73] To these are then added the theological virtues of faith, hope and charity.
[74] L16, fr. 1.
[75] *Ibid.*
[76] L16.
[77] *Enneads*, I.2, 16.
[78] O'Meara, "Patterns," 79.

The following descriptions of the virtues are by no means exhaustive. Instead, they represent what remains of Iamblichus' writings on the subject. The primary sources for this are the fragments of his surviving letters and the sixth book of his Pythagorean Corpus, *On Arithmetic in Ethical Matters.*[79] The latter of these relies heavily on Aristotle's *Nicomachean Ethics.*

Wisdom

The highest of the virtues is wisdom. Wisdom takes two forms: theoretical wisdom, *sophia*, and practical deliberation, or prudence, *phroníseos*. Theoretical wisdom is the chief of the virtues, utilizing them all. Iamblichus connects virtue to Nous, the divine Intellect, giving it the power to organize the virtues into the most useful arrangement. Wisdom comes from Nous and is perfected by it by fully participating in the divine mind. Through our participation in this virtue we are most connected and assimilated to the gods.[80] Aristotle says through *sophia* we are able to grasp true "beings" or *"realities whose fundamental principles do not admit of being other than they are.'*[81] In his Pythagorean work, Iamblichus relates this form of wisdom to the monad *"which sees what is known in a unitary way.'*[82]

Through prudence we can discern between what is good and noble and what is not. By being able to discern what is noble we can then act nobly.[83] In short, wisdom is the divine model upon which all life should be based, from the daily activities of the average person to the decisions of the *Republic*'s philosopher-kings and queens.[84]

Significantly, Iamblichus describes wisdom as an *"eye of intellect,'*[85] reflecting imagery from the metaphor of the sun in the *Republic.*[86] Just as the eye needs light to discern what is around us, we need wisdom, which flows from a spiritual light,[87] to discern the proper ordering of the virtues. Also, through wisdom, this eye of intellect, we can turn our gaze upwards towards the source of illumination, which is also the source of wisdom.[88]

---

[79] The nine, or ten, volumes of Iamblichus' *On Pythagoreanism* remain largely untranslated. There is a critical edition of Book I: *The Pythagorean Life* by John Dillon and Jackson Hershbell, and at least one amateur translation of Book II: *Proteptic to Philosophy*, published as *The Exhortation to Philosophy* by Thomas M. Johnson in in 1907. Dominic J. O'Meara's *Pythagoras Revived* is, at the time of writing, the best source on the un-translated and unpublished portions of *On Pythagoreanism*, including *On Arithmetic in Ethical Matters* (70-76).

[80] L4. Cf. *Rep.* 501b-c

[81] *Nich.*, VI.1139a.

[82] *Theo Arith.*, 33-35.

[83] L4.

[84] L4. Cf. *Rep.* 501b-c.

[85] L4.

[86] 507b-509c.

[87] In classical pagan Neoplatonism this takes the form of the god Helios.

[88] Cf. L4: "[Wisdom], then, receives its existence principally from the pure and perfect Intellect. Once generated, however, it contemplates the Intellect itself and derives its perfection from it . . . ."

We gain an extended view of the nature of wisdom through Emperor Julian's *Hymn to King Helios*. While in his letter to Asphalius Iamblichus relates wisdom directly to Nous, Julian, reflecting a fuller version of Iamblichean theology, relates wisdom to Athena, the virgin goddess of wisdom and war. In this *Hymn* Julian claims Athena does not spring from the head of Zeus, but instead *"was sent forth from Helios whole from the whole of him, being contained within him.'*[89] This isn't as contradictory to the more common myth as it might seem; Julian considers Helios and Zeus cognates.[90]

In the *Hymn*, Athena is Helios', who is Nous, perfect intelligence, the mind of the divine Mind, as it were. Further, Athena is responsible for *"unifying the gods in Helios".*[91] She also servers to order the gods represented by the seven planets and all the stars in the heavens, known as the visible gods, and to fill them all with practical wisdom. She also gives to humanity the blessing of wisdom.[92] Athena's role is identical to the function of wisdom in Iamblichus' letter, and in the *Republic*. Importantly, wisdom is associated with Athena, but is distinct from her. The gods, in their perfection and participation the Good, have no need of virtue. Rather, it is humanity that benefits from participating in the virtues emanating from the divine realm.

Exercise: Two Contemplations on Wisdom

In this practice we employ part of Iamblichus' letter to Asphalius on the subject of wisdom:

> *It is wisdom, which dominates all the other virtues and makes use of all of them, like an eye of the intellect ordering well their ranks and proportions according to the most apt arrangement that discourse displays before our gaze at the present.*[93]

Find a comfortable place to sit and allow yourself to become still and silent. You may count breaths, focus on heart beats, repeat a simple mantra to yourself, or whatever other method you may have to attain inner silence. A benefit to this practice is to clear your mind of any preconceived notions you might have about the meaning of the passage. Approaching the reading in this manner allows you to view it with new eyes and an open mind. This allows for new insights into the reading, which might otherwise be blocked by the belief you already know its meaning. When you are ready, engage in *lectio divina* using this passage as your focus. If necessary, review the instructions for this practice in the previous chapter. This concludes the first contemplation on wisdom.

---

[89] Julian, *Hymn*, 409.
[90] *Ibid.*
[91] *Ibid.*
[92] *Ibid.*, 411.
[93] L4.

The second contemplation is a visualized *theoria.* This exercise employs one of the most well-known scenes from Plato's *Republic*: the allegory of the cave. Note that in the following visualization the focus is not on the blinding sun, but its light. The light, like wisdom, allows us to discern truth from falsehood. Just as the sunlight is not sight, but that which allows for sight, wisdom is not discernment, but without wisdom, discernment is impossible. The visualization follows:

You are standing in a cave. Your neck is held tight by a shackle. Breathing is easy, but you cannot move your head to look around. All you can see is what is in front of you. At the far end of the cave is a wide screen, like a movie theater. The cave is dark, but somewhere behind you is a flickering light source, casting images onto the screen. As you watch, strange shapes pass before you. As you watch, fabulous creatures march from one end of the screen to the other. A minotaur. A dragon. A goddess. A demon. A human. Other shapes, some fantastic, some mundane, traverse before you as well.

The shapes on the screen are not all you perceive. Sound is everywhere around you, bouncing off the cave's walls. The wavering, echoing sounds are familiar to you. One voice tells you of the secrets of the creation of the world. Another voice whispers prayers. A third screams about the unfairness of life. A fourth cries aloud in pain or ecstasy. The fantastic images upon the screen make sounds as well, so the cave is filled with noise.

This is life in the cave. You experience it as the whole of the world. It is normal. It is safe. It is home. The shackle around your neck does not confine you, it protects you. There is nothing to see, nothing worth seeing, that does not pass before your eyes. This is life.

Without warning, something shakes the chain at your neck and soon the shackle falls away. Gentle hands firmly turn you away from the screen and you see myriads of others around you. None of them are like what you have seen before. Life on the screen is dark and blurry, those standing around you, though shrouded by the cave's gloom, are clear and sharp to your eyes. So much so that they are difficult for you to properly see. Each is chained, as you were, and none are aware of you. All they see is the screen. You are taken from your place.

As you walk, gentle hands on your arms, the cave becomes brighter, soon filling with intense, flickering light and heat. The intensity of the light is blinding and you turn away. As you pass the bonfire you see your own shadow cast upon the cave's wall, flickering with the movement of the fire. You look from the shadow to your body and back, seeing for the first time your true shape, even if poorly illuminated by the light of the fire. What you have seen all your life is like this: a shadow of a veiled truth.

You pass the fire, but instead of the light fading, it grows. The gentle hands lead you closer towards the light and soon push you out of the cave. Light streams down from above, blinding in a way that causes the intensity of the bonfire to be forgotten as nothing. You close your eyes and try to return to the safety of the cave, but firm hands prevent you from entering again. You are turned away and stumble into the light.

You try opening your eyes, but the brightness is too intense. You try again, looking at the ground, away from the unknown source of brilliance and warmth above you. You find it difficult to see at first, but soon your eyes adjust to the relative dimness of the ground at your feet, shaded as it is by your own shadow. As your eyes adjust, you discern individual blades of deeply green grass. The tiny blades move in a soft breeze, but unlike the wavering forms of the screen, what you see is clear and true.

As your eyes become more accustomed to the light you slowly look up. There is grass all around you, and the deep brown of tree trunks. The dark grass is highlighted in places by bright spots of light filtering through the trees tops. Nearby, you see a pond. Approaching it, you find yourself reflected in the clear, still water. This is the first time you have ever seen your face. Pause to take in your beauty, even as your realize that what you see before you is only a little more real than the familiar shadows. Though the reflection is crisp and comprehensible, it is clear to you the reflection is only an image of the truth.

Finally, you lift your eyes higher. Trees of all kinds fill the sky; leaves of different hues blow in the breeze. Each leaf stands out clearly to you, and discerning the different kinds of trees comes easily to you in the sunlight. Beyond the leaves is a brilliantly blue sky. Soft white clouds dot the azure heaven and soon, though you cannot view it directly, you see the sun. The brilliant orb makes everything clear to the eyes of your soul. For a time you rest, basking in the light, and the awareness of a Sun beyond the sphere in the sky, which brings with it the illumination of a higher Truth, and beyond that great Sun lies Eternity, quietly fills your being.

But behind you is the cave. Its entrance is no longer guarded and a set shackle keys hangs from a hook next to the entrance. You may return as you will.

Bravery

Bravery, or courage, *andreías*, is the second virtue and again there are two kinds: "manly" courage and constancy.[94] The first form of bravery consists of daring and fortitude.[95] Further, such bravery is valorous and majestic.[96] People with this type of bravery endure pain because it is noble to do so.[97]

---

[94] O'Meara, *Pythagoras*, 74.
[95] *Symp.*, 192a.
[96] *Laws*, VII.802e.
[97] *Nich.*, 1117a.

The bravery of constancy, the truest form of the bravery,[98] is typified by a brave person whose high spirited nature, regardless of plain and pleasure, functions under the rule of reason concerning what should and should not be feared, or that which is real and that which is not.[99] High spiritedness is one of the three parts of the soul, and is led by reason and followed by the appetitive.[100] Iamblichus, in a letter to Olympius, expands upon this, describing bravery as an *"unshakable intellectual potency."*[101] Bravery is a kind of mental activity, the *"self-identity of intellect"*[102] which brings about an unwavering state of mind, existing within itself. Further, bravery may exist on its own or may be ruled with wisdom.[103] Through this combination of virtues, the individual not only knows what is or is not to be feared, but is able to discern what is for both the individual and common good.[104]

Iamblichus[105] expounds upon Plato's description of bravery as the source of discernment between what is to be feared and what is not. Bravery, when attached to reason, gives us this power, and also allows us to stand against that which should be feared. Bravery helps us stand up for that which we believe in. Through courage and reason we can live noble lives, full of courageous actions, performed for the sake of doing what is right, regardless of common opinion. Further, bravery allows us, for the sake of the common good, to carry out these noble activities, even through adversity and pain, with composure and balance.[106] This suggests a high, perhaps spiritual kind of bravery rooted in the Form of Virtue.

This view of bravery, as the highest of intellectual activities, is quite different from our modern understanding. Typically, we do not think of bravery as an intellectual activity. Who hasn't heard the saying "there is a fine line between courage and stupidity"? What are the Platonists telling us about this virtue? One important implication is that thoughtless acts of "bravery" are not brave, merely thoughtless. Any animal can act in such a way. As a faculty of discernment, bravery allows us to fully understand when a situation is to be feared or not. Moreover, courage enables us to act in the face of danger, opposing public opinion, and even the threat of death. Acting from the virtue of bravery is not mindlessness, but movement from purpose. Further, Iamblichus suggests brave activities are ones performed solely *"for their own sake."*[107] Acts of courage and bravery are carried out because that is what brave people do.

---

[98] L10, fr. 1.
[99] *Rep.*, 442c1.
[100] *Rep.*, 436a-437d. See chapter fourteen for more on this subject.
[101] L10, fr. 1.
[102] *Ibid.*
[103] Cf. L10, fr. 1 and *Rep.* 442c3.
[104] *Rep.* 442c3.
[105] L10, fr. 2.
[106] *Ibid.*, C.f. *Nich.*, 1117a
[107] L10, fr. 2.

Exercise: Two Contemplations on Bravery

The first contemplation on bravery is a discursive dialogue with yourself. You may do this aloud, silently or through writing. Have a conversation with yourself about the nature of bravery. Begin from your personal understanding of bravery. Take time to define what bravery means to you, and to explain your definition. Why does it mean what you think it means? If you are aware of other understandings of bravery, what are they, how do they differ from your own, and why do you reject those? Next, include Plato's and Iamblichus' definitions of bravery. How are they similar to yours? How are they different? What do the differences say about how you have thought about bravery in the past? What do Platonic understandings of bravery reflect upon bravery as a virtue?

These are only a handful of topics you may include in your dialogue. Do not feel you must include them all, and do not be limited to them. The nature of discursive dialogue is to explore a topic broadly and fluidly, not to be bound by formality. However, in all instances it is important to apply reason to everything you discuss. If a thought cannot be supported by reason and logic, discard it until it can. This holds for Plato's and Iamblichus' definitions as well. Socrates often offers explanations he will readily discard if proven unreasonable. We should hold ourselves to no lesser standard. However, it is also important to remember that just because we cannot find the logic or reasoning in a statement that does not mean there is none. An idea that we reject now may be reclaimed once our understanding of it is improved.

The second contemplation is another *lectio divina.* Once again you will explore a passage from Iamblichus, here from his letter to Olympius on courage:

> *Let courage in the most proper sense be understood to be such as is an unshakable intellectual potency, and the highest form of intellectual activity, and which constitutes self-identity of intellect and a state of mind steadfast within itself.*[108]

Temperance

The third virtue is *sophrosýnis*, literally "sound-mindedness," and variously translated as temperance, moderation, and self-control. As before, there are two kinds of temperance, one related to harmony, the other to symmetry. Just as wisdom informs bravery, harmonious temperance moderates and orders all the virtues.[109] A temperate person works harmoniously with reason,[110] making them sober, reasonable and fit for guidance.[111]

---

108 L10, fr 1.

109 *Rep.*, 430e.

110 *Nich.*, 119b.

111 *Rep.*, 431e

Symmetric temperance gives proper order and rank to the three parts of the soul so that reason holds sway over the other parts in due proportion.[112] A person in possession of this virtue is fully their own master,[113] with reason controlling their spiritedness and desires. The virtue of self-control allows us to become perfect through the subordination of the passions which incline us towards generation and away from the mental or spiritual realms. More importantly, temperance partakes of the ordering nature of the cosmos, preserving a proper way of living. Through this virtue, the other three are harmonized and focused, and because of this we become more like the form of the gods.[114]

Temperance takes the role of moderator of the virtues. It is not a mean, partaking of the nature of that which its moderates, but a coordinator. Through self-control, a virtuous person is able to act appropriately as the situation dictates. This is accomplished by the coordination of the parts of the soul. The "worse parts," spiritedness and desire, are not extinguished by virtue but are employed appropriately, rather than in excess, self-indulgence being the very opposite of temperance.[115] Likewise, the virtues are brought together through moderation, and applied appropriately, under the guidance of reason, the vehicle of wisdom.

Exercise: Two Contemplations on Temperance

For this first exercise you will keep a journal about your actions and behaviours for at least a week. Use a journal, rather than mentally keeping track of how you react to the situations you find yourself throughout the day. By writing down events, thoughts and emotions are both clarified and more easily reviewable over time. Be honest with yourself through this, and in fact all of the exercises. Without self-honesty cannot we grow as intellectual, moral, and philosophical people.

Be certain to record how you react to both the situations you find yourself in and the thoughts that arise in your mind, especially those which may cause you stress or bring about strong emotions. Do you find yourself acting reasonably when someone disagrees with you? In tense situations do you act emotionally first? Are your reactions in proportion to the situation? Do you find yourself carrying a grudge? There are other questions to ask yourself, and these will occur to you as you engage with this exercise.

Why do this? In order to gain temperance, we must know how we act and react to any given situation. If we do not know this, how can we know about our ability to self-control? By watching our reactions and thoughts, we better understand ourselves. Not only will we be better able to see how we react, but

---

112 L3, fr. 1.
113 *Rep.*, 430
114 L3, fr. 4.
115 L3, fr. 5.

why. This is important: the virtues are never mindless, they are ruled by reason. This means that acting moderately, but mindlessly, is not acting through the virtue of moderation. Also, perform the exercises for an extended period, not just once, and revisit them occasionally as a philosophical self-checkup.

The second contemplation is a *lectio divina.* Here Iamblichus, in his letter to Arte,[116] speaks of the nature of self-control, saying it harmonizes all the virtues to work together. It is this quality of temperance, in relation to the other virtues, Iamblichus writes of when he tells Arte:

> *This being its nature, it both provides a stimulus to all of them to come into being and, when they are established, assures their firm preservation.*

Justice

The last of the cardinal virtues is *dikaiosinis,* justice. Once more this virtue is divided into two kinds: distributive and reciprocal.[117] According to Iamblichus, distributive justice is the summation of, or resides in, the virtues.[118] This means when wisdom and bravery are harmonized through temperance the result is justice. Justice consists of what is proper to feelings of community, the observation of legal obligations, working towards the betterment of the people and not only oneself, and generally working towards the greater good.[119] Through justice the natures of all things are preserved and exemplified.[120]

Iamblichus bases his definition of reciprocal justice on that of the Neopythagorean mathematician Nicomachus. Reciprocal justice is the *"reciprocity of the equal and appropriate."*[121] This is derived from Aristotle's discussion of friendship and politics in chapter eight of the *Nicomachean Ethics*, which states when people are friends there is justice. Friendship is superior to other kinds of justice, as distributive justice alone does not necessarily include friendship. Reciprocal justice, which is justice in the fullest sense, always guarantees a non-diminishing, base-line status of the people, even if the status of some increases,[122] and always includes a facet of friendship.[123] This element of friendship is important because it is only in friendship that true equality and reciprocity are possible.[124]

---

[116] L3, fr. 6.

[117] Aristotle denotes three kinds of justice; distributive, rectificatory and reciprocal. Iamblichus does not appear to deal with the middle form.

[118] L2, fr. 1, *Rep.*, 443b.

[119] L2, fr. 2.

[120] *Rep.* 434a-435b.

[121] *Theo Arith.*, 46-7

[122] Ambrosi, "Justice," 19. This actually differs from Pythagorean justice, which is in the mode of *lex talionis*, which Aristotle rejects.

[123] *Nich.*, VIII 155a.

[124] C.f. *Nich.*, VIII 156b5-25., 1159b25-1160a1-30.

Exercise: Two Contemplations on Justice

It is time for another self-dialogue. Hold off this conversation until you engage in the first three sets of exercises for at least a month. Also, I encourage you to read further about these virtues. The *Republic* is an excellent place to begin, but Plato is hardly the only philosopher to write about virtue. Compare different expressions of the cardinal virtues through the writings of various philosophers and theologians. What do Aristotle, Augustine, Ibn Sina or Kant have to say on the subject?

In this conversation you will talk about justice. This is, in the tradition of Socratic dialectic, a fairly free formed conversation. Begin by defining justice. Not necessarily as how you've read it here or in some other work of philosophy, but how you really think about the subject. Then, as always, ask yourself why this is justice and not something else. Justify your definition. Do so reasonably and logically and, if you cannot, be honest about that. In the beginning, it is fine if you cannot justify your position. This means more thought on the subject is in order, and this self-conversation is an excellent beginning towards that end.

Also, explore other definitions of justice with which you may be familiar, and attempt to explain them logically and reasonably. Again, if you cannot do so, why is that the case? As you progress with your understanding of justice, discuss how this virtue connects you to wisdom, bravery and temperance. If it does, how, if not, why? There are, as always, other areas to delve in your conversations about justice. These are only a few with which you can start.

The second contemplation is a *lectio divina*. You will again consider a passage from Iamblichus. Do not feel confined to the passages given here. As you progress in your studies you will find other passages, either from Platonists or other philosophers and theologians, which inspire or to which you are otherwise attracted. I encourage you to contemplate these as well. The following passage comes from Iamblichus' letter to Anatolius[125] on the subject of justice:

> *It is to the very culmination of all the virtues and the summation of all of them, in which, indeed, as the ancient account tells us, they are all present together, that one would come by being led to justice.*

The virtues are the foundation of human moral activity. Through them we are able to live harmoniously, not only with our fellow humans, but with the ordering of the cosmos[126] and, if you so believe, the gods or God and all the heavenly hosts. The practice of the cardinal virtues is an integral part of the philosophical life, and goes beyond contemplations. Take what you understand and have experienced of the virtues and live them every day. Through them we are able to

---

[125] L2, fr. 1.

[126] This ordering is known as Fate amongst the Neoplatonists.

walk the philosophical path, keep our spirits and souls on target and, ultimately, move our love of wisdom towards the divine work of theurgy.

The Scale of Virtues

The scale of virtues is a ladder of different ways the cardinal and subsidiary virtues are applied. The idea of the four virtues operating in a hierarchical scale originates with Plotinus and is formalized by Porphyry. This scale is not in relation to one another, one virtue compared to another, but in relation to the mental and moral development of a person. Each level after the lowest, the natural virtues, builds upon and includes the levels below it, and each level contains all four virtues. However, having obtained one level in full does not mean the next level will be achieved.

Iamblichus, in his now lost *On the Virtues*,[127] builds upon the four levels developed by Plotinus and Porphyry, adding to both the top and bottom of the scale for a total of six levels of virtue. This scale of virtues, which becomes normative for later Neoplatonism, is as follows: natural virtues, ethical, political or civic, purificatory,[128] theoretical,[129] and theurgic virtues. Each level of virtue may be associated with one of the cardinal virtues more than the others. For instance temperance is especially associated with the level of ethical virtue.[130]

Natural virtues, which Iamblichus bases on Aristotle, are natural extensions of a particular kind of being's essence. One does not need to learn the natural virtues of one's species; they are inborn, though they can be improved with training. For example, lions naturally have the virtue of bravery. This can include bodily virtues, such as keen senses, and intellectual virtues associated with the soul, such as memory. With these can come natural vices, such as being greedy or unneighbourly.

Through proper education, natural virtues can be raised to ethical virtues and natural vices can be eliminated. Moderation is the cardinal virtue most closely associated with the ethical virtues, especially in the form of chastity. Temperance is not limited to sexual moderation, and includes the ability to moderate the spirited and volatile aspect of the soul.[131] Neither the natural nor ethical virtues require the ability to reason. As we saw, the temperance of the ethical virtues only necessitates the calming of an overactive spirit, but not the domination of the rational aspect of the soul associated with wisdom. The natural virtues simply

---

127 Fragments of this, and other pieces of Iamblichus' corpus, survive in the writings Damascius, the last head of the Athenian Academy, as well as the eleventh-century Christian Neoplatonist Michael Psellus.

128 The political and purificatory virtues were first developed by Plotinus in *Enneads*, I.2.

129 This, along with a paradigmatic level, is developed by Porphyry. Iamblichus exchanges the paradigmatic level of virtue in favour of the theurgic level.

130 O'Meara, "Patterns," 81.

131 *Ibid.*

reflect the way we are from birth and the ethical virtues a matter of training and habituation, not reason. This is not, however, the same as saying they are unthoughtful; the irrational soul is also capable of a manner of thought.

However, to possess the political virtues the ability to focus the rational part of the soul is absolutely necessary. Because of this, the political virtues are uniquely human; other kinds of animals can possess the lower two levels. The benefits of the political virtues are two-fold: they help the soul in its progress and are beneficial to other people through their practice. Based on justice, the political virtues *"are a principle of order and beauty in us"* as long as we live in generation.[132] Justice takes the form of inner harmony and symmetry (ethics) or extends to include the ordering of the households (economics) or the state (politics). Justice is associated with philanthropy, which is connected to friendship.[133] The possession of political virtue is the highest level of human virtuousness. Above this level, the philosopher lives a divine life,[134] the achievement of which requires engaging in contemplation and theurgy.

The purificatory virtues mark a movement away from human virtuousness and a movement towards divinity. Plotinus sees these virtues allowing us to rise above our entrapment in the world of matter, bringing us closer to the gods and God.[135] Engagement with the virtues on this level bring about the purification of the soul so that it may fully remember itself as a divine being and, ultimately, rise above and withdraw from physical manifestation, if only temporarily.

> *He used to say that when the soul . . . (is) at first disengaged from the body, it concentrates on itself; then it abandons its own habits, withdrawing from discursive into intellect's thought; finally, at a third state, it is possessed by the divine and drifts into an extraordinary serenity befitting gods rather than men.*[136]

For Plotinus, the purified soul does not need to remain at this high level, and, while still incarnate, may descend to employ the civic virtues in a perfected way.[137] For Iamblichus this descent is a necessity of the dual-natured human soul.[138]

The theoretical virtues represent a level of intellectual perfection as the soul ascends to fully participate the divine Intellect. Damascius' teacher, Isidore, describes some of the theoretical virtues, which are separate from the intellectual virtues associated with discursive reasoning. This is the level of divine knowing or absolute gnosis, rather than the partial knowing of the human mind. These virtues include *"absolute efficiency"*, *"aloofness from the obvious and habitual conformity"* with the

---

[132] Plotinus, *Enneads*, I.2, 17.
[133] O'Meara, "Patterns," 83.
[134] *Ibid.*
[135] See O'Meara, *Platonopolis*, 40-44.
[136] Damascius in O'Meara, "Patterns," 84.
[137] *Ibid.*, 43.
[138] See chapter fourteen.

herd of humanity, and an *"unswerving impulse towards that delight in intelligible beauty."*[139] Where the purificatory virtues are those representing the movement of focus from the body to the soul and intellect, theoretical virtues are those associated with a fully purified soul.[140]

The highest level on the scale of virtues is the theurgic virtues. Few descriptions of this level remain. This is most likely because almost no one reaches it, something to which Iamblichus attests in his description of the rare theurgic sage in *De Mysteriis*. One possible candidate for this level is the priest Heraiscus. Heraiscus, despite not being perfect in natural talents, has both ethical and political virtue and is extremely close to the gods in such a way that he knows everything Proclus knows, Proclus representing the nearly perfect Platonist, while Proclus does not know everything known to Heraiscus.[141]

There is nothing beyond this level of virtue. One might argue for a fully divine set of virtues above those of a divinized human. Remember, however, that the gods have no need of virtue. Being the source of the Form of Virtue, and with certain virtues associated with particular deities, the gods transcend virtue in all ways. We might also argue for a scale of vice. Vice, however, is more connected with evil than the good inherent to the virtues. Evil, as we will see in the next chapter, has no existence of its own, and therefore has no place upon which to rest a scale.

---

[139] O'Meara, "Patterns," 85.
[140] O'Meara, *Platonopolis*, 32.
[141] O'Meara, "Patterns," 86.

Chapter Five

On Evil

As complex as the subject of Virtue and the virtues is, evil is even more difficult. The crux of the problem is explaining how evil can exist when everything that exists comes, ultimately, from the Good, which has no evil within it. In other words, what is the Platonic approach to the "problem of evil"? For Iamblichus, the problem is worse than this, as not only is the Good all good, but so are the gods, the archangels and angels, and at the very least the Demiurges. The source of reality and the creating gods are good, want good for everything else, and are perfect. So from where does evil come? All Neoplatonists admit to the existence of evil, but how does it fit into this scheme?

Plotinus and Absolute Evil

Plotinus, possibly due to his contact with the Sethian Gnostics, and the influence of the Middle Platonist Numenius, says matter is evil. In *Ennead* I.8, Plotinus develops an elaborate rational for this conclusion. Having posited the existence of the Good as that which is not only the source of all, but that which is beyond everything which it emanates, Plotinus admits evil cannot have existence or being in the formal sense of the word. We speak of the existence of evil only as an accident of language, not as a true description of evil. Instead, evil's nature is the opposite of existence; it is non-Being, a mere image of Being, if even that.[142]

Just as we may differentiate between that which has Being and the source of that Being, we must also differentiate between that which participates evil and the source of evil, what Plotinus calls "absolute evil." Absolute evil is the very opposite of the Good. For Plotinus, despite his defense of the Demiurge, the shaper of the material world, and the cosmos as not being evil, matter is evil. *Ennead* I.8 says matter contains untrue form, that it is lifeless, a hindrance to the proper functioning of the soul, always changing, an absolute lacking that has no part in the Good.[143]

Plotinus' description of evil is, unfortunately, more powerful than his argument. Although Plotinus relies heavily on the *Phaedo* and *Phaedrus*, which

---

[142] *Enn*, I.8.2-3, 57-8.
[143] *Ibid.*, I.8.4-5, 59-60.

represent matter and the soul's descent into matter negatively, his argument ignores the Demiurge's role in the *Timaeus*.[144] For a general argument about the nature of evil and its relationship to matter this may not be a big deal, but for a Platonist's argument about the same, it is of enormous consequence.

Iamblichus and the Reconciliation of Matter

Unfortunately, whatever Iamblichus wrote on this subject, such as in his *On the Virtues*, is largely lost. The few complete works we have of his are not dedicated to the subject of virtue, or evil, and, along with the fragments of Iamblichus' Platonic commentaries, offer only a little on the subject. What seems clear, given Iamblichus' relatively positive view of incarnation and matter, is that he did not equate matter with evil. Or, at least he did not do so in the same manner, or to the same degree, as Plotinus.

In the *Timaeus*, the Demiurge, *Demiurgos*, or "Craftsman," creates the world of generation because the Demiurge itself is good, *"and the good can never have any jealousy of anything. And being free from jealousy, he desired that all things should be as like himself as they could be."*[145] Which is to say "good." However, the phrase "as they could be" is important. Late Platonic metaphysics is emanatory, and each level of emanation is ontologically less, has less Being, than that from which it proceeds. Although matter cannot be absolute evil, as it must participate the Good through the Demiurge, it is at the bottom of the chain of being and therefore matter's capacity to hold the influences of the Good is significantly less than everything preceding it.

There is, however, another important implication in this passage from the *Timaeus*. Iamblichus tells us the presence of higher powers extends to the lowest levels, with the influence of the immaterial levels being *"present immaterially to the material."*[146] If this is case, matter cannot be the ultimate source of evil, Plotinus' "absolute evil." However, matter isn't exactly good, either. As the farthest removed from the Good, even though it participates the Good to some extent, that extent is not very great. Matter may not be evil, but, when it comes to the anagogic progress of the soul, it also isn't good.

The reason for this is the nature of matter. Iamblichus uses Aristotle's word for matter, *hylē*, which is the "stuff of matter," as it were. Matter and the cosmos are under the direction of the Demiurge, the creative god. The cosmos, both the physical and immaterial levels, are penetrated by the Demiurge's, and the gods', thoughts or "reason-principles," *logoi*. These *logoi* inform the *hylē*, a receptive substance, and direct it toward shape. *Hylē* itself is matter, but not form or shape, but rather matter *qua* matter. Only once matter receives the *logoi* does it take shape

---

144 *Tim.* 36d-37a, 41a-46c.

145 *Tim.* 30a.

146 DM V.23, 267. C.f. DM VIII.3, 313.

and form and so relate to matter as it is normally understood. *Logoi* are lower manifestations of higher, causal principles, such as the Forms. More poetically, given the alternative translation of *logos* as "word," we can say the Demiurge speaks the world into its form, or perhaps is continuously singing it into existence.

The effect of matter on anything surrounded by it is powerful and potentially harmful. Not everything is affected by matter in this way. The gods, even those labeled "material" and "sub-lunar" are above the influence of matter. Entities with less Being, especially those whose activities primarily take place in the material world, such as some daimons, and of course humans, are not so fortunate. Around such beings matter can accumulate, forming a kind of shell around the being's "pneumatic vehicle," or interface between the spiritual and physical levels.[147]

Still, matter itself is not evil. The effect matter has on certain kinds of spiritual beings cause evil. The accretion of *hylē* around the spiritual vehicles of human souls, and some daimons, makes it difficult for the emanating power of ontologically prior beings to penetrate the vehicle. This, in turn, makes it difficult for such beings to participate the Good, the ultimate source of Being, and its envoys, the Demiurges, gods, angels, and the rest of the greater kinds of spiritual beings. Due to this, such afflicted entities deviate from their essence. Going astray like this produces evil.

Proclus on Evil, or Why Plotinus is Wrong

Proclus' view of evil clearly reflects Iamblichus'. However, where there is little remaining of Iamblichus' thoughts on ethics and evil, an entire treatise of Proclus' on the subject survives, entitled *On the Existence of Evil.* Like Plotinus, Proclus sees evil as a lacking, a negative, describing it as a "parasitical existence,"[148] and having no existence of its own.

In his description of evil, Proclus first says evil, like good, has two forms: pure and unmixed, and impure mixed. Pure good, or the Good, is an absolute, ontological reality for all Platonists, and Proclus does not deviate from this. Mixed good is ultimately the same as mixed evil, Being mixed with privation. However, absolute non-Being is impossible:

> *"And non-being itself, too[, is twofold] . . . that which absolutely does not exist – it is beyond the lowest nature whose being is accidental – as it is unable to exist either in itself or even accidentally, for that which does not exist at all does not in some respect exist, and in another not. . . . what absolutely does not exist and has no share whatever in being has absolutely no being."*[149]

[147] See chapter eighteen.

[148] Chlup, "Proclus'," 28.

[149] Proclus, *Evil*, 8.20-9.4.

Just as absolute Good is beyond Being, absolute evil is beyond non-Being,[150] and is not. This means entities, including people, we might describe as "evil" are, at worst, mixtures of good and evil, existing because of the good that is the source of their Being.[151]

Evil, then, is a privation, to varying degrees, of good. But what is the cause of evil? The cause of evil is the upsetting of the proper ordering of the parts of a whole. As such, only certain kinds of beings can engage in evil. Intelligible beings, for instance, which are perfectly ordered above the divine Intellect, do not have this problem, nor do universals, such as gods. Only particulars, such as particular souls or bodies, can participate evil, such as when wisdom fails to properly order the parts of the soul.[152]

Proclus sees three kinds of evil: evils of the rational soul, of the irrational soul, and evils of the body. Of evils of the soul, there are two kinds: the evil described as "disease" and the evil called "foulness."[153] "Disease" of the soul is caused by disorder within the soul and a failure of the soul to live a life of reason. Foulness is described as "'ignorance' and privation of intellect."[154] In either case, the soul fails to follow after that which is ontologically superior. In the case of disease, this is an internal failure: the rational part follows the irrational rather than the other way around. In the case of foulness, the soul fails to participate the divine Intellect, from which the Whole Soul and, ultimately, individual human souls emanate.[155] Evil in the body occurs when the body does not follow the dictates of nature.

Importantly, evil is not found in any of the parts of the soul, or even in bodies. If it was, evil would have a kind of positive existence. Instead, evil is found only in the relationships between the parts of the soul or between bodies and universal nature. Evil "exists" not within the things themselves, but within the processes connecting those things. More specifically, evil is found only when there is a failure of relationship within those processes.

The way to cure a being of its evil has already been intimated, both in the previous and present chapters. Foremost, evil is cured through the proper relationships between ontologically inferior and superior beings. Bodies, for instance, are subordinate to nature and the World Soul and should maintain a proper relationship with the natural world. Disease takes root when this fails to occur, and this is the evil of the body, which can lead to its destruction. For souls, the proper internal relationship is between its parts, and between a soul and Intellect. The body is maintained through an understanding of its nature as part of

---

150 *Ibid.*, 9.5-14.

151 This idea is more fully developed by our Dionysius, see below.

152 Chlup, "Prolcus'," 28-9.

153 C.f., *Soph*, 228E-230E.

154 Proclus, *Evil*, 56.5-7.

155 *Ibid.*, 55.5-15.

the natural world, and is protected through the proper use of medical arts, exercise, etc. As we saw in chapter four, the correct associations of the soul are maintained through the virtue of wisdom.

Dionysius on Why Proclus and Iamblichus are Right

Pseudo-Dionysius devotes nearly half of the fourth chapter of *The Divine Names* to the topic of evil.[156] This part of the work, based largely on Proclus' *On the Existence of Evil*, offers some areas of deep insight and is worth examining.

Dionysius begins by taking up the problem of evil demons. If everything comes from the Good and has its source of Being in the Good,[157] how is it that *"demons whose origins lie wholly in the Good are themselves not shaped like goodness? . . . What is it that made them evil? What in fact is evil?"*[158] At first this may appear somewhat far removed from pagan Neoplatonism. There are, after all, no demons or fallen angels in the system of Iamblichus and the later Neoplatonists. However, Iamblichus posits that some daimons, working closely with the physical realm, are capable of becoming evil, even though this is not their initial state. Also, although human souls are also not naturally evil, they can incline towards the physical realm where evil occurs. Dionysius affirms the Platonic idea that evil cannot come from the Good. If evil comes from the Good then it participates the Good and is not fully evil.[159] Instead, following Proclus, he says that there is no absolute evil, only mixed good and evil[160]

From where does evil come? Dionysius has already affirmed it cannot come from God, and goes on to say it does not *"inhere in beings"*[161] because all beings come from God, and if they exist at all, they are participating the Good. Being of the Good, they cannot be the source of evil. An extreme example of this are devils. Certainly devils are evil, but they are not evil by nature. Such a thing is impossible because devils exist, have Being, and therefore must come from the Good. Yet the Good cannot create evil. The answer to this riddle is that devils fall from their participation of the Good. However they do not do so completely, otherwise they would cease to be. In terms of Christian thought, this presents a new and radical understanding of demons. The implication, which Dionysius spells out in full, is that devils are not evil by nature and their evil is also impermanent, as only God is eternal.[162] We may use this same principle to understand how some daimons may become evil and then be purified.

---

[156] DN IV.18-35.

[157] This reflects standard Platonic metaphysics, and is established by Dionysius in the first half of the chapter.

[158] DN IV.18.716A.

[159] DN IV.19.716B-C.

[160] DN IV.19.716C.

[161] DN IV.21.721C.

[162] DN IV.23.725A-B.

The same holds true for humans. Certainly, humans can engage in evil activities, but does that make those humans evil? Not in the capital E "Evil" sense of the term, no. A person may lack in some element of the Good, abandoning for some time, even their entire life, one or more of the virtues. But evil, as evil, is not in that human. Nor is it in irrational animals, nor even part of nature, nor in our bodies. Furthermore, contra Plotinus, bodies are not the cause of evil, neither is matter.[163] None of these things are evil or the source of evil, because they all have existence and therefore come from the Good, which has no part in evil.

So where is the evil? There is no evil *qua* evil. Evil is a lacking of the Good. To whatever extent something fails to participate the Good, that is its evil. In this way, anything that is capable of not participating the Good to some degree is capable of evil.[164] This aptly reflects the *New Testament's* understanding of sin as *hamartia.* In Greek tragedies, *hamartia* represents an action performed thinking the results will be for the better and which turn out for the worst. In the *New Testament*, *hamartia* often means to miss the mark. In both cases the word suggests having fallen away from our soul's purpose and in so doing acting inappropriately, even when our intentions may be good.

So what is evil? Evil, as Dionysius puts it, is an accident, its source lying outside of itself.[165] As a lacking in the Good, evil activities occur when we try to do what seems right and virtuous, but is in fact not. Evil occurs when we misunderstand the Good and attempt to apply our faulty knowledge. This is true even for activities that seem purposefully evil. A person may mistake wealth for what is Good and therefore attempt to amass wealth at any cost. Even at the most basic level, an apparently evil being, such as a demon, still desires the Good in as much as it desires existence, and will do whatever is necessary to maintain that existence.

Like Proclus, Dionysius sees specific kinds of lacking in relation to the evils of particular beings. For spiritual entities, such as devils, and presumably daimons, *"evil is contrary to the good-like mind."*[166] For human souls, evil is being *"contrary to reason."*[167] For the body, evil *"is to be contrary to nature."*[168] So, in Dionysius, we find a reflection of Proclus' understanding of evil, which itself may have its origin in Iamblichus. But Dionysius goes beyond by helping us understand evil in practice.

---

[163] DN IV.25-28.729B

[164] DN IV.20.720D-721A.

[165] DN IV.32.732C.

[166] DN IV.32.733A.

[167] *Ibid.*

[168] *Ibid.* Both this and the evil of the soul echo Proclus perfectly.

Exercises: Contemplating Evil

At first it may seem that a spiritual exercise on evil is both oxymoronic and either dangerous or impossible. What can a spiritual exercise have to do with evil? Evil has no real existence, how can there be an exercise on a not-thing? Negative exercises are actually an important feature of Dionysian spiritual practice. There is a difference, however, between this and that. Dionysian apophatic theology focuses on God as God exists before or beyond Being. The negative we are exploring is the very opposite of this. This evil is not simply at the terminal end of the chain of being, but not a link on the chain at all.

Also, the point of this exercise is not, unlike the other exercises, to improve a quality in ourselves. Instead, it is to understand a lack of quality within ourselves. All but the loftiest of sages allow the irrational parts of themselves to sometimes rule the rational. We also want to better understand the nature of evil so as to better recognize it in ourselves. To these ends, here is a spiritual exercise concerning the evils in which we engage.

This exercise focuses on understanding evil and takes the form of a meditation, similar to the *Meditations* of the Stoic emperor Marcus Aurelius. These meditations are somewhat similar to *lectio divina*, but also have qualities similar to guided meditation. For example, the Roman Stoic, Seneca the Younger, writes: *"Place before your mind's eye the vast spread of time's abyss and embrace the universe; and then compare what we call human life with infinity . . . ."*[169] The purpose of these meditations is to mentally expose you to a concept, experiencing it through the imagination under the direction of the intellect. For Iamblichus, imagination is a powerful tool and connected to the divine realm.[170] The following contemplation is partially derived from Proclus' *On the Existence of Evil*[171] and draws upon imagery from the allegory of the chariot from Plato's *Phaedrus*.[172]

As you engage in this meditation, it is important to be brutally honest with yourself. This is not a time to hide our imperfections. Instead, it is time to discover as many of them as possible. Only through this kind of honesty can we come to understand ourselves as we truly are, and through this become better people. As with the other contemplations, take some time to quiet your mind before proceeding.

Place before your mind's eye, so far as possible, a realm existing in the beatitude of perfection, where no suffering or evil exists. Take time for yourself to develop this image, leaving out no detail of what perfection might entail. Find yourself grasping for this realm, following luminous spheres of perfection in an eternal orbit. Now examine yourself closely and carefully. You will find your

---

169 Quoted in Hadot, *Philosophy*, 182.
170 DM II.14, 155.
171 23-24.
172 246a-254e.

illumination flawed in comparison to that which leads you. Do you act in perfect wisdom at all times, allowing only the rational to rule the irrational? Do you fear what need not be feared? Are you temperate in all considerations and just in all actions? For every deficiency you find a corresponding deficiency in your brilliance and as your illumination grows dimmer so, too, do you fall from your orbit, crashing into yourself as you stand upon the ground in a world lacking all that you do.

The point of this exercise is not to focus on the crash, your soul's coming into incarnation due to its imperfections. The point is to understand, as intimately as possible, the reason for those imperfections. Your plummeting into generation occurred outside of time, there is no reason to rush from your faults to your incarnation. A secondary meditation can be developed wherein you explore a world filled with your deficiencies and the moral effects such a world has upon its occupants.

Chapter Six

Political Philosophy

A chapter on politics in a book on theurgy may seem out of place. This is at least partially due to the modern conception of politics and politicians, which has taken on a negative connotation. It is also partially due to Plotinus, who is sometimes described at Plato without politics,[173] and his influence on our understanding of Neoplatonism. To the Platonic philosopher, however, the heart of politics, political philosophy, is something far different from modern conceptions, and may be seen as one of the highest points of Platonic philosophy.

As the name implies, the focus of political philosophy is the state and its citizens, the *polis*. Plato writes extensively on the subject of the perfect city-state and its inhabitants, as well as lesser forms of governance, in the *Republic* and *Laws*, as well as in some of his letters. Together, these texts present three levels of political reform. The first level is that of moral reform on the level of the political virtues discussed in chapter four. The second level is derived from the *Laws*, which differentiates between three different forms of constitution. These are a city wherein all property and family are held in common, a city where it is understood common property is the best way but allows private property and family units, and a lower city where there is private property and family units, which is thought to be an adequate form of governance given the circumstances of a non-philosophical citizenship. The best form of governance, which Plato mythologizes as having originated from the titan Kronos during the golden age of humanity,[174] is identified with the perfect city-state of the *Republic*, and is described as a *"city of gods or of children of the gods"*, placing it outside the grasp of normal humans.[175]

Plato's connecting of the ideal city-state, ruled by divine daimons rather than human kings or even philosophers[176] to the titan Kronos is no accident. In the *Cratylus*, Socrates gives the etymology for Kronos as coming from a word meaning pure, *koros*, and the word for mind, *nous*.[177] Kronos, the son of Ouranos, the heavens, and the father of Zeus, is the pure mind, the divine intellect, or absolute

173 O'Meara, *Platonopolis*, 4.

174 *Laws* 713c-714a.

175 *Laws* 739d. C.f. O'Meara, *Platonopolis*, 92.

176 See *Rep* V.473d.

177 *Crat.* 396b.

reason. Whether taken literally or allegorically, this is the model for Platonic politics: political philosophy is ruled by reason above all else. From the perspective of the Neoplatonists, the perfect city-state of the *Laws*, and subsequently the *Republic*, is perfect not only because it is ruled by reason, but because in doing so it is based on a divine model, and is therefore a reflection of Demiurgic principles.[178]

What is political philosophy, and why, given Platonism's tendency towards reason and intellect over the passions, will any Platonist take an interest in a political life?[179] Following Dominic J. O'Meara's insightful consideration of the subject,[180] we must look not at modern notions of politics but at ones with which the Platonists are familiar. In Aristotle's *Nicomachean Ethics* we find the student of politics studying *"virtue above all things"*,[181] which includes what is good for both body and soul and so must include a study of not only the body but the soul.[182] Such a study goes beyond the virtues, including other sciences such as strategy, economics and rhetoric, including the purpose or goal of those studies within its own. This ultimate goal, *telos*, is the good, the chief good, for humanity.[183] Political philosophy is therefore the study of the means and sciences of politics towards the end of achieving not only the chief human good, but that good for everyone within the politician's sphere of influence.[184]

As do many answers in philosophy, this leads us to more questions. Here, the primary question is "what is the chief human good?" Socrates provides the answer to this in the *Theaetetus*: *"becoming like the divine so far as we can."*[185] This end is the ultimate purpose behind Neoplatonic practice: philosophical, religious and theurgic. Only the divinized human can fully participate in the divine work of the universal organizing principle called Nous, the divine Intellect and noeric Demiurge. That this is the chief human good has a profound effect on political philosophy. Rather than erroneously viewing politics as a *"treatment of irreducible disagreements and conflicts over 'goals and policies' within a community,"*[186] politics is a means towards the divinization of not just a single human, but the finer and *"godlike"*[187] goal of achieving the divinization of humanity.[188]

---

178 Shaw, *Theurgy*, 8-9.
179 For examples of the later, see *Apology*, 31d-32a and *Rep.*, 496c-e.
180 *Platonopolis*, 7.
181 *Nich.*, I.13, 950.
182 *Ibid.*
183 *Ibid.*, I.2, 936.
184 C.f. O'Meara, *Platonopolis*, 7. Traditionally the city-state or nation, though this might now be applied to a global community.
185 *Theat*, 176b.
186 O'Meara, *Platonopolis*, 7
187 *Nich.* I.2, 936.
188 C.f. L6, fr. 1.

The Role of the Philosopher

Iamblichus, and various members of his school, are not afraid to hold political opinions, or even political office. Iamblichus' top student, Sopater, becomes a member of Emperor Constantine's court.[189] Iamblichus' student Eustathius works at an embassy to the Persian king Sapor.[190] Iamblichus writes on the subject as well. For instance, in a letter to Dyscolius, possibly the governor of Syria, Iamblichus expounds at length on the qualities of a ruler, including amongst them high-mindedness and generosity.[191] However, the question remains: What is the role of the philosopher in politics?

To answer this we must return to Plato's *Republic* and the allegory of the cave. I introduced you to many elements of this in the second contemplation on wisdom in chapter four. In the allegory, the soul is freed from its bonds and is able to experience the divine realm. However, this experience is not the end of the individual's journey. Rather than basking in noetic quiescence, the soul willingly returns to the cave to free others. This Bodhisattva-like responsibility belongs to the philosopher and might be seen as a prelude to, or reflection of, the work of the theurgic sage.[192]

The role of love in the philosopher's return to the cave[193] is highlighted in the *Symposium* and the writing of Hierocles, an important Alexandrian Neoplatonist. In his work *On Providence*, Hierocles discusses the distinction between philosopher and lover. Whereas the philosopher engages in a life of pure contemplation, the lover works to imitate the acts of the divine, acting through philosophy to bring benevolence to the world. The philosopher may represent the ascent of the soul, but the lover is the soul engaged in demiurgy, divine behaviour in the physical and spiritual worlds.[194]

It is the lover, characterized by philanthropy, an important quality of justice, who becomes the philosopher-king, or queen, of the *Republic*. From this perspective, the philosopher above all other humans is most fit to rule. Through the study, and living, of the virtues, the philosopher's love of wisdom expands to encompass a desire for their own well-being and for those around them. The study and life of philosophy, in time, becomes identical to the goals of political philosophy: the achieving of the chief good of humanity. After all, how can a

---

189 Albeit with, ultimately, fatal consequences.
190 O'Meara, "*Republic*," 202.
191 L6, fr. 2. See also L1, *On Ruling*
192 This reading of the *Republic* relies on explanations also given in the *Symposium* and *Timaeus*, wherein the philosopher returns to the cave, or civilization, due to love of wisdom and an imitation of the goodness of the Demiurge. See O'Meara, *Platonopolis*, 73.
193 The cave may here be seen not only as a metaphor for the physical world, but also as civilization away from the contemplating work of philosophy and the academy.
194 O'Meara, *Platonopolis*, 76-7.

virtuous person live in the greatest happiness while knowing others suffer? The teachings of the Platonists suggest they cannot.

But what does it mean to be a philosopher-king or queen? It seems clear that at some point the idea is understood literally. Plotinus approaches Emperor Gallienus with the aim of building a *"city of philosophers"* in Campania,[195] possibly to be based on the *Republic* or *Laws*. Also, as we've seen, some Neoplatonists enter into politics, to varying degrees of success. While entering into governmental office with Platonist attitudes is perhaps a worthy endeavour, we are in no way required to take the idea of the philosopher-king or queen literally. Instead, we may take from this idea the importance of the philosopher living a life amongst people, rather than a sequestered life of contemplation and study. While quiet study and contemplation are an integral part of philosophical education, they are not enough. They are means, not ends. The end is human happiness. Read that again: human happiness. This is not merely the happiness of the individual, of the philosopher, but the happiness of humanity itself. As Hierocles writes, this requires love as well as philosophy. In this we find that philosophy and political philosophy are ultimately the same.

Exercise: Contemplation on Leadership

The role of the philosopher in Neoplatonism is not only that of a thinker, but also that of a leader. While the later Platonists think on grand scales, and at least one Roman emperor thinks of himself in terms of Plato's *Laws*, it is unlikely that many of us will ever become emperors or their modern political equivalents. It is equally unlikely that many of us will be in positions where we can influence such people. This does not mean we never take on leadership roles or cannot make a difference in the lives of others. This means cultivating the qualities of a leader.

Iamblichus leaves two letters on ruling, of which only fragments remain. I mentioned one of these letters, written to the Syrian governor Dyscolius, in which Iamblichus describes the qualities of a ruler as including high-mindedness and generosity, to which we can add benevolence. A letter on the same subject to an Agrippa,[196] possibly, like Dyscolius, a Syrian official,[197] also expounds on leadership qualities.

The most beloved form of leadership is one that tempers *"the solemnity and austerity of rule"* with *"nobility of character and sympathy for one's fellow human beings."*[198] A ruler should also be insightful and free from, and immune to, corruption of any sort. Only in this manner is it possible to apply the law in all cases. However, the application of the law should not be cold and calculated. Iamblichus' letter

---

[195] Porphyry, *Life*, cxi-cxii.

[196] L1.

[197] Dillon and Polleichtner, *Letters*, 59.

[198] L1, fr. 1.

suggests following the law should be guided by the beauties of the virtues.[199] Without wisdom, courage, temperance and justice, the law is a dead and lifeless thing.

The basic qualities of a ruler or leader are as follows: virtue, insight, high-mindedness, benevolence, generosity, and incorruptibility. These are the qualities of a leader, but also the qualities of a philosopher. As such, these are also the qualities necessary to cultivate before engaging in the cathartic and anagogic practices of theurgy. Also, remember that Platonists believe the perfect city is modeled after the divine. This means the ruler is likewise acting upon a divine model. This hexad of qualities reflects divinely derived attributes, and is a beginning step towards divine imitation.

Some of these, such as the cardinal virtues, have already been discussed. If you have stopped engaging in the contemplations on the virtues, now is a good time to revisit them. Instead of contemplating the other qualities as you have the virtues, take some time for self-assessment. Think about each of them in turn. How do they exist in your life and how do you live by them? Are you generous when you can? Do you easily turn your back on your claimed principles? Under what circumstances might you do so and what does this mean for you and your principles?

Recall that evil is an absence of good, or the Good. The above qualities ultimately stem from the Good and the Form of Beauty.[200] Where one lacks in these there is an absence of that Form. This is not to say that if you lack any of these qualities in any way you are evil. Almost everything beneath the highest divine levels is missing some element of these qualities. It does mean, however, it is important to be aware of the qualities we have and in what ways we are deficient in them.

Individual vs. Communal Happiness

In the above discussion of the role of the philosopher in politics, it seems the philosopher must subordinate their happiness, and possibly well-being, for the sake of the whole. The *Theatetus*, in describing the experiences of the *"leaders in philosophy"* when engaged in the generative world, makes them quite miserable, misunderstanding what common people understand with ease.[201] If this is the philosopher's fate when amongst what Plato calls the great herd of humanity, why descend?

One answer is found in the writings of the Neoplatonist, senator, and eventual praetorian prefect of Italy, Macrobius. According to Macrobius, this question

---

[199] L1, fr. 2.

[200] See chapter seven.

[201] *Theat.* 174b-175b.

arises from a misunderstanding of the relationship between the philosopher-ruler and the virtues. This happens especially when we understand the virtues as being only purificatory in nature. If virtues lead to happiness, and virtues are purificatory, that is to say lead from the physical to divine or intellectual realms, how can any philosopher-ruler be happy when focusing on their duties to their fellow humans? But there is more than one rung to the ladder of virtues. A ruler also must engage in the lower, political virtues. If the philosopher-ruler can engage in the virtues at this level, they will find happiness.[202]

This answer is somewhat problematic. While the political virtues may bring some kind of happiness, they are lower on the scale than the purificatory virtues. At best, such happiness is of a lower level than those of higher forms of virtue. The average person may be content with a kind of political happiness. But we are not discussing the average person; we're talking about the philosopher-ruler. Happiness at the lower level is, to the Platonic philosopher, a mere shadow of the happiness found at the higher levels of virtue. [203]

Perhaps the answer is found with Plotinus. In the last chapter of *"On True Happiness,"* in *Enneads* I.4, Plotinus places true happiness above mere welfare or prosperity.[204] For Plotinus, true happiness cannot be found in existence or life alone, but in *"Reason and Authentic Intellection,"* which is the perfect life of a human being, of which *"there exists no single human being that does not either potentially or effectively possess this thing which we hold to constitute happiness."*[205] A philosopher-ruler, the Plotinian Sage, operating at the level of theoretical or paradigmatic virtue, even when engaged in the physical realm, is always happy. Nothing on a lower level, such as the suffering of the body, can truly affect such a person.[206] And, while *"the Sage would like to see all men prosperous and no evil befalling anyone; but though it prove otherwise, he is still content."*[207]

This is all well and good, but Plotinian Sages are few and far between and, typically, Iamblichean philosophy disagrees with most of Plotinus' notions concerning the undescended soul, which the above passages reflect. As expected, Iamblichus repudiates the untouchable Plotinian Sage. Instead of the wellbeing of the philosopher-ruler's subjects being, ultimately, irrelevant to the ruler's happiness, quite the opposite is true: *"[f]or this . . . is the aim (telos) of a good ruler, to cause his subjects to flourish."*[208] The connection between the ruler and the ruled is extraordinarily close, because *"the common good is not to be separated from the individual*

202 O'Meara, *Platonopolis*, 81.
203 According to O'Meara, they do not even bring happiness, but are merely a prerequisite for the happiness attained at the purificatory level.
204 *Enn*, I.1.
205 *Enn*, I.4.4.
206 *Enn*. I.4.5. c.f. O'Meara, *Platonopolis*, 82.
207 *Enn*, I.11.
208 L6, fr. 1.

good; . . . the individual advantage is subsumed within that of the whole, and the particular is preserved in the universal.'[209] As in a marriage one must pay attention to the *"common interests of both'*[210] parties, in this case the philosopher-ruler and those whom she or he governs.

We may conclude from the above that the good of the ruler is not subordinate to the good or happiness of their subjects. Instead, the happiness of the ruler and the ruled are intrinsically linked. We have established the *telos* of political philosophy as, in the words of Plato, *"becoming like the divine, so far as possible."* Successful engagement in political philosophy, which has the same *telos* as all philosophy, means divinization cannot be limited to the Plotinian Sage but must extend to everyone, so far as possible. Divinization means participating in universal orders. It is, however, *"impossible to partake as an individual of the universal orders, but only in communion with the divine choir of those who, with minds united, experience a common uplift.'*[211] The divinization of one, such as the philosopher-ruler, depends on the divinization of those they govern.

There is another ramification to this idea, related to communal and theurgic worship. If the individual is to attain to universal consciousness, it is not done alone. The apex of all universal orders is a monad embracing multiplicity. The individual is part of a multiplicity, and only through unity with others can any person return to the monad from which they originate. Political philosophy is the apex of Platonic dialectic, engaging in the bringing together of many into a single whole.

---

209 *Ibid.*

210 L19.

211 *In Phileb.* fr. 6.

Chapter Seven

Beauty

We will conclude this first section by discussing two subjects with which we could very well have begun: beauty and love. These are frequently tied together in the dialogues as the basis of all philosophy. As we will see, they are also important, driving theological and theurgic factors.

What, then, is beauty? This is a question Socrates asks people while wondering around Athens. He never receives a reply he likes. The Greek word usually translated as "beautiful" is *kalon*. As is often the case with translation, "beautiful" and "*kalon*" do not mean exactly the same thing. While there are times in the dialogues where there is congruence between the words, such as in the description of a grassy, tree-shaded resting place,[212] this is not always the case. Also, Plato is more likely to describe a work of art or the beauty of a face as *kalon* than nature.[213]

In other places, translating *kalon* as "beautiful" seems out of place to modern aesthetics. Sometimes *kalon* has the connotation of "noble" or "admirable." In the *Symposium*,[214] wisdom is described as *kalon*, giving the word an ethical connotation different from conceptions of physical beauty. Sometimes the word "fine" is used to translate *kalon* instead of "beautiful,"[215] but so is "loveliest"[216] and "delightful,"[217] which can serve to muddy the waters as much as purify them. Instead of approaching the word philologically, let us examine it philosophically instead.

Two Views of Beauty: Form and Symmetry

In the course of the dialogues, Plato forms two apparently conflicting theories of beauty. In the *Greater Hippias*, or *Hippias Major*, Plato develops the idea of beauty as an intelligible Form. The Forms are an integral part of Platonic metaphysics, representing elements of idealized, archetypal, or divine reality. For

---

212 *Phad.*, 230b.
213 Pappas, "Aesthetics," Beauty.
214 *Symp.*, 204b.
215 Pappas, "Aesthetics," Beauty.
216 *Symp.*, 204b, Michael Joyce, trans.
217 *Phad.*, 230b, R. Hackforth, trans.

instance, there is a Form of Justice and Wisdom, of which human justice and wisdom are but mere images. Of the Forms, however, the Form of Beauty holds a unique place.

As a Form, Beauty must be understood as existing outside of any beautiful thing. Instead, everything that has beauty, which is, to some degree, everything, participates the Form of Beauty. This provides an answer to Socrates' question to Hippias, how does he know what things are beautiful and what are ugly.[218] Certainly, if it is through Justice one is just, through Wisdom one is wise, then it must be through Beauty that something is beautiful.[219] These Forms are, for Plato, *"really existent things"*[220] rather than metaphorical or psychological constructs.

But the Form of Beauty is not exactly like other Forms. The Forms are found on the noeric or intellective level of being, below the intelligible realm, and are frequently the products of the gods. But the *Symposium* describes wisdom, which is itself the product of a Form, as beautiful. This implies that Beauty is somehow greater than Wisdom. In more technical language, Beauty is ontologically prior to, or comes into being before, Wisdom. If this were not so, Wisdom would have no need to participate in Beauty as it apparently does, nor would we describe wisdom as beautiful, as wisdom would be beyond beauty, or at the very least co-equal but still distinct. The reason Beauty is superior is due to its connection to the Good, one of the ways Platonists understand God. This connection is found in the nature of beautiful things also being beneficial or good:

Socrates: *So we reach the conclusion that beautiful bodies and beautiful rules of life, and wisdom, and all the things we mentioned just now, are beautiful because they are beneficial?*

Hippias: *Evidently.*[221]

The *"things we just mentioned"* are *"the powerful and the useful."*[222] Are the powerful and the useful beautiful? Yes, or at least they can be, but they are not, in and of themselves, beautiful. Only when they are also good or beneficial are they beautiful. Because Beauty is connected to the Good, which in its lowest extreme is found at the height of the noetic realm, Beauty is superior to all other Forms.

Although the cause of beauty is the Form of Beauty, this is not Plato's only definition. In the *Philebus*, Plato has Socrates give a somewhat unusual description of beauty:

> *The beauty of figures which I am now trying to indicate is not what most people would understand as such, not the beauty of a living creature or a picture; what I mean, what the argument points to, is something straight, or round, and the surfaces and solids which a lathe, or a carpenter's rule and square, produces from the straight and the round. . . .*

---

[218] *GH*, 286d.
[219] *Ibid.*, 287c.
[220] *Ibid.*, c.f. 287d.
[221] *Ibid.*, 296e.
[222] *Ibid.*, 296d.

Things like that, I maintain, are beautiful not, like most things, in a relative sense; they are always beautiful in their very nature, and they carry pleasures peculiar to themselves which are quite unlike the pleasures of scratching. And there are colours too which have this characteristic.[223]

Socrates' examples of beautiful things includes plane figures, possibly the Platonic solids representing the four elements of fire, air, water, earth, and the World Soul, all of which have a high level of symmetry.[224] The round object a lathe produces suggests a cylinder and cylindrical symmetry. This is reflected in the *Greater Hippias*, where Socrates describes beauty as that which is "*appropriate.*"[225]

How is appropriateness related to symmetry? This is an element common to Hellenic aesthetics, and is built into the language. There are several Greek words used to describe the world. The most common, *kosmos*, has the meaning of arrangement and is the word used for world, realm or universe, suggesting the universe has a particular arrangement to it. The *kosmos* is ordered, especially in Neoplatonism, through *logoi*. *Logos* has several meanings, including "word," "argument," "reason," "intelligence," and "proportion." These, especially the last, suggest a kind of symmetry or harmony, *harmonia*. *Harmonia* comes from a root word meaning "to join," which in this case suggests a proportional and intelligent joining of parts into an appropriately arranged whole, the *kosmos*.[226] The use of proportion and harmony are also found, in detail, in the omni-benevolent Demiurge's creation.[227] Although the *Greater Hippias* uses *prepei*, "is appropriate," and *to prepon*, "what is appropriate," rather than *harmonia*, this still allows us to understand how Socrates and Hippias entertain an idea of beauty as appropriate.[228]

The question remains, if Beauty is a Form, how can beauty be symmetry or proportion? This question reflects the apparent contradiction in these two assertions. A Form does not depend on anything physical for its existence. We can say the Form of Chair exists regardless as to whether or not there are, have been, or ever will be any physical chairs. A chair is simply a particular, and imperfect, image of the Form of Chair. Proportion or symmetry, however, typically requires physical things. The left side of something may be symmetrical with its right side. A group of objects may be placed together in such a way as their proportions are beautiful.

---

223 *Phil.*, 51c-d.

224 Lloyd., *Symmetry*, 457.

225 *GH*, 290c-d.

226 C.f. Proclus, who *"maintains that every metaphysical entity which has order and symmetry, also comprises the qualities of justice . . . and beauty."* (Terezis and Polychronopoulou, "Beauty," 54.)

227 *Tim.*, 30a-53e.

228 Sider, *Early*, 469.

Recalling that Plato is a Pythagorean, or that he is at least interpreted as such by the later Neoplatonists, this problem is easily resolved. The central feature of Pythagoreanism is its use of numbers, specifically the decad. As noted, Plato's use of geometric figures relates to the five Platonic solids. However, there is a further significance to the use of such figures. By using geometric figures, Plato implicitly connects the ideas of harmony and symmetry inherent in the Platonic solids to numbers, the basis of geometry.[229] According to Iamblichus, there are several kinds of numbers. One of these is "idea numbers," which are identical to the Platonic Forms.[230] The apparent contradiction is now resolved. While symmetry and proportion are properties of physical things, the bases of these are found in the world of Forms.[231] Proportion and harmony, as the essence of what is beautiful, find their origin in the Form of Beauty.

What is Beautiful?

Beauty has its roots in the Form of Beauty, and that which is beautiful is that which has harmony, proportion and symmetry. This does a great deal to help us understand Beauty in its most abstract form, but does not necessarily help us with what is, and is not, beautiful, in the sensible world. Plato discusses the nature of beauty, and what is and is not beauty, in several of the dialogues, including the *Greater Hippias*, the *Symposium* and the *Republic.*

In the *Greater Hippias*, Socrates begins by hailing Hippias as *"beautiful and wise."* This is later contrasted with the physical ugliness of Socrates, especially in the *Symposium.* Yet the *Greater Hippias* sets the foundation for Plato's thoughts on beauty. Certainly this is true for the setting out of Beauty as a Form, when Hippias asks *"You are looking, I think, for a reply ascribing to beauty such a nature that it will never appear ugly to anyone anywhere?"*[232] This is exactly what Socrates wants, and he finds it in the Forms. Hippias, however, understands beauty on the physical level: wealth, health, fame, to reach old age, to have an expensive tomb, and the so forth.[233] This is the kind of physical beauty in which we are now interested, and, importantly, Socrates does not deny these things are beautiful, only that they are not Beauty itself.

In the *Symposium,*[234] Plato's erotic treatise, Socrates relates what he, as a young man, learns from the Mantinean priestess Diotima. While this leads once again to a theory of the Form of Beauty, there is a discussion of the role of poets and

---

[229] In Iamblichus' *On Pythagoreanism*, the study of geometry is placed just beneath the study of arithmetic, the study of numbers and the decad, meaning the study of geometry is dependent on the study of number itself. See O'Meara, *Pythagoras*, 46.
[230] O'Meara, *Pythagoras*, 78.
[231] C.f. Lloyd, "Symmetry," 457.
[232] *GH*, 291d.
[233] *Ibid.*, 291d-e.
[234] *Symp.*, 201c-212b.

artists and their search for beauty. Diotima's *"hierarchy of beauty"* begins with the beauty of bodies, beginning with a particular body before moving on to the beauty within all bodies.[235] This love of the beauty of bodies then becomes expressed as a beautiful verse.[236]

However, although poetry and art is related to beauty in the *Greater Hippias*, it is so almost nowhere else. Instead, the opposite is true. For instance, in the *Republic*, poetry, especially narrative poetry, is banned from the ideal city, as is all mimetic art. This is because such art is deceptive; appearing to be something it is not. Such creations are tertiary, falling beneath the Form employed by the Demiurge and an object based on the Form created by a craftsman. A painting is merely an image of an image. A painting of a chair is not a real chair; it simply looks like a real chair, which is itself based on the Form of Chair.[237] Tragedies and comedies are the same, presenting to the audience not the actual people involved, such as Agamemnon or Achilles, but only surface versions of them, taken out of context and with their natures blown up, acting contrary to reason. Worse, such performances present themselves as being the actual words and activities of real people in such a way that they may be emulated, bringing their irrationality,[238] which is the contrary of philosophy and wisdom, into someone's everyday life. Such things, so far removed from truth,[239] and appealing to the irrational part of one's soul or mind, can contain no real beauty.

This is not to imply these things are ugly. Plato never goes that far, nor can he. While mimetic art may be at a far remove from the pure, good, and beautiful work of the Demiurge,[240] it is still based on something based on a Form. It is clear from people's reaction to beautiful poems, songs, sculptures, and paintings that Beauty is present in these things. At best, Plato can point out the ways in which there is a greater privation of Beauty in such works of art.

From all this we may make at least a tentative statement as to what is beautiful. That which participates the Forms, all of which being under the supervision, if not actually having been created by, the Demiurge, also participate, to some extent, in the Form of Beauty. That is, anything and everything posterior to the Forms has some element of beauty, as do the Forms themselves. The *Timaeus*, however, gives us a clue as to what is the most beautiful. In describing the creation of the physical world, *Timaeus* says the Demiurge, intending *"to make this*

---

235 *Ibid.*, 210a-b.
236 *Ibid.*, 209b-c.
237 *Rep.* 597d-598d.
238 *Ibid.*, 603e-605e.
239 *Ibid.*, 598b.
240 Almost by definition, the works of the Demiurge, or at least what we will later define as the celestial Demiurge, are good because the Demiurge itself is not only good (*Tim.*, 29e) but incapable of evil. As there is a direct connection between the Good and the Form of Beauty, anything good must also contain beauty.

world like the fairest and most perfect of intelligible beings,'[241] creates what the Neoplatonists call the "Essential Living Being"[242] in the likeness of the beings of the intelligible realm. This Essential Living Being, as an image of the beauty of the intelligible realm, and as a direct creation of the Demiurge, is the most beautiful of things, as is everything contained within it, which, according to Iamblichus, is *"all the other living beings.'*[243] With this, we see that living beings are the most beautiful of all things in creation.

Reclaiming Art – It's not Just Pretty, it's Good

Plato's critique of imitative art is fairly damning. For Plato, nothing good can come of such practices and they are banned from the perfect city of the *Republic*. But why is imitative art bad? This is because it plays upon the irrational and appetitive aspects of the soul, strengthening them while weakening the rational part. The various examples given throughout the Platonic dialogues give ample demonstration of this. Poems incite people to emotional outbursts, plays present themselves as repeating the words and actions of heroes and cause people to imitate irrational activities, songs encourage the emotions to take control of rational thought, paintings pretend to be what they are not, and so forth. In every instance the art pretends to be something other than what it is and because of this deception the rational mind is put in abeyance and the irrational comes to the fore.

Yet we find examples of imitation that do not have derision heaped upon them. The carpenter, for example, fails to reproduce the Form of Sofa in the creation of his or her particular sofa. A particular sofa is merely an imitation of the Form of Sofa.[244] It is not the Sofa we're looking for, although it may pretend to be so. The craftperson's eyes are "fixed" on the Form[245] and, through making, or using, such crafts, can be said to have some knowledge or relationship with the Form from which it is derived, which is not true of the imitator, who only knows the surface of a particular and never the universal.[246] What, then, distinguishes the imitator of the Forms from the imitator of the imitator, and why is the former good and the later not?

The answer lies in a combination of the level of remove of the imitation and the subsequent relation with the Forms this allows the imitator. Imitation allowing for no knowledge or experience of the Forms, such as Plato discusses, affects the irrational side of its audience, because it is based solely on the sensible realm.

---

241 *Tim., 30d.*

242 See, for instance, *In Tim.*, fr. 43.

243 *Ibid.*

244 *Rep.*, 596b.

245 *Ibid.*, 596a.

246 *Ibid.,* 601e-602b.

These things contain a beauty, but that beauty is greatly marred by the accretions of the irrational. This sensible beauty, corrupted by irrationality, has a negative effect. While outwardly alluring, the attraction, which begins with our soul's love for the Form of Beauty, and which it hopes to find in physical appearance, is not anagogic but genagogic.

For Plato, all of what we call "fine art" is a form of mimesis, imitation. However, even he allows for some kinds of poetry, such as hymns to the gods or praise poems to heroes.[247] How are these forms of poetry different from other, banned kinds? The answer is that fine art, contra Plato, is not the product of mimesis but of phantasia, imagination, an inference drawn by the Sophist Philostratus.[248] This idea is already common in the time of Ammonius Saccus and is found in the works of the Middle Platonists such as Numenius and Nicomachus,[249] who are influential on Plotinus and Iamblichus. Plotinus, referring to fine art,[250] writes that such art works with the Forms or *logoi* and is therefore beautiful,[251] and by extension, good. Further, Plotinus says we should not condemn imitative art for the very reason that which art imitates is itself an imitation, and because art makes recourse to the Forms. This is possible because the artist relies upon their phantasia which, in its intelligible aspect, connects the artist with the Forms rather than the sensible world.[252] Fantastic or imaginative art, even if it engages in imitation, becomes the basis for saving art from the trash bin, but it does not save everything. Works such as pseudo-historical plays might still be considered taboo, except for those portions engaging in hymnody or praise, which has an inspired[253] and imaginative nature.

The emphasis on divinely located imagination and imaginative art becomes highly influential. By engaging with the Forms and their *logoi*, fine art and poetry become a kind of token or symbol of the divine realm. This ideology is at the root of traditional, astrological talismancy, the creation of talismans, as presented in texts such as *Ghayat al-Hakim*, or, *Picatrix*,[254] and Thabit Ibn Qurra's *De Imaginibus*.[255] These books of magic use astrological timing to empower the talismans they describe, but also fantastic imagery representing the powers of the planets and stars. When taken together, such talismans become microcosmic tokens or signatures of the divine realm.

---

247 *Rep.*, 607a, *Ion* 533d-534e.

248 Finberg, "Filiation," 150.

249 *Ibid.*, 149.

250 But, importantly, excludes portraits.

251 *Enn.*, V.8, 410-11.

252 C.f. Iamblichus in Priscianus, *Metaphrasis in Theophrastum* 23.13-24.20, in the appendix to *DA*, 241.

253 Works of art or poetry considered divinely inspired are also safe from Plato's critique, as they come from the gods or God and are not considered the products of a human mind.

254 *The Goal of the Sage*, more popularly known as *Picatrix*, written in Arabic in the 9th century CE.

255 *On Images*, 9th century CE.

The Neoplatonic aesthetic transcends magical or theurgical applications. The ideology behind the iconography of the Orthodox Christian Church is an excellent case in point. An icon is a painting usually depicting Christ, the Virgin Mary, a saint or archangel. Unlike western images of the same, Orthodox icons do not typically attempt to be realistic in their portrayal of these figures, opting instead for a stylized depiction instead, frequently drawing upon Byzantine aesthetics, which are influenced by Neoplatonic thought.[256]

Icons are not merely pieces of art, and may be seen as a continuation of Hellenic pagan tradition, where a god or goddess is understood to be present within their statue. They are *enyla eida*, Forms in matter, manifestations of the *logoi* of the Forms,[257] and may be understood to participate the image they represent,[258] an idea fully attested by pseudo-Dionysius.[259] For this reason icons are traditionally said to be "written," rather than painted, as they are seen as forms of divine scripture. They are also unsigned by the artist, as the icon writer is understood to merely transmit the holy reality that is at the heart of the icon.

The idea of beauty in Platonic thought is, as we have seen, of great importance. However, by itself, beauty seems to serve no function. Only when *kalon* is connected to *eros* can beauty lead upwards to Beauty and the divine realm. This section's next and final chapter joins love and beauty, which leads the philosopher to the realm from which the virtues originate, in completion of the philosophical life.

Exercise: Contemplating Beauty

This exercise is more active than previous exercises, and will stimulate your mental faculties and physical senses. Find an image that is beautiful to you. This may be any kind of image, though for our purposes, sacred images are more useful than *Whistler's Mother*. Your image does not need to be a painting. Statuary is just as good. If you do not have access to such images, the internet houses thousands of them.

Once you have chosen your image, spend at least ten minutes looking at it, taking note of any thoughts or feelings that arise in relation to your viewing. As you do this, ask yourself some of the following questions: Why are you drawn to this image? Why is it beautiful to you? How is it beautiful to you? Are there aspects of it that are not beautiful to you? Do the imperfections mar the image's overall beauty? Why or why not?

---

256 Stern-Gillet, "Neoplatonist Aesthetics," 44.

257 DM V.8, 236-9.

258 Alexandrakis, "Influence," 77-8.

259 EC IV.3.473C-476A.

Spend time contemplating these questions, as well as any others that occur to you. After you have done this, let these thoughts fade from your mind. With your mind clear, allow yourself to simply take in the image's beauty, allowing it to inspire you in any way it might. When you are finished basking in the image's beauty, be sure to take note of any thoughts or feelings that may have arisen during that time.

Chapter Eight

Love

Beauty, connected as it is to the Form of the Good, is the highest goal of philosophical practice. However, beauty can be obtained only through love, which binds together everything we have discussed. Although there are several Greek words that may be translated as "love," within the scope of traditional Platonic thought, the most important of these is *eros*. In Christian Platonism, especially the Neoplatonism of Marsilio Ficino,[260] the word *eros* is replaced by *agape*, but as we'll see, without a significant change in meaning. That there is little distinction between *eros* and *agape* in Platonic writing is important, as some writers, especially Christian apologists, attempt to portray *eros* as primarily sexual love and *agape* as a kind of spiritual love, making Christian love superior to pagan love. In either case, it is love that raises the philosopher, and the theurgist, to the heights of their art.

Plato's theory of love is found primarily in the *Symposium*, which we discussed in relation to beauty. Once again we turn to Diotima's speech, where she expounds upon the nature of beauty and, and perhaps more importantly, the nature and function of love. Diotima's love is an innovation in relation to common Greek notions of love. These are presented by those attending the symposium, a dinner and drinking party held by Agathon and attended by Socrates. The kinds of love described ultimately follow Diotima's hierarchy of beauty, going from the love of a particular person, to the love of all people and then upwards to love of the intelligible realm.

Plato's theory of love rejects romantic ideas. Diotima denies that Eros is a god, and neither beautiful nor good. Instead Eros, as the offspring of Penia and Poros, Resource and Need, is a daimon, holding a median position between the divine and human realms.[261] Eros can be neither beautiful nor good because nothing desires what it already has, only that which it lacking. Eros desires beauty and goodness and leads people to them. But Eros does not only lead upwards, and is not simply *"a longing for the beautiful."*[262] Love is procreative, a longing *"for the*

---

[260] Though, as we'll see, not in Pseudo-Dionysius, who uses *eros*.

[261] *Symp.* 203b-204a. The later Neoplatonists restore Eros to his deific position and Ficino (DAm, VI.4, 112) combines the two, saying love comes from both the divine and daimonic realms, and is therefore both a god and a daimon.

[262] *Ibid.* 206e.

conception and generation that the beautiful effects," and, ultimately to hold the Good forever, which is to say, immortality.[263] Love may be directed towards procreation when centred on the level of generation, but on the level of the spirit it is the virtues to which we are turned.[264] Ultimately, through love of beauty, the philosopher's soul rises upwards to a vision of the Form of Beauty itself.[265]

What is the nature of Plato's love? Is it not, ultimately sexual and selfish, as denoted by the word eros? There is clearly a sexual element to the *Symposium*'s eros, but is love selfish, and if so, how can it be something worth venerating? It seems hard to deny a certain selfishness to love. Love is, after all, the desire to have something for oneself and is therefore egocentric, even if spiritualized. Worse, Plato's love uses people as a means to an end. One does not love a beautiful person; one loves the beauty in a person in order to gain a better understanding of beauty and the Form of Beauty. The person is never really the object of love and is left behind when a new level of beauty is attained.[266]

This, at least, appears to be the case, but is it so? Is it possible to want beauty for myself while simultaneously wishing the best for the person in whom I see that beauty? Can I not desire for both myself and for the object of my love? Also, if what I desire for myself is a virtue, which is of the higher aspect of beauty, is that not also desiring something good for someone else? For an individual to possess the virtue of justice, one of the most important virtues,[267] is of benefit to everyone, not just the one who possess it. That is, to desire justice as a virtue is to desire justice for everyone.[268] There is no need for love to be selfish, and at its highest levels, it cannot be selfish. The conclusion, it seems, is that Plato's love simultaneously adores its immediate inspiration and the ultimate source of beauty in the intellective realm.

The Later Neoplatonists

The later Neoplatonists greatly value the anagogic aspect of Eros. Following the *Chaldean Oracles*, Iamblichus sees Eros as a primordial power and the first creation of the Demiurge.[269] The Demiurge then fills each soul with a "deep love" to bring it back to the gods.[270] In the *Timaeus*, the gods have the task of creating all that is mortal in the human soul. The Demiurge creates what is immortal.[271] That is, the gods are responsible for the irrational soul and the Demiurge for the

---

263 *Ibid.* 206e-207a.
264 *Ibid.* 207d-209d.
265 *Ibid.* 211c-d.
266 See Levy, "Definition," 286.
267 *Symp.* 209b.
268 Lewy, "Definition," 287.
269 CO. fr. 42.
270 Shaw, *Theurgy*, 123-4.
271 C.f. CO. fr. 39.

creation of the rational soul. Love, as a product of the Demiurge, is part of the rational soul, rather than the irrational. Love, intelligible love rather than generative love, is a kind of reason, drawing us to the intelligible realm. Rather than being distinct, the lower love leads to the upper and, just as love brings forth life, in the body and in the soul, and is the work of love in the *Symposium*, so it is also in theurgy. Where in generative love the source of inspiration is the beloved person, in theurgic love the sources are divine tokens, symbols, the gods and Demiurge, placed in matter to raise us to their source.[272]

Iamblichus' theurgic love is not mono-directional. Theurgic religious ritual ritualizes the cosmos.[273] Through these practices the theurgist ascends in theurgic love to the gods. When performed correctly these rites transform the theurgist into the likeness of the object of the sacrifices, and raises him or her to the gods at the heart of their theurgic love.[274] This higher kind of love, which attaches us to the divine tokens and Forms, is the source of inspired beauty and imaginative art. The higher love is the ultimate source of the icons of Orthodox Christianity and, as we'll see in section three, an integral component of theurgic talismancy.

Iamblichus' divine Eros is also found in the works of Proclus. In his commentary on *Alcibiades*, Proclus, describing what he calls in his *Cratylus* commentary *"pronoetic love,"* says *"Eros descends from above from the intelligible sphere down to the cosmic, and turns all things toward the divine beauty."*[275] To connect lower and higher forms of love, Proclus makes great use of the two forms of Aphrodite found in Plato, the earthly or encosmic Aphrodite Pandemos, Aphrodite of all the people, and Aphrodite Ourania, the heavenly Aphrodite born of sea foam.[276]

Proclus examines Eros and the source of Eros, which he finds in the noeric form of Aphrodite. According to Sallustius, following Iamblichus, Aphrodite is one of the three harmonizers of the universe and the source of harmony and beauty.[277] While this only examines Aphrodite in a single aspect, as one of the visible gods, Proclus' complex theology explores Aphrodite on many levels, from the height of divinity to the daimonic level.[278] Eros is Aphrodite's constant companion, and her ultimate form is the source of Eros in its fully godly, rather than daimonic, aspect. Proclus also uses Sallustius', or Iamblichus', idea of Aphrodite as a source of harmony, causing the union of opposites, and strengthening the weaker or lower of the two in its union with the upper. Once again we see the anagogic power of love and its connection, here made explicit, to beauty. Also, and importantly, due to the high placement of Aphrodite and Eros

---

[272] *Ibid.*, 125.
[273] Shaw, *Theurgy*, 124.
[274] C.f. DM V.9-10, 241.
[275] Quoted. in. Richardson, "Love," 183-4.
[276] *Symp.* 180e. The most well-known image of Aphrodite Ourania is likely Botticelli's *The Birth of Venus*, unfortunately known as "Venus on the Half-Shell."
[277] CGU, VI, 13.
[278] Lankila, "Aphrodite," 26-40.

in Proclus' system, we find not only the anagogic theurgic love, but also the descending love that triggers the uplifting response in those below.[279]

From this footing Pseudo-Dionysius further expands upon the Neoplatonic idea of love. At first, it is surprising that Dionysius uses *eros* rather than *agape* in his writings, especially in *The Divine Names*, where Eros is a name of God. This is because the *New Testament* uses *agape* rather than *eros*, and there is often a sense within Christian writings that *eros* refers to physical love, while *agape* refers to a kind of spiritual love. Dionysius denies this, saying they are equivalent terms, and that using *eros* rather than *agape* is no different from explaining *"the number four by twice two, or straight lines by direct lines, or motherland by fatherland, or any other, which signify the self-same thing, by many parts of speech.'*[280] For Dionysius and his contemporaries, *eros* is a cosmic power, an idea not usually connected to *agape*. As he is writing a kind of cosmic theology, it makes sense he prefers *eros* over *agape*.[281]

Although Dionysius departs from the pagan Platonists by considering physical *eros* a kind of false love,[282] he builds on other important ideas. The divine Eros is ecstatic in nature, causing the lover to no longer belong to him or herself but to the object of their love. This ecstatic love both ascends and descends and, like Aphrodite, is a harmonizing force in the cosmos.[283] The ascent is rather typical of Neoplatonic thought, expressed through the reversion of the soul to its source. The descent is in the form of divine providence, a theme prominent in Iamblichus' *De Mysteriis*. Dionysius, however, adds a third kind of love, that which occurs between equals.[284] Whereas the first two forms of love are those between the divine and the soul, this new form of love between equals goes outside of pagan Neoplatonism, representing the love of the persons of the Trinity for one another,[285] or of the connection all beings on the same ontological level may have for one another,[286] although it is possible this is inherent to Iamblichus' gods existing as a single form.

In Platonic thought we cannot say the Good itself loves, has love or is love because it is the ultimate source of love, and therefore transcends love. Why does love, in the form of Aphrodite or Eros, not appear until a much lower ontological level rather than at, for instance, the intelligible? This is likely because the higher gods, who Proclus describes as *henads* or unities, have no need for this striving upwards; they are already at the summit of existence and fully participate the One and the Good. Instead, the genagogic and anagogic powers of love are only

---

[279] Rist, "Note," 236.
[280] DN IV.11.708C-D.
[281] Rist, "Note," 237.
[282] DN IV.11.709B-C.
[283] Rist, "Note," 240.
[284] DN IV.13.712A.
[285] Rist, "Note," 241. However, see Kupperman, "Eros and Agape in Dionysius the Areopagite," http://www.jwmt.org/v3n25/kupperman.html, for alternative understandings of this.
[286] Kupperman, "Eros and Agape," http://jwmt.org/v3n25/kupperman.htm.

necessary at lower levels, this is why Proclus' Aphrodite descends to the level of daimons, overseeing the beautiful embodiment of the Forms in matter.

Ecstatic Love, Erotic Mania and Divine Inspiration

Plato's particular form of anagogic love has been with us nearly twenty-five hundred years. Only in the fifteenth century, however, is it given the name "Platonic love." The great Renaissance Neoplatonist and translator Marsilio Ficino, first in a letter to Alamanno Donati in 1476, and then more fully in his book *De Amore*,[287] coins and explains the term. In *De Amore*, Ficino carries on Dionysius' rejection of physical love, seeing Platonic love as intellectual and non-sexual, or even anti-sexual.[288] While the intellectual status of Platonic love is representative of Platonic and Neoplatonic thought, Dionysius' and Ficino's anti-sexual positions are quite far from the original Platonic ideas of love and beauty, apparently coming from preoccupations within their religious traditions. For the earlier Neoplatonists, love is always love; a matter of degrees, not kind.

Despite the anti-sexual position of Ficino's love, his description of the ontological realms is in keeping with Neoplatonic thought. For instance, Ficino describes four circles or realms as manifestations of God's Beauty, which is a divine ray emanating from the Good.[289] The beauty in the intellectual and sensual realms excites love in all who experience it. For Ficino, as in the *Symposium*, love may be defined as *"the desire for Beauty.'*[290] Unlike Plato, Ficino does not expound upon various forms of beauty, such as in poetry or art. Possibly inspired by the *Philebus*, he focuses on human beauty as the object of love.

While we have already seen a connection between love and intellect or reason, Ficino is explicit about it, describing them as the two wings which must be developed in order to fly back to the soul's homeland described in the *Phaedrus*.[291] While reason, stemming as it does from the divine intellect, is of extreme importance, Ficino recognizes the equal importance of mania or divine inspiration and rapture, which Proclus and Dionysius recognize as ecstatic love. The importance of mania is recognized by Plato. In the *Phaedrus*, a philosopher's soul is described as such that to the masses philosophers seem deranged or out of their wits.[292] The philosophical soul is one *"who has sought after wisdom unfeignedly, or had conjoined his passion for a loved one with that seeking.'*[293] Earlier in the same dialogue, Socrates describes four kinds of *mania*: prophetic, telestic, poetic, and erotic.

---

287 Finished and presented to Lorenzo de' Medici as part of Ficino's *Platonis Opera* in 1482, the first print edition appearing in 1484 (Devereux, "Textual," 174).
288 Hanegraaff, "Mantle," 175.
289 DAm II.3, 47, II.5, 51.
290 *Ibid.*, I.4, 40.
291 Rees, "Consciousness," 10.
292 *Phaedr* 249d.
293 *Ibid.*, 249a, emphasis added.

Prophetic frenzy is what the Sibyl at Delphi and other such temples experiences when in the grasp of the god.[294] Iamblichus considers this kind of prophecy, one where the prophet is completely possessed by a god, the only true form of divination.[295] Telestic frenzy has to do with the performance of sacred rites and sacrifices for the purposes of healing.[296] Ficino understands this to be "*a powerful stirring of the soul, in perfecting what relates to the worship of the gods, religious observance, purification and sacred ceremonies.*"[297] Plato tells us true poetry has nothing to do with the skill of the poet. Only poetry inspired by the Muses makes a person a good poet.[298] Of erotic frenzy we have already spoken, this is the love that ultimately raises one so smitten by the vision of the Form of Beauty.

Each of the frenzies has at least two things in common, commonalities strong enough to lead Ficino to assert that the four frenzies are actually four aspects of the same frenzy. First, the frenzies are anagogic and ecstatic, lifting the soul upwards and outwards towards participating ontologically prior realities. Iamblichus, especially, sees divine inspiration as a kind of total possession by the god.[299] Second, these frenzies all come from without the soul. Prophetic frenzy is inspired by a god, Apollo according to Ficino. Dionysos causes telestic frenzies. Poetic frenzy comes from the Muses. Aphrodite or Venus is, of course, the source of erotic frenzy.[300] Here we can see the hand of Proclus, his theology of Aphrodite and her various levels of existence, and the transference of the soul from the lower, daimonic, Aphrodite to the fully divine Aphrodite Ourania.

Ficino also orders the frenzies differently. Poetic mania is first because through poetry and music the sleeping parts of the soul awaken and harmonize. The worship brought through telestic frenzy unifies the soul, reducing it to "*intellect alone.*"[301] Prophetic mania leads the intellect back to unity with itself, and is caused by and causes prophecy. This soul is now able to recall the One above it and turns itself towards the Good through the frenzy of love.[302] Ficino also relates the activities of the frenzies to the Allegory of the Chariot in the *Phaedrus*, each mania influences the unruly horse that causes the chariot to crash and the subsequent incarnation of the human soul. Through the frenzies that horse is corrected and placed under the rule of the obedient horse until, through love, the

---

[294] *Ibid.*, 244a-b.
[295] DM III.26, 185; III.28, 189. Ficino's understanding is quite similar.
[296] *Phaedr* 244d-e.
[297] In Hanegraaff, "Frenzies," 558.
[298] *Phaedr* 245a. Ficino's description of this frenzy echoes Plato's.
[299] According to E. R. Dodds, this was an accepted understanding of true prophecy. See, Sheppard, "Inspiration," 140.
[300] DAm VII.14, 170.
[301] *Ibid.*
[302] *Ibid.*

head of the charioteer, representing the noeric quality of the soul, is fully purified and returns to its heavenly home.[303]

Expanding on Plato, Ficino also differentiates between true and false versions of each frenzy. There is true prophecy and then there is *"foresight or inference."*[304] Against the true mysteries is superstition. The true poet, and Ficino here includes musicians, is contrasted against "superficial" and "vulgar" music and poetry that relies on the cunning of the poet's wit and technique. Against true erotic love is carnal love.[305]

As we have seen from Iamblichus and Proclus, and following Ficino's notion that the frenzies are elements of one kind of divine inspiration, all the frenzies are elements of theurgic love. For a Neoplatonist, this kind of *eros*, an *eros* that allows the theurgist to demiurgy, is the highest kind of love. It is a love that transcends the individual so completely as to raise the theurgist to divine levels and activities.

The goal of Platonic political philosophy is to bring to all people the chief human happiness: becoming like God, so far as possible. For the philosopher-ruler, bringing this chief good to those they rule may mean a company, a congregation, a town, or a country. However, for the theurgist, this means all of creation. In both cases, the seeking after the good comes from love.[306]

The impetus behind the drive upwards towards the divine is Eros.[307] Behind Eros is the harmonizing activity of Aphrodite who, in turn, imitates the unifying activity of the One. Ficino shows us that erotic frenzy is the highest phase of divine inspiration. Therefore, becoming like the divine so far as we can, though ultimately pointing towards the Good and the One, points us first towards Eros and the highest Aphrodite. For the later Neoplatonists, the ontological gap between the human soul and the One is too great a void to cross. Unlike in Plotinian Neoplatonism, here absolute union with God is impossible. Although not every soul is placed within the orbit of Aphrodite,[308] like Athena who fills the other gods with wisdom, Aphrodite harmonizes the gods and fills them with harmony, and is herself their synthesis,[309] just as Justice is a synthesis of the virtues. In fact, Ficino shows love exists within the cardinal virtues,[310] as we would expect if Aphrodite harmonizes all the gods. This being the case, it comes as no

---

303 *Ibid.*, 171.

304 Hanegraaff, "Frenzy," 559, c.f. DM III.26, 185.

305 *Ibid.*

306 C.f. DAm, I.3, 40.

307 C.f. Ficino, *"The grace of this world or ornament is Beauty, to which that Love, as soon as it was born, attracted the Mind [the noetic-noeric realm]; and it led the Mind , formerly ugly, to the same Mind made beautiful . . . . Who, therefore, will doubt that Love immediately follows Chaos, and precedes the World and all the gods who are assigned to the parts of the World, since the appetite of the Mind precedes its receiving of the Forms, and it is in the already formed Mind that the gods and the World are born?"* (DAm, I.3, 39.)

308 See chapter twelve: The Greater Kinds, the Gods, and Theology.

309 Julian, *Hymn*, 411.

310 Ficino, DAm, V.8, 96-8.

surprise that Ficino says all disciplines are governed and mastered by love.[311] Whether or not we are innately aligned with love is irrelevant, love, like wisdom, fills all things.

Exercise: Contemplating Love

The following contemplation, which draws its inspiration from the work of Marsilio Ficino,[312] is similar to the second contemplation on wisdom given in chapter four, though it employs imagery from the *Phaedrus'* Allegory of the Chariot, rather than the *Republic*'s Allegory of the Cave. Like that exercise, what follows is in the mode of a guided visualization. These two contemplations are also similar in that they use the metaphor of sight and vision. In the former, vision is akin to wisdom and the ability to discern. In what follows the focus shifts somewhat from vision, to that which makes vision possible: the eye and light and their relationship to beauty and love.

As always, take some time to calm yourself, relaxing your mind and body, before beginning. It is also appropriate to have soft music in the background. Such music should be soft, uplifting and energizing rather than morose and heavy.

Imagine yourself standing in a great forest. Sunlight filters through gently wind-blown leaves, creating a dizzying display of constantly shifting shadow and light. Stumbling forward you catch yourself from falling. Your body is heavy, heavier than it has ever been, your thoughts fragmented and assaulted by the body's sensations. Examining your hands you see they are of flesh and blood, not spirit and light as you once remembered. Around you is the wreckage of a once celestial chariot, now mired in matter. Debris marks a path away from you towards a lessening of trees. Slowly, careful of your embodiment, you follow the chariot's remains.

As you leave the forest's shadowy confines your eyes begin to adjust to the brilliant sunlight. The trail of debris leads you away from the crashed chariot and, as you follow, soft, unearthly music comes to your ears, stopping you in your tracks. Complex harmonies play amidst a bright, uplifting melody. Nine resonant notes sound out against your scattered thoughts, each one as bright in your mind's eye as the sun in the sky. Lifting your inner ears towards the sound you lose sight of the trail of debris and follow the blissful music.

Following the heavenly music clears your mind. Under each shining note your thoughts illuminate and unify. The dizziness of the light and shadows leaves you and you remember your crashing descent into the wooded glade and your subsequent embodiment. Despite the chaos it has brought, you do not feel like a

---

311 *Ibid.*, III.3, 66-7.

312 Drawing from the final book of the *Platonic Philosophy*, a letter to King Ferdinand of Argon, and *De Amore*, as well as from Julian's *Hymn to King Helios.*

foreigner in the body. The body is home, or at least one of your homes, but the body you have now is too heavy, too mired in old habits and false opinions. The music engulfs you and as your mind unifies you lightly step into a clearing.

In the centre of the grassy plain is a flat-topped, rough-hewn stone. Three objects rest on the stone: a silver vessel, a plate of incenses, and a tripod of fire. The music leads you forward. In the silver vessel is crystal clear water. You feel a sense of purity from the water, as though simply by standing near it you could cleanse yourself. On the plate are many piles of incense and a place to burn them.

The music draws you towards the water. As you plunge your hands into the cool liquid a new sound occupies you. Words, sounding not in your ears but your mind, flow in a steady rhythm, like a chant or prayer. The words are familiar to you, yet indecipherable, as though spoken in a language you have since forgotten. Pulling your hands from the water you find they feel lighter, that you feel lighter. There is a shining quality to your skin that does not come from the glistening liquid.

Turning your attention to the incense, you stop and contemplate each of the dozen piles. Perhaps you are drawn to one set of sweet smelling herbs or fragrant resins. Each pile brings out a certain sensation within you: a deep contemplative mood; the call to serve the people and lead them upward; a great swelling of courage and vitality; a compassion towards healing and a clarity of senses; love; the gift of speech, interpretation, and possibly magic; a movement towards procreation, be it in body, soul or mind; perhaps other feelings as well. Regardless of the personal feelings you encounter with each incense, listen also to the words spoken in your inner mind. Contemplating this higher sense, you choose the most appropriate incense and burn it.

Smoke curls upwards and the scent of incense fill you, raising you upwards towards the sunlight in a body of light and spirit. As your rise towards the heavens the land spreads out beneath you. In the sunlight you see the whole of the land, everything that is happening, has happened, and will happen. You begin to remember your other, heavenly abode and all illusion falls from your celestial body as words not your own flow from above and spill from your lips, speaking of what was, what is, and what will be. You become lost in the words and absorbed into them. There is nothing now but the Voice which speaks and the blinding light of the sun.

As the words cease you come to yourself once again. You are in a field of spring grass, standing in a luminous chariot to which are harnessed two winged horses, one light, one dark. Above you is the celestial sky, the divine abode. The sun beams down upon you, filling your eyes. Your crystalline mind reflects that light outward, touching everything, everywhere, every-when. The sun's rays illuminate you and everything else they touch so their true beauty becomes manifest to you. The abundant beauty calls to you, and, at its heart, the Form of Beauty. But there is something still deeper. As love blossoms within your mind a greater call, one that has always been present but until now inaudible, beckons.

Firmly grasping the reins, you set the chariot in motion. Powerful wings set you aloft as you rise towards the object of true Love, and your place in the heavenly abode. As your spirit vehicle rises into the heavens a light beyond light engulfs you and all is brilliance.

Theologia

Chapter Nine

First Principles – The One

The whole of Platonic cosmology centres on a single, simple concept, the subject of the first Paramedian hypothesis: the One. As it is the foundation of Platonic thought, we will spend some time trying to understand something that is ultimately beyond understanding.

The Ineffable One – That Which Is Not

The One is utterly simple, utterly singular, utterly transcendent. It is also the sum total of everything that exists. Everything exists undifferentiated in the One and the One exists unified in everything. The One is beyond essence, *ousia*, and beyond Being, *on*, the basic constituents of most existing things, followed by power, *dunamis*, and activity, *energeia*, on the one hand, Life, *zoe*, and Intellect, *noesis* on the other. These two sets of characteristics are the basis for existence as we understand existence. The One does not exist as we understand existence.

This basic proposition concerning the One appears in Plato's *Parmenides*. The *Parmenides* contains eight hypotheses that, through a series of proofs, describe reality and its contents. Iamblichus understands the first four hypotheses to describe the One, the gods, the greater kind, and the human soul. The first hypothesis is concerned with the One: if it is one, is outside of time, neither a whole nor a part, has no limits nor shape, no location, etc.[313] This absolutely "not-this-ness" of the One leads Iamblichus to call it the "entirely ineffable," *pantelos arrheton,* One.

This basic proposition also presents us with a number of questions. I will express only three: First, why is the One called "one" if it is in fact none? Second, how are we to approach or discuss something described as having negative Being, something that is by definition beyond description, and why bother doing so in the first place? Finally, how does the ineffable One relate to the many?

The first question is a matter of linguistics and context. Iamblichus is a Pythagoreanising Platonist. A peculiar element of Pythagorean theological arithmetic is that the monad is not the same as the number one (1) in modern mathematics. Instead, a monad transcends number and is the *"non-spatial source of*

---

313 *Parm.* 137c-141e.

number.'[314] Number, as such, comes into being with the dyad, where there are two things, or difference. Without difference there is no number: one is different from two, two is different from three, etc.

Without difference there are not many things. Perfectly identical things must coincide in every way and are therefore the same thing, not separate from one another. This is not simply a matter of numerical verses qualitative identity. Two things that have qualitative identity, such as identical twins, are not completely identical. Their DNA is distinct, they have different finger prints, they have different atoms, they do not exist in the same space and time, etc. Here we have a One that is none but also the first of a series of things that are different from, but dependent upon, the One for their Being. Even so, in deference to the ineffable One's "negativeness" it is not even referred to as a monad.

The second question is not frequently answered by the pagan Neoplatonists. Plato shows nothing can be said about the ineffable One:

> *And if a thing is not, you cannot say that it 'has' anything or that there is anything 'of" it. Consequently, it cannot have a name or be spoken of, nor can there be any knowledge or perception or opinion of it. It is not named or spoken of, not an object of opinion or of knowledge, not perceived by any creature.*[315]

If this is so, then it makes sense the Neoplatonists don't bother with the issue. Plotinus gets around the question by combining the first and second hypotheses of the *Parmenides*, making the One both nothing and something,[316] and so allowing him to describe the One as necessary. Iamblichus and the later Neoplatonists, however, keep the Ones distinct and so are silent on the subject. After all, if the ineffable One is beyond everything, what is there to discuss?

But for Dionysius there is much to discuss. Dionysius recognizes the divine names given in scripture as being accurately descriptive of the transcendent God in manifestation. But Dionysius' contemplative practices require more than understanding and experiencing God in creation. By systematically proposing and denying everything attributable to God, the mind moves, so far as possible, beyond creation. Dionysian apophatic theology forms the basis of a type of "negative contemplation," a way to *"know and to celebrate super-essentially the Superessential, through the abstraction of all existing things.'*[317] Without contemplating God as nothing, understanding God as something, though not useless, does not allow us to reach God in God's fullness.

But what of our final question? If the One, or God, is entirely ineffable, what is the relationship between the One and the many? In other words, if the One is

---

314 Waterfield, *Theology*, 35.
315 *Parm.* 142a.
316 Dillon, *Commentaries*, 30.
317 MT II.1.1025A.

beyond all things, beyond the basic constituents of existence as we know them, then how does all that comes from the One come into being?

Plotinus avoids the question more than he tries to answer it. Porphyry makes the One the first part of the first of the divine hypostases. Porphyry develops, based on the teachings of Plotinus, a triad of Being-Life-Intellect, called the intelligible triad. For Porphyry to place the One, the source of being, at the head of this triad makes sense. But in doing so the One can no longer be ineffable; it can now be described as, if nothing else, the source of being.

Iamblichus solves the problem by positing the existence of not one One but three. At first this seems contradictory to the idea of the One being *one*. In order to understand this it is important to first understand Iamblichus' idea of time in the spiritual realms.

A Brief Divergence: Time – But Not as We Know It

What is time? How long it takes for something to happen? Action in space? An illusion, lunch time doubly so? All of the above? In *Physics*, Aristotle defines time as *"number of movement in respect of the before and after,"*[318] with which we all might generally agree. Iamblichus, however, denies that time and movement are identical. Movement, he says, exists within a relationship to something that is not moving or to some other motion. Time, however, does not need rest and exists in and of itself, not in relation to something else.

This view of time is necessary in order to apply it beyond the physical realm. Iamblichus denies that even the lowest part of divine realm, the noeric realm, exists in *"a spatial and dimensional sense."*[319] If this is so of the intellective, how much more so of the higher noetic realm, which transcends even the Mind of God? If time is movement and change, how can we speak of time in the divine realms as described by Iamblichus? Realms within which reside beings that do not change. Can we tell time in a "place" where there is no space for an action to occur and no bodies to perform them?

Time is not Iamblichus' primary concern at this point. Time exists in the psychic and physical worlds. Before time is Aion, Eternity, which acts as a measure for the noetic realm. In his *Alcibiades* commentary, Iamblichus approaches the intellectual triad as occurring in an ontological procession: Being precedes Life and Life precedes Intellect, *"[f]or we strive for Being more basically than Life, and for Life more basically than for Intelligence."*[320] Everything posterior to the One has Being, but not everything with Being has Life, and not every living thing has Intellect. Anything that has a mind is also alive and exists. In his *Timaeus*

---

[318] Aristotle, *Physics*, IV.11s.

[319] *In Tim.* fr. 50.

[320] *In Alc.* fr. 8. Compare to Proclus: *"For either [a being] alone possesses being from its cause or life with being, or it receives from thence a gnostic power."* (ET, §34).

commentary,[321] Iamblichus connects this procession to an idea of three "moments" within the noetic realm, stemming from Aion. These moments are the different ways in which the divine realm is approached, from an ontologically "earlier" moment to a "later" one.

The first noetic moment is the hypostasis, or divine reality, as it exists in itself, or in its purest form. This moment is called unparticipated, *amethektos*, and is the source of Being. The second moment is the participated, *metachomenos*, hypostasis. This is how ontologically posterior beings view and experience the hypostasis in question. This is the source of Life.

Participation, *metalipsis*, is an idea we have already seen, and of which we will see much more. It suggests the dependence of ontologically posterior realms and being upon superior realms and beings. Participation is necessary because of the differences between secondary entities and their primary sources.[322] If the primary and secondary beings are identical there is no need for participation. However, there would also not be primary and secondary beings, a state that is necessitated by the existence of the simply One and described in the *Timaeus* myth.

The final moment, the source of Intellect, is the hypostasis as it is reflected in those lower being, called "in participation," *kata methexin*.[323] There is no movement implied in these moments, they exist simultaneously, and there is no change from one state to the other, they are eternal, disconnected from befores and afters. These measures are by Aion. Aion appears as a deity in a number of contemporary religions, including the Hermetic texts, Gnosticism, and the *Chaldean Oracles*.[324] Aion appears in the form of a lion-headed man with wings, entwined by a serpent rising above his lion's head.

The Simply One and the Dyad

The noetic moments, described as Aion, do not, strictly speaking, apply to the One, which is ontologically prior to the realm of the divine intellect. But it is clear the basis of the three moments is found in the Iamblichean triadic One. We can see the ineffable One as corresponding to the first noetic moment. The ineffable One is the One in and of itself, unconnected to anything posterior to it. It is the unparticipated One.[325]

Following this One is another One. This One is variously called the "simply One," *ho haplos hen*, and "that which is before duality," *pro tos duados*. This second One is necessary because the ineffable One, the first moment of the One, is completely contained within itself. If the ineffable One is eternally ineffable there

---

321 *In Tim.* fr. 65.

322 DM 54.13-55.2.

323 Dillon, *Commentaries*, 33.

324 Dodds, in Proclus, *Elements*, 228.

325 C.f. Finamore, *Vehicle*, 41.

can be nothing outside the One, which, as you are reading this book, you know there is. The simply One is the creative first principle, or the One in activity, as opposed to a passive One in repose.

The simply One is derived from Iamblichus' reading of the second hypothesis of the *Parmenides*.[326] Whereas the first hypothesis concludes that a One cannot be, the second hypothesis begins by saying that *"[i]f a one is, it cannot be, and yet not have existence."*[327] Although it is tempting to describe this One as a One with Being, the One, all three of them, is beyond Being and essence. All we can say about the simply One is that it exists.

Before leading to the One-Being, the final "moment" of the One, there is a second consequence to Iamblichus' separating the ineffable and simply Ones: the development of the dyad. The dyad is in between singularity and multiplicity and has characteristics of both.[328] The dyad at this point represents *"Limit and the Unlimited, or …One and Many."*[329] "One" and "Many" can be understood as the existence of opposites.

The introduction of the dyad here is a logical necessity stemming from the second Parmenidean hypothesis. For the Pythagoreans, multiplicity begins with the triad, but Plato makes it clear that plurality must exist if there is a One that is, so the One and Many are not only opposites but the beginning of number in the Platonic system.[330] In placing the dyad ontologically after the simply One, rather than at the same time, Iamblichus tells us about duality being a natural result of the existence of the simply One.

First, he says the Parmenidean hypotheses are not just logical propositions. They represent something real. Beyond this, however, Iamblichus tells us about necessity. The level or mode of reality we're talking about here might be described as "ontological." That word has been used several times already. The root of the ontology is *ontos*, meaning "that which is." Ontology is the study of real things, and ontologically prior things are "more real" than what comes after them. The One is as real as real gets. The One is necessary in a way like nothing else. If there is no One, there is nothing, and there is clearly something. You, me, this book, etc. These things are, and they are because the simply One is. What Iamblichus is saying is that at this level things that must be are. If something must logically follow from a proposition such as the simply One, then that something exists. Not only does it exist, but it exists ontologically posterior to that which it must follow. The dyad must be, and it must be after the simply One, and following the dyad is the One-Being.

---

326 Dillon, *Commentaries*, 30.

327 *Parm.* 142a.

328 Waterfield, *Arithmetic*, 43.

329 Damascius, quoted in Dillon, *Commentaries*, 31.

330 *Parm.* 144a-e.

The One-Being

The final One is called the One-Being or One-Existent, *to hen on*. The One-Being sits at the lowest point of the realm of the One. The One-Being acts as the bridge between the realm of the One and the noetic realm, and simultaneously exists in both. This is part of an Iamblichean axiom, found also in Proclus, that the lowest principle of one realm is also the highest principle of the next. The One-Being is prior to both oneness and Being, both of which it gives to the noetic realm.

Once reflected into the noetic realm, the One-Being becomes Aion and Paradigm, the monad of that realm, unifying and ruling over the Being-Life-Intellect triad.[331] Or, more specifically, Aion and Paradigm represent a vertical extension of the One from its place into the noetic realm.[332] This means Aion and Paradigm occupy the same ontological place as the One-Being, but, as they exist at the top of the noetic realm rather than at the bottom of the realm of the One, are functionally different. Strictly speaking, there is no difference between the One-Being, Aion or Paradigm. However, as they fulfill very specific roles in Iamblichus' cosmology, it is convenient to speak of them as though they were distinct.

As the Paradigm, the One-Being is the model upon which the Cosmos is based and is described as the "Essence of Being"[333] from which all Being stems. That the Paradigm is the cosmic model is important, because it tells us about the nature of the cosmos. This fact tells us the cosmos is modelled by the Demiurge upon something eternal, unchangeable, good, and beyond generation: *'Everyone will see that [the Demiurge] must have looked to the eternal, for the world is the fairest of creations and he is the best of causes.'*[334]

The Good

Before moving on to the noetic-noeric and noeric realms, we must discuss the Idea of the Good, *tou agathou idean,* or simply the Good, *tou agathon.* The Form of the Good is illustrated in Plato's *Republic*, and described as that *"which just things and all the rest become useful and beneficial,"*[335] and the Good itself, which is the One, is the source of that Form, which is closely connected to the Form of Beauty. For Plato, the exclusion of the Good from our lives is the exclusion of everything. The Good is the foundation of all things.

---

331 *In Tim.* fr. 54. This likely stems from Iamblichus' interest in the *Chaldean Oracles.* Compare with *'In every cosmos there shineth a Triad, over which a Monad is source"* (CO. fr. 27 in Mead, *Echoes*, 321).

332 Clark, "Egyptian," 184.

333 *In Tim.* Fra. 35.

334 *Tim.* 29a.

335 *Rep.* 505a.

What is the Good? The Good is that which every soul peruses, and does so for the sake of everything it does.[336] This, of course, tells us relatively little, and that's the point. The Good, like the One, is almost impossible to describe in useful ways. Because the Good is beyond Being and essence there is no single thing to point to in order to describe it. In order to describe the Good, Plato uses analogy.[337]

Plato's Socrates begins by discussing the nature of sight, the greatest of the five senses. Sight is not possible if there is only the organ of sight and the object to be seen. Sight is only possible with light. The source of light is linked to a divine source. In Platonic thought, and especially Neoplatonism, the planets, moon and sun are the bodies of the visible gods. The sun is the body of the Titan-god Helios.

When our eyes are trained on objects fully illuminated by the sun, we have full, clear, powerful vision. The Form of the Good is like the sun, which is a visible reflection of the invisible Good. When the soul is trained on the noetic realm, *"where truth and reality shine resplendent,"*[338] it can have knowledge of those things and attain to reason. If, however, the soul turns towards generation, its vision of truth is blunted, just as though the eye were turned away from illuminated objects.

However, while light and vision are like the sun they are not the sun itself. This is also true of the Good. Though truth and reality are revealed by the presence of the Good, they are not the Good. The Good is beyond that which it allows us to know. Much like the One, we may not truly know the Good, but we may know of it. The similarities between the Good and the One are not surprising: the Good is the One.

That the Good is the One is a basic Neoplatonic tenant, and is perhaps best explained in Proclus' *Elements of Theology*.[339] Here he says all things desire the Good. Therefore, in the logic of Platonic ontology, the Good must be beyond all things because nothing desires to attain what it already has. That the Good illuminates the whole of the noetic realm means it exists prior to that realm, and so is not only beyond entities but beyond Being. Also, the Good is such that it is fully self-contained. Nothing can be added to it because if something can be added to the Good to improve it, then that thing is be the Good all things desire.

Now, all things come from the One, the single cause of all. How can the Good be the One? Proclus may answer "how can it not?" What, after all, can be better than the Good? If something is better than the Good, would not the soul turn towards that instead? Further, the nature of the Good is to unify things and

---

[336] *Ibid.*, 505e.
[337] The complete analogy is in *Rep.* 507c-509a.
[338] *Ibid.*, 508d.
[339] ET §VIII-XIII.

perfect them. We see this in the *Republic*, where the Good makes all things beneficial and useful and therefore beautiful. But the principle of unity belongs to the One-Being as monad above the noetic realm. This means that anything failing to participate the Good also ceases to have the power of union, and anything that ceases to have the power of union ceases participating the Good. *"Goodness, then, is unification, and unification goodness; the Good is one, and the One is primal good."*[340]

This is the height of divinity within Platonic thought. This is the height of divinity within Platonic thought. The One is God, though the God of mystics rather than conceptions more popular to the Abrahamic religions. As such, the One, in all its modes, is not directly knowable. As with the analogy of the sun in the *Republic*, we are able to see truth by the One's divine light, but we should not mistake the truth for that which illuminates it. And without the One, there is no truth. But Hellenic philosophy is supposed to be practical. What use is knowledge of an unknowable One?

The One is the very foundation of everything. Yes, the One exists beyond all things. But also exists in or to all things. Of this principle, the Divine Iamblichus says:

> *"In the highest levels of beings, the abundance of power has this additional advantage over all others, in being present to all equally in the same manner without hindrance; according to this principle then, the primary beings illuminate even the lowest levels, and the immaterial are present immaterially to the material."*[341]

The One is with us all the time. The unity and goodness it brings is what we all strive for, even if we don't always succeed in meeting its measure. All acts of love are imitations of the Good, for Eros is the perpetrator of unions. Finally, and importantly, as the source of unions, the presence of the Good in the material world is what allows for the practice of theurgy, *theosis* and, ultimately, *henosis*.

---

340 ET §XIII

341 DM V.23, 267.

Chapter Ten

The Spiritual and Natural Realms

In the last chapter I mention a number of "realms," but do not discuss them at any length. The nature and interplay of the spiritual realms, such as the noetic, the noetic-noeric, and the noeric realms is complex and exists only as fragments within the Iamblichean corpus. While later Neoplatonists, especially Proclus, develop these ideas in some depth, it is impossible to determine exactly how much they share in common with Iamblichean thought, though evidence suggests the later work is based on Iamblichus. Where others, such as Julian the Philosopher, are known to have had access Iamblichus' now lost writings, frequently those writings are simplified for the purpose of the writer's project, and sometime reinterpreted to fit into the writer's metaphysics. A basic understanding of the chain of being is still important, as it is the means through which theurgy works.

The Noetic and Noeric Realms

The place of the Ineffable and Simply One is no place at all, and certainly no "realm" in any sort of common usage of the word. The Ineffable One is nowhere at all and the Simply One might be understood as pre-existing everywhere. Plotinus discusses four realms, the non-realm of the One, the realm of Intellect, the realm of Soul and the sensible realm. Later Neoplatonists expand upon this. For Iamblichus, to speak of the One having a realm makes little sense, and in truth, Plotinus thinks the same. We may call this a realm only for convenience.[342]

The first of the Iamblichean spiritual realms is the "noetic" realm, which Ficino calls the "Angelic Mind." It is at the head of this realm that the One-Being rests as its Monad in the form of the Aion and Paradigm. It is also from this realm that the "noetic" or "intelligible" triad is found. The intelligible triad is what ultimately gives rise to all beings, their lives and intellects at lower levels in a rich interweaving of the three parts of the triad at three different levels. These three levels make up the noetic or intelligible, noetic-noeric or intelligible-intellective,

---

[342] C.f. Ficino, DAm, I.3, 38. "The "realm" of the One, or God, is not properly called a realm at all because *world* means *ornament, composed of many*, whereas God must be completely simple." (*Ibid.*)

and noeric or intellective aspects of this realm. Intellective refers to that which thinks. Intellective thinking grasps the intelligibles, or that which are thought of.

But what does this mean? The three moments discussed in the previous chapter come into play here. Each part of the triad has its own set of moments, with the last moment of one triad being the first moment of the next. The highest part, the noetic, belongs to Being. The middle or noetic-noeric, belongs to Life, and the noeric to Intellect. But again, what does this mean? What does it mean to be "intelligible" or "intellective" or both?

Intelligible means that which can be thought of, and can be used to describe both this and the noeric realm, which may be considered a "sub-realm" of the noetic. They are not thoughts in that the mind creates them. Instead, they are what the mind grasps when thinking, pre-existing the thoughts created by the mind. Using the three moments model, we describe this part of the realm is the "unparticipated" moment, the intelligibles before being grasped by the mind. The intelligibles are like the contents of the mind. However, in Plato's way of thinking, the contents of the mind pre-exist the mind itself. In other words, the mind is not a *tabula rasa*; learning is remembering. The act of remembering, or the use of the intellect to grasp the intelligibles, is posterior to that which is being grasped. Being originates from Aion in the noetic part of the noetic-noeric realm. As an extension of the One-Being, Aion has non-Being, existing before the rise of the quality of Being.

"Being" is what gives entities their existence and their ultimate nature and preserves their order, making it close to the nature of essence, *ousia*.[343] That is to say Being is what defines a being as itself and not something else. Being is closely connected to thought. If something can be thought of then it is thought of as being, as existing. Because of this, like the One, Aion, Eternity, cannot truly be thought about. What we think about Aion reflects ourselves more than it does Aion. Beings ontologically closer to Aion have more Being, have more existence, than those farther away. As such, Being denotes a kind of limitation or demarcation, something the One, in any of its forms, does not have. Being is the primary composition of existence in the noetic realm and below. As the first moment of the first part of the intellectual triad, Aion is both prior to Being and Being's source.

This is common to late pagan Platonic thought. The source of something does not contain that element within itself, but is instead beyond it. Everything occurring posterior to the source participates the source to varying degrees. But nothing has it fully, or else they would have no need of participation. Thus Aion does not have Being, and has no need of it. Everything after Aion does to varying degrees, and needs Being because it is ontologically posterior to Being's source, therefore lacking it to some degree. The ineffable One is beyond everything. One

---

[343] DM, I.5, p21.

can say of it neither that it is God or not God, nor can we say, in reference to the One, that there is a God or that there is no God. The One cannot be thought of at all.[344]

The closer something is to the source, the fuller it has what comes from that source. In this case, the gods or divine intelligibles of Iamblichus' system have the most Being.[345] They are the most well defined beings that exist. Pure human souls, on the other hand, are the farthest from the source, and are so the least well defined as unique beings, filled with the attributes of the gods and Forms. Practically, this means the gods know precisely what they are, without mistake, without question, without seeking. Human souls, however, have a hard time understanding themselves, knowing what they are, and why they exist.

In typical Iamblichean fashion, the noeric or intellective realm[346] does not directly follow the noetic. Instead, there is a mean in the form of the noetic-noeric realm. This realm between the noetic and noeric is not a mathematical affectation, used merely to fit in with other trinities within his system. The mean is an important link in the chain of being. The mean functions as the connector between what comes before and what comes after. It is a melding of the two aspects, allowing the higher mode to affect the lower. Without the mean there is no way for the mind to grasp the intelligibles. Instead, the intelligibles will always be above and beyond everything posterior to them. This means, for example, the gods cannot affect in any way the physical cosmos and our minds will be empty of thought. So the noetic-noeric portion of this realm, like all means, is as important as what comes before and after.

The intelligible-intellective realm is not simply a bridge, however. This is the realm where the quality of Life holds sway. Life has already formed in the noetic realm, as a sub-quality of Being, but here we find Life as Life and not as an aspect of noetic Being or noeric Intellect. It is at this level the "*monads of the Forms,*" the noetic-noeric gods, are found.[347] The Forms themselves are only in the noeric level.

The intellective or noeric realm is that of Intellect proper. This is where noetic reality is grasped by the divine mind. It is not surprising, then, that the Platonic Forms, rendered alternatively as *eidos* and *idea*, are found at this level. The Forms, the realities the physical world reflects, are fully present at here. This *idea* is represented in the *Republic*'s famous Allegory of the Cave.[348]

The allegory is presented in the contemplations on wisdom. We are like beings in a dark cave, chained so that not even our heads can move. We all face a wall

---

[344] C.f. Perl, *Theophany*, 13-14

[345] *Ibid.*

[346] We may call this a realm for convenience, as it may also be seen as a part of the whole noetic realm rather than something distinct.

[347] *In Phil.*, fr. 4.

[348] *Rep.* 514a–520a.

where we see shadows moving around. We can hear, but what we hear is distorted by echoes and distance. But we don't see the shadows as shadows and we don't recognize the sounds as distorted, because this is all we experience. For us, the shadows are the real things, the distortions are what is normal and right. We don't know we're in a cave being illuminated by a fire behind us. We don't know the wavering shadows are not true reality.

Even if we are freed, a horrible experience for any of us, being ripped out of what we thought was real and thrown into a strange and unfamiliar world; we still do not experience reality. We see, once our eyes adjust to the fire light, solid bodies casting those wavering shadows, and a flickering source that makes the shadows possible. We can walk up to a chained person and hear the sounds they made without distortion. In time we might even come to understand what we hear and see. But we're still inside the cave.

Most of us fight not to be taken from the cave. Inside the cave is a known reality. Even when we are free we are in a place we know, even if we experience it differently. But outside the cave? Anything can be out there. So we must be dragged out, kicking and screaming, and are sun-blind as we emerge. We cannot look up at the true source of light. So we look down, and again, as our eyes adjust, we see shadows. But this time the shadows come from a clear source in a fully illuminated world. And, after a time, we begin to look around. We see the grass and the trees and a lake and our reflection, and, slowly, we turn our gaze upwards until we see the sun itself.

This is what our lives are like. The cave is the physical world, which is as far away from the source of Being as possible. This is a world we think is real, but in truth consists only of shadowy reflections. Reflections based on the Forms, but ones far below the Forms, just as the fire is only a dim reflection of sunlight. Our freedom from the shackles of the cave is analogous to the beginnings of the practice of philosophy and theurgy. We see the Forms manifested in the physical in the mode of "tokens" or "signatures" and the world of the soul. But then we go outside, dragged by our daimons, or guardian spirits, who want what is right and good for us. And we are blinded by the world of intellect. Only now do we begin to grasp true reality. The things we see around us are real things, the Forms upon which what we saw in the cave were based, and they are illuminated not by a flickering, weak fire but by the source of all fire, the sun itself. And in this light true reality is grasped, so far as possible.

There is one final part to the allegory. In the end the free soul, the theurgic sage, voluntarily returns to the cave. It is hard for us to see there, as we have the light of the sun in our eyes, but we have come to free others, and do so with love. And, just like us when we were chained there, no one wants to be free.

Much as Being is the primary mode of the noetic world and Life that of the noetic-noeric, Intellect is foremost in the noeric. The lowest portion of the noeric, which contains intellect of Intellect, is Nous, the divine Mind. This lowest part of the overall noetic realm is also the top-most portion of the next hypostasis, that of psyche or soul.

The Psychic Realm

The psychic realm, the realm of the soul and the World Soul,[349] sometimes referred to as the celestial realm or Heaven, is the last of the spiritual realms above the realm of generation and the physical cosmos. Iamblichus is vague on this point, sometimes treating this as a distinct realm and sometimes as part of the noeric realm. Here we may see Nous reflected into this realm as the monad of the Soul, or the unparticipated Whole Soul, which exists as a whole in the form of the World Soul, and as parts or individual souls.[350] Because Intellect is the monad of the Soul, Soul participates Intellect, and so is able to grasp the intelligibles and be joined to higher levels. So, once again we find the three moments present throughout the noetic realm, which continue into the psychic. The Whole Soul is *"transcendent and hypercosmic and independent and exerting authority over all,"* and *"imparticipable and placed over all the souls in the cosmos as their monad."*[351] Following the established pattern, the participated from of the Whole Soul is the World Soul, and the soul in participation are individual souls.

The creation of the body of the World Soul is described in the *Timaeus*.[352] In this cosmogonic myth the World Soul is described as being modeled after Aion, and is given the form of the Greek letter chi (X), holding within itself the powers of Sameness and Difference, together with their mean or mixture, which are reflections of the dyad in the realm of the One. The bands of the X are brought together as a sphere composed of two crossing circles, with the outer circle of Sameness rotating horizontally to the right and the inner circle of Difference turning diagonally to the left. The circle of difference is divided into seven sections, carrying the pneumatic vehicles of the planetary or visible gods. Finally, Soul is connected to this body, being diffused evenly and throughout from the centre to the extremities, making the World Soul as an image of Aion.

Time and Space begin in the psychic realm. This is not mundane, but transcendent Time and Space. Transcendent Time, *chronos*, rather than Aion, is described as an image of Aion in the psychic realm, the celestial realm of the soul:

> *"Wherefore [the Demiurge] resolved to have a moving image of Aion, and when he set in order the heaven, he made this image Aion but moving according to number, while Aion itself rests in unity, and this image we call Time."*[353]

---

349 DAm I.3. 38.
350 Cf. Shaw, *Theurgy*, 62.
351 *In Tim.* fr. 50.
352 34b-37c.
353 *Tim.* 37d, with modifications.

In this realm Time is instantaneous, there is still no "before" and "after," no measurement of change of state. Cause and effect are simultaneous. Time here is not ordered, but ordering: *"there is an order of time, not however an order which is ordered, but one which orders . . . .'*[354] The ability for transcendent time to function in this way comes from Nous.[355]

As we have established that transcendent Time is not a measurement of change or motion, then what is Time and from where does it come? As an image of Aion, Time is established in the psychic realm, modeled on the three moments. Time is an image of Aion by way of Time's *"cyclic unfolding and continuity and successiveness, and by distinguishing beginnings and middles and ends and in not to any extent being found wanting to any of the things encompassed by it . . . .'*[356] Ultimately, Time is an image of Aion because Time participates Aion.

Things that participate an ontologically prior reality preserve within themselves something of what they participate, an image or imprint of the higher essence.[357] Time is also the first image, as Aion cannot be said to be an image of the One, because the One has no image. Given this, the nature of Time and its relationship to the psychic realm, we might conclude that the psychic realm is itself an image of the noetic, just as Psyche participates Nous. Likewise, the cosmos is an image of the Essential Living Being, or the Whole Soul, Nous in the psychic realm.[358] The human soul, then, exists as an image within an image of an image of Aion.

As an image of Aion, Time also has three moments and is related to Being, Life, and Intellect. The three moments or qualities Time receives from Aion are *"the idea of 'was' and 'will be,'" "becoming younger and older,"* and *"coming to be at the same time or having now come to be or destined to be on another occasion.'*[359] The first quality comes from Being, the second from Life, and the third from Intellect. The first quality, coming from Being, is the granting of Being. The second, becoming younger and older, denotes the idea of growth from Life. The third, where we'd expect the granting of intellect, instead suggests the idea of individuation,[360] which is related to Nous. Time, however, does not so much contain these within itself, but passes them along to the physical world and mundane time, acting as a mean between the highest and lowest realms.

Even when Time is not seen in a direct relation to motion, we still find a connection between the ideas of Time and space. Once again, Iamblichus is not concerned with physical space, but of a kind of transcendent or psychic Space.

---

354 *In Tim.* fr. 63.
355 *Ibid.*
356 *Ibid.*, fr. 64.
357 *Ibid.*
358 *Ibid.*
359 *In Tim.* fr. 65.
360 Dillon, *Commentaries,* 349-50.

Space comes into being at the same time as bodies, inextricably linking them together, but the bodies under discussion are divine and ethereal, not mortal and physical. To think of Space as merely physical is a *"perverting [of] its essence into bounds of surfaces"* and fails to link *"Nature to the activity of the Demiurge."*[361]

Space is linked directly to the causative forces of creation, and cannot be removed from that cause to be understood in merely physical terms. This is a rejection of Aristotle, which is fitting as we have already rejected Aristotle's mundane notions of time. Instead of seeing space and bodies as separate, Iamblichus says in the psychic realm space and bodies are connatural. Space is *"a corporeal power which supports bodies and forces them apart and gathers them up when they fall and collects them together when they are scattered about, at once completing them and encompassing them about from all sides."*[362] Space is a completion of bodies, and a unifying force, rather than simply where bodies exist.

The Phenomenal Realm, Fate and Providence

The final link in the chain of being is the phenomenal cosmos. Like the world above, the phenomenal world has three portions: hypercosmic, encosmic, and a hyper-encosmic mean in between. Unfortunately, Iamblichus tells us little about the hypercosmic realm except that it cannot be conceived of through the human mind and that it is the home of the hypercosmic or invisible gods. This does not mean it cannot be thought of, only that we cannot think of it. The hypercosmic realm may be seen as a reflection of the noetic realm in the created cosmos. The hyper-encosmic and "liberated" realm is a reflection of the noetic-noeric realm, connecting the upper and lower levels as a mean and is home to the liberated gods.[363]

The encosmic realm, home of the visible gods, consists of the spheres of the a fiery and eternal ether, which may include the fixed stars, the seven planets and the physical or "sub-lunar" universe, called by Marsilio Ficino *"the whole machine which we see,"* and the *"World Body."*[364] Iamblichus divides the sub-lunar realm into three sections, the aether, ruled by Kronos, the air, ruled by Rhea, and the sea or water ruled by Phorcys. Beneath this is the Earth itself,[365] which may be symbolic of the material universe. In the Allegory of the Cave, the physical world is the cave and its chains. Iamblichus' understanding of this world is drastically different from not only his Middle Platonist forbearers, but his Neoplatonic forbearers as well. Whereas earlier Platonists see the world as either evil or the cause of evil,

---

[361] *In Tim.* fr. 90.

[362] *Ibid.*

[363] C.f. Darrow, "Orphism," 200.

[364] DAm, I.3, 38.

[365] *In Tim.* fr. 77.

Iamblichus condones neither view as properly Platonic. The difficulty lays in the differing ways the material world is treated in the Platonic dialogues.

In the dialogues, especially the *Phaedo* and the *Timaeus*, the descent of the soul into the body is considered alternatively negative and through force (the *Phaedo*), or positively and through an act of free will (the *Timaeus*). This seemingly dual approach to incarnation, which we will discuss further in chapter fourteen, has repercussions concerning ideas about the nature of matter, or that which is incarnated into. Ultimately, Iamblichus' solution is that in and of itself, matter is not bad, but the accretions of matter around the soul can have negative spiritual effects.

The late Platonic notion of matter, or *hylē*, is not composed of atoms or molecules or, in fact, connected to any scientific conception of matter. Instead, *hylē* can be thought of as an empty form, waiting to be filled. The filling of *hylē* by the Platonic Forms and their *logoi* creates the impression of all the things we experience in the physical world. These things are neither distinctly themselves nor distinctly the Forms but something in-between, being real, but not "really real" as are the Intelligibles. *Hylē* itself is empty, but when filled with *logoi* it becomes like "matter" as we normally understand the word.

Matter is not created by the Demiurge. Instead it comes from the One and is understood to be eternal, making the cosmos eternal. The Demiurge only directs the *logoi* and thereby shapes matter. Even if the purely physical aspects of the cosmos change, the cosmos itself will continue in some form.

The rejection of matter as evil leaves us with a problem. If matter is evil, we can easily understand why there is evil in the world. But what happens when matter is not evil? How do we understand the cause of all those unfortunate things that happen? As we'll discuss in the next chapter, we cannot blame the gods or the higher beings. For the most part, their connection to the Good prevents them from being able to act in an evil manner. Part of the issue is our own diluted relationship with the Good. But that cannot account for everything. The final piece of the puzzle is the role of Fate.

Fate, *Eimarmei*, according to Iamblichus, is *"the one order that comprehends in itself all other orders."*[366] By this, Iamblichus means Fate is the ordering force controlling all other orders in the sub-lunar realm and all things subject to generation.[367] This includes the incarnate, impure soul. While under the sway of Fate we are also subject to the necessities of nature, which include living, dying, pain, suffering and a host of other ills that are good for nature and its functioning, but not necessarily perceived as such by us.

---

[366] L8, fr. 1.

[367] L12.

This ends the first part of our discussion on the chain of being. Each of the worlds forms a link, or several links, in this chain, stretching from the One to physical matter. Every part of this multi-cosmic structure is interconnected, and this is an essential component of Iamblichus' theology. If there are links missing anywhere in the chain, that which exists below the break cannot receive from that which remains above. This describes a desolate universe, devoid of meaning and spirit. The universe Iamblichus describes is one filled with meaning and life. This meaning inherent to the universe, placed there by the Demiurge, gods and other divine beings, gives us our meaning and our means to return to the One.

In the next chapters we will fill the wonderful, life-filled creation with beings, from a god beyond the gods down to human souls. It is only right, then, that we begin with the first being, the primary servant of the One: the Demiurge.

Chapter Eleven

The Demiurge

The various realms are filled with beings, from gods to souls. But no being is quite as enigmatic or controversial as the Demiurge. Even talking about "the Demiurge" presents a difficulty, and later Neoplatonism posits multiple Demiurges, in various schemes, without always differentiating between them in title.

What is the, or a, Demiurge? The English word comes from the Greek *Demiurgos*, variously translated as "craftsman" or "public worker." The Demiurge is mentioned throughout the Platonic corpus and holds an important role in the *Timaeus* and *Phaedo*. Still, the nature of the Demiurge is open to interpretation, and two major themes concerning the Demiurgic essence have come down to us, one from Neoplatonism and one from Neoplatonism's older cousin, Gnosticism.

Yaltabaoth vs. Helios, or What's in a Name?

For some, the Gnostic Demiurge may be the more familiar of the two. In classical Gnosticism the Demiurge, sometimes named Yaltabaoth or Yaldabaoth, is an evil and arrogant creator, a false God, brought forth in error by the aeon or hypostasis Sophia, divine Wisdom. This is well portrayed in the second century Sethian Gnostic text *The Apocryphon of John*.

> *"And because of the invincible power which is in [Sophia], her thought did not remain idle and a thing came out of her which was imperfect and different from her appearance, because she had created it without her consort.*[368] *And it was dissimilar to the likeness of its mother for it has another form.*
>
> *And when she saw (the consequences) of her desire, it had changed into a form of a lion-faced serpent. And its eyes were like lightning fires which flash. She cast it away from her, outside that place,*[369] *that no one of the immortal ones might see it, for she had created it in ignorance. And she surrounded it with a luminous cloud, and she placed a throne in the middle of the cloud that no one might see it except the holy Spirit who is called the mother of the living. And she called his name Yaltabaoth.*
>
> …

---

368 The aeon Barbello or Christos.

369 The Pleroma or divine realm analogous to the noetic realm.

> *And when he saw the creation which surrounds him and the multitude of the angels round him which had come forth from him, he said to them, 'I am a jealous God and there is no other God besides me.'"*[370]

Together Yaltabaoth and the "angels," otherwise identified as evil archons or celestial governors, create Adam and Eve, though humanity's life-giving essence comes from beyond this Demiurge and his archons. Though this is not the only Gnostic interpretation of the Demiurge, some depict him as simply ignorant, deluded or deranged, and not actively evil, it is still representative of the general view of classical Gnosticism: the Demiurge is bad.

While Gnosticism derives some of its theological and philosophical elements from Middle Platonism, it is not limited to that. The image of Yaltabaoth, a lion-headed serpent, suggests the same Persian and Mithraic origin as Aion. The references to Adam and Eve place the Gnosticism of this period fully within the realm of Abrahamic religions, and with Christ taking the starring role, Christianity. Given all the concerns with which Gnosticism deals, and all its various sources, it is not surprising when the *Apocryphon* speaks of the Demiurge, it talks about something different from what Neoplatonists mean by the same word, even though both share a basic formative function.

There are Platonic aspects in the Gnostic view of the Demiurge, but there is also clearly something different. For instance, how does the description in the *Apocryphon* fit with *Timaeus'* description?

> *"Let me tell you then why the creator made this world of generation. He was good, and the good can never have any jealousy of anything. And being free from jealousy, he desired that all things should be as like himself as they could . . . [The Demiurge] desired that all things should be good and nothing bad, so far as this was attainable."*[371]

The Neoplatonic Demiurge is a far cry from its Sethian counterpart. From where do the differences come, and are there any similarities? The differences likely originate in the discrepancies between Gnostic and Neoplatonic understandings of incarnation and the nature of matter. The classical Gnostic view is almost entirely negative. This is reflected in the thought of Plotinus and Porphyry, and rejected by the later Neoplatonists. If descent into matter and generation is inherently bad, that which creates matter and generation is also bad. As God can't be evil, God cannot have created the physical world. Yaltabaoth becomes the perpetuator of the realm of generation and our subsequent enslavement to false gods. Only through the aeon Christos, or Barbelo, can we learn of our true nature, that we possess the divine spark, and return to the pleroma or noetic realm.

What of the Neoplatonic Demiurge? If God is good, and the physical world is good, why need a Demiurge? There are at least two reasons. First, although God

---

370 AJ, 10.1-.19, 13.5-10.
371 *Tim.* 29e-30a.

is good, and the Good, God is also utterly transcendent and so creates nothing. The *Timaeus* describes the physical world as a creation, not an emanation. It must have another cause. Second, though the physical world isn't evil, it is also not exactly good.

There are some other important differences. First, in Gnostic cosmology, the Demiurge is not responsible for the creation of souls in anyway. In the *Apocryphon of John*, Yaltabaoth and his archons are only able to create human bodies, but not rational souls. Only by bestowing the divine sparks Sophia accidentally puts into her creation upon them are the bodies brought to life.[372] Yaltabaoth is only the means through which souls come into bodies. However, the World Soul and rational souls proceed from the Neoplatonic Demiurge.

Second, Yaltabaoth declares himself the one true God, which suggests to the archons he is in fact not God, otherwise why bother declaring it?[373] The Platonic Demiurge does not declare itself to be the one true God, nor is it understood as such, and is known only as the god of gods or second god beneath the Good and the One. This fits its role in the *Timaeus*. There is no deception on the part of the Demiurge, for the Demiurgic nature is not just good, but of the Good itself.

Despite these wide ideological differences, there are still similarities between the two Demiurgic views. The primary parallel is that they are both creator deities. There is no denying that the Neoplatonic Demiurge shapes and forms entire realms and their spiritual inhabitants. That incarnation is generally positive and a necessity in later Neoplatonism, and not in Gnosticism, does not detract from this.

The Three-Fold Demiurge

At some point Iamblichus writes the now lost *Peri Theon*, or *On the Gods*. However, there are elements in book VII of *De Mysteriis* that appear[374] to do for the Egyptian gods what *Peri Theon* likely did for the Greek divinities. Though *De Mysteriis* gives certain details as to the nature of the Demiurge, the fullest report of Iamblichean Demiurgic theology comes to us through Emperor Flavius Julianus Augustus' *Hymn to King Helios*. This, along with relevant portions of Iamblichus and Plato, especially the *Timaeus* and *Phaedo*, help form our views of this first child of the One.

Emperor Julianus or Julian, also known as Julian the Philosopher,[375] is often credited as the last pagan emperor of Rome. A near contemporary of Iamblichus, Julian asks one of Iamblichus' senior students, Aedesius, to become his teacher.

---

372 AJ 15.1-19.33

373 *Ibid.* 13.10-.13

374 Clark, "Egyptian," 200.

375 Or derisively as "Julian the Apostate," for his conversion to a Neoplatonically influenced Roman paganism from his native Christianity.

Aedesius turns down the appointment and offers his own student, Maximus of Ephesus, in his place.[376] Julian also has in his collection of Iamblicheana Sallustius' *Concerning the Gods and the Universe*, which is inspired by *Peri Theon*.[377] Given this, it is likely Julian's own theological writings reflect Iamblichean theology as well.[378]

So far, we've discussed "the Demiurge," but that isn't an accurate approach to the subject. Although Plotinus postulates a single Demiurge at the lowest point of the Intellectual Triad, Iamblichus has three: one ruling over the noetic realm, one ruling the noeric and encosmic realms, and one over the sub-lunar world.[379] In Iamblichus, each Demiurge may be represented by several different deities, or several deities subsumed into a single god.

Eternity, the Pre-Essential Demiurgos

Iamblichus describes the first Demiurge as pre-essential, *proousios*.[380] This Demiurge is further described with a series of theurgical epitaphs: "father of himself," *autopater*; "principle of himself," *autarchis*; "god of gods," *theos theon*; "father of essence," *ousiopator*; "principle of intellection," *noetarchis prosagoreoetai*; and "monad from the One," *monas ek tou enos*.[381] To these, Julian adds "supra-intelligible," *epekeina tou nou*, and "Idea of Being," *idean ton onton*.[382] These titles fit well with the idea of the One-Being, rather than a Demiurge, yet we are assured of the existence of a pre-essential Demiurge.

Who is this Demiurge, and what is its nature? Iamblichus says the pre-essential Demiurge *"gathers into one and holds within himself"* the entire noetic cosmos.[383] Proclus takes this to mean the pre-essential Demiurge is the entire noetic realm. However, this seems unlikely. If nothing else, Iamblichus' cosmology is consistent within a given text. The other Demiurges do not follow this model and there is another Demiurge at the lowest extremity of the noeric realm. Instead, it seems more likely Iamblichus describes an intellectual act of *"noeric self-thought."*[384] The pre-essential Demiurge, as the transcendent and hypercosmic "Father of the Demiurges," *patros ton demiourgon*, is not thinking itself into existence but the other two Demiurges, described as "demiurgic thoughts" in

---

376 Dillon and Polleichtner, "Introduction," in *Letters*, xiv.

377 Clarke, et al., "Introduction," in *De Mysteriis*, xxiv.

378 Clark, "Egyptian," 183.

379 *In Soph*, fr. 1. Proclus, possibly following *Peri Theon*, posits triads of Demiurges at each level.

380 DM VIII.2.

381 *Ibid.*

382 *Hymn*, 359.

383 *In Tim.* fr. 34.

384 Clark, "Egyptian," 189.

Iamblichus' commentary on the *Sophist*,[385] the first of which is identified as Zeus, whom Julian equates with Helios, and the second as Hermes.[386]

Who is this Demiurge that is higher than even Zeus and Helios? Iamblichus says the Paradigm, the monad or highest principle of the noetic realm, is contained within the Demiurge and is identified with *"the first Zeus,"*[387] above Julian's noeric Zeus. The Paradigm is also Aion, lion-headed Eternity, the vertical extension of the One-Being in the noetic realm.[388] This association places the Father of Demiurges at the summit of the noetic realm, as an intelligible aspect of the One, hence the first Demiurge's pre-essential nature. In this respect, Proclus' interpretation of Aion encompassing the whole of the noetic realm has some merit. Aion is the three noetic moments existing at the noetic, noetic-noeric, and noeric levels, as well as the encompassing monad and henad, the unifying divinity, of the noetic realm.

The identification of Aion/Paradigm with the pre-essential, noetic Demiurge is supported in book VIII of *De Mysteriis*. Iamblichus, using the Egyptian pantheon to fit his Abammon persona, identifies the celestial Demiurge as the god Kmeph, over which is set *"the indivisible One and what [Hermes] calls the 'first product,' which he also calls Ikton."*[389] The implication is that the pre-essential Demiurge set over the celestial Demiurge is this *"Ikton," the monad of the noetic realm.*[390] Dennis Clark identifies Iamblichus' Ikton, more properly Heikton, as the Egyptian god Heka.[391] Heka is both the god of magic and the personification of magic or, as Iamblichus puts it, the *"first act of magic."*[392] Though Heka might only be associated with the idea of time through the connection of magic with Djehuti or Thoth, Aion and Heka both represent cosmogonic forces, further tying them together.

Aion and Heikton preside over essence and Being. They are both before essence and the source of essence and essentiality.[393] Both come into existence before the gods. As god of magic, Heikton is an excellent choice for pre-essential Demiurge, from which all theurgy ultimately descends. This may seem confusing at first, as theurgy is not magic. But the Egyptian *Coffin Texts* describe Heka/Heikton as the primordial creative power used by Atum-Re in the act of creating the cosmos, which well describes theurgy. Heikton comes into being before duality from/as the One-Being/pre-essential Demiurge, before the Word

---

385 *In Soph.* fr. 1.

386 Julian, *Hymn*, 391.

387 *In Tim.* fr. 36.

388 Finamore, *Vehicle*, 139.

389 DM VIII.3, 311.

390 *Ibid.*, n. 410.

391 Clark, "Egyptian," 173.

392 *Ibid.*, 166, n. 3. Clark's "first act of magic" is an restoration of *mageoma*, which Clark *et al* replace with Gale's alternative translation *maieoma*, "first product." See DM VIII.3, 311, n. 409.

393 DM VIII.2, 309.

of creation is spoken.[394] Because of this, Iamblichus informs us the only appropriate way to worship the pre-essential Demiurge is through silence.[395]

In Gnosticism and Jewish Kabbalah are concepts similar to Aion/Heikton. The Gnostic *Apocryphon of John* describes a three-fold descent of saving power in the form of three figures. The first is the Autogenes Christos, the Self-Generated Saviour, or the Mother-Father, who causes Yaldabaoth to place the divine essence into the Biblical Adam.[396] That Autogenes is an aspect of Barbelo or Pronoia, Forethought, the first Gnostic hypostasis, is clear from a Gnostic text called *Marsanes*.[397] Though in *Marsanes* Autogenes Christos holds the final position within Barbelo in the *Apocryphon* Autogenes is the first descending power, linking it more closely with Aion.

Amongst the Kabbalists the divine name Eheieh holds a similar position to that of the pre-essential Demiurge. The name is derived from *Exodus*. Moses asks God whom should he tell the Hebrews sent him, Moses, to rescue them. God tells Moses "eheieh asher eheieh," which may be translated as "I am that I am" or, more tellingly, "I will be what I will be." Eheieh, "I will be," well represents the pre-essential nature of Aion. This name is located at the top of the Tree of Life at the sefira Keter, the Crown, and directly below the ultimate, negative form of God called Ain, Nothing, analogous to the One. As neither the divine names of the sefirot, nor the emanated sefirot themselves, are considered God in Kabbalistic thought, there is a close correlation between the names and their sefirot to the Neoplatonic hypostases beneath the One.

Neoplatonism is brought successfully into Islam, and especially into Sufism. However, unlike the Kabbalists, Muslim mystics do not always give new appellations to many of the figures. As such, though various forms of the Demiurge are found within Islamic Neoplatonism, they do not necessarily have specific names such as those found in Jewish, Christian or pagan Neoplatonisms. A possible exception to this is the angel Shahrivar, derived from Zoroastrianism and brought into Sufism by the Kurdish philosopher Shahab al-Din Suhrawardi, who identifies Shahrivar with Prince or Lord Hûrakhsh, a solar angel. This figure is best identified with the noeric rather than the noetic Demiurge.

All this describes the pre-essential Demiurge very well, but what does it do? One of the primary activities of this Demiurge is thinking. In that it is the monad and henad, the power of unity in the whole of the noetic realm, it is the source of that which is thought, and therefore Being, in the noetic realm. This principle of intellection thinks the other Demiurges, and Being itself, into existence. The Demiurge acts as the source of the intelligible triad, and so is also the source of

---

394 Clark, "Egyptian," 176.
395 DM VIII.3, 311.
396 AJ 19.15-19.32. Cf. Turner, *Gnostic*, 326.
397 *Mar* 3.25-3.27.

Being, Life, and Intellect and represents the first movement of the One from the universal to the particular.

The Leader of the Leader Gods – The Noeric Demiurgos

When the phrase "the Demiurge" is used without exception, it usually refers to the celestial Demiurge. This is the main subject of Julian's *Hymn to King Helios*. As an outline of Demiurgic theology the *Hymn* is highly informative. The noeric Demiurge holds the position of the third moment of the noetic realm and is usually identified as *Nous*, Mind or Intellect.

Julian describes an entire solar, Demiurgic theology: a transcendental Helios who rules over the noetic cosmos, Helios, "king of all," *vasilea ton olon*, the ruler of the noeric realm intellective gods, [398] and finally the visible sun ruling over the world of generation.[399] Helios is the mean between the noetic and sensible realms[400] and their corresponding gods, an important position for the working of theurgy. Julian may have been aware of this important role when he defined "mean" as *"that which unites and leads together things that are separate."*[401]

Elements of Julian's solar theology, though based on the lost *Peri Theon*, are also found in Iamblichus' Egyptian theology in *De Mysteriis*. Here, Iamblichus lists five gods: Heikton, Kmeph, Amoun, Ptah and Osiris.[402] We've already seen the connection between Heikton/Heka and Aion, but this is also relevant in connecting Julian's Hellenic solar theology to Iamblichus' Egyptian theology. The *Coffin Texts* describe the power of Heikton as of the highest order, pre-existing and requisite to the creative power of Atum-Re, who like Amoun, is associated with the solar god-king Re, just like Helios.[403]

Iamblichus does not mention Atum-Re in his theology, but he is familiar enough with Egyptian theology, much of it coming through the Hermetic rather than classical Egyptian sources, to make the above connection. He does mention Amoun and Kmeph, who are placed a step lower than the ontologically prior Heikton.[404] Amoun, an Egyptian solar deity often connected to the god-king Re, is called the "demiurgic intellect," or "creative mind," *dimiourgikos nous*, and "master" or "protector of truth and wisdom," *alitheias prostatis kai sofias*.[405] Amoun is well-known to the Greeks as Amoun Zeus, a significant connection for Julian's theology.

---

398 Julian, *Hymn*, 359, 361, 375, 385-7, etc.

399 Clark, *Egyptian*, 183. Julian is largely silent on the sub-lunar Demiurge. See, *Hymn*, 369.

400 *Ibid.*, 359.

401 Julian, *Hymn*, 377.

402 DM, VIII.3, 311-313.

403 Clark, "Egyptian," 176.

404 DM, VIII.3, 311.

405 *Ibid.*

Unlike Amoun, Kmeph is less well known. Iamblichus calls him "the leader of the celestial gods," *epouranion theon igoumenon*, and an "intellect thinking himself," *noun einai aton eaton noounta.*[406] "Leader of the celestial gods" is exactly how Julian refers to Helios. As an "intellect," Kmeph is firmly connected to Amoun in the noeric realm, again like Helios.

Though Heikton is not found in other Greek texts, Kmeph is identified in Greek writing with the Egyptian god Kematef, which means "one who has completed his moment, his time," possibly referring to time as it exists before creation,[407] analogous to the transcendent Time of the psychic realm. Through Kematef, we find our connection to the sun, as Atum-Re is described as the "Ba," the soul or lower manifestation, of Kematef.[408] This may link Atem-Re with the sub-lunar Demiurge, the visible sun in Julian's theology, but it also definitively connects Kmeph with solar symbolism and, with his other epitaphs, Julian's noeric Helios. Also, the *Papyri Graecae Magicae*, or PGM, explicitly associates Kmeph with Helios: *"PERTAOMECH PERAKONCHMECH PERAKOMPHTHOAK KMEPH, the brilliant Sun, who shines throughout the whole inhabited world."*[409]

Julian's Demiurgic theology is somewhat more complex than it may otherwise seem. Though his association of Helios with the noeric Demiurge is clear, Helios is also connected to other deities as well. We will discuss some of this in the next chapter, where Iamblichus' tendency towards a form of panentheism is made clear. There we will see how the phenomenal gods are subsumed within the essence of their noeric Demiurge. Here, however, something different occurs. While gods such as Dionysos and Athena are subsumed *into* Helios; Zeus, the king of the Olympic gods, is made identical *with* Helios.[410]

Zeus' Demiurgic nature goes back to at least Plotinus,[411] and it is in part through the association of Zeus with Helios that we learn some of the Demiurge's functions. The noeric Helios-Zeus has dominion *"over the separate creation which is prior to substances,"*[412] or the psychic realm. The Demiurge's ordering power over the psychic realm stems from Plato's *Timaeus*,[413] where the Demiurge is described as creating the World Soul and the phenomenal realm. *Timaeus'* Demiurge, the "creator of the universe," addresses the visible gods, tells them how the universe should work, and sets them to their tasks.[414]

---

[406] *Ibid.*, 309.
[407] Clark, "Egyptian," 178.
[408] *Ibid.*
[409] PGM III.141-143.
[410] Julian, *Hymn*, 393.
[411] Dillon, "Theology," 110.
[412] Julian, *Hymn*, 393.
[413] 29d-40d.
[414] 41a-d.

What we see is that Zeus/Helios/Amoun/Kmeph, the noeric Demiurge, is a god of formation and order. This is the Demiurge who fashions the World Soul and mixes the souls of the phenomenal gods, the greater beings and humanity and orders the gods to place the physical realm in its proper order.[415] All of these creations are eternal in nature, and so it is not surprising to find Kmeph depicted as the Ouroboros,[416] which is similar to what Plato uses to describe the "eternal living being" or World Soul.[417] As divine mean, the noeric Demiurge connects the physical and intelligible realms.

In Jewish mysticism the creative Demiurgic force is aptly associated with the so-called Tetragrammaton, Hevayah, Yahweh or YHVH. As the central-most divine name within Jewish Kabbalah, Yahweh fits perfectly with Julian's Demiurgic "mean."

Unlike the pre-essential Demiurge, we may turn to Neoplatonism, rather than Gnosticism, for a Christian Demiurgic analogue. In this instance, we look towards Pseudo-Dionysius. In the *Celestial Hierarchy*, Dionysius describes Jesus as the one *"through Whom we have access to the Father."*[418] That is, Jesus is the mean between God the Father, whom we may identify with the One, and the realm of generation. Further, Jesus is described as establishing and revealing the celestial hierarchy,[419] much as does *Timaeus*' Demiurge. To further this connection, we turn to Iamblichus' placement of Heikton in the role of pre-essential Demiurge. Egyptian myths describe Heikton, or Heka, *"as a power even before the first utterance of the Logos."*[420] Logos, Word, is a title of the Christos from the *Gospel of John*: *"In the beginning was the Word, and the Word was with God, and the Word was God."*[421] So, specifically, it is Jesus as Logos, following after the Autogenes Christos, who holds this position.

An Encosmic Demiurgos?

Julian's theology describes the visible sun as a third demiurgic power. Helios is the sun itself and the Greek word for the sun as well. But do we really need an encosmic Demiurge? We do not, because we already have one. Noeric Helios is described as the leader of the celestial gods. The celestial gods are the encosmic or visible gods of *De Mysteriis*. As such, noeric Helios is the Demiurge of both the noeric and phenomenal realms, acting through his pneumatic vehicle in the psychic realm, which appears as the visible as the sun in the phenomenal.

---

[415] *Tim* 39e-41a, 41D-42e

[416] Clark, "Egyptian," 178.

[417] *Tim* 33.

[418] CH I.2.121A, quoting Jn 1:9.

[419] *Ibid.*, I.3.121C-124A.

[420] Clark, "Egyptian," 176.

[421] Jn 1:1. Ἐν ἀρχῇ ἦν ὁ λόγος καὶ ὁ λόγος ἦν πρὸς τὸν θεόν καὶ θεὸς ἦν ὁ λόγος.

The Sub-Lunar Demiurgos

Though Julian is very helpful in identifying and understanding the noeric Demiurge, he is not as useful when it comes to the sub-lunar Demiurge. Part of the difficulty is that Julian names a number of gods in association with Helios who appear as though they should be encosmic deities. However, two of them, Dionysos and Asklepios, upon further reflection, are better fitted to the sub-lunar realm and, strictly speaking, the sub-lunar realm is encosmic, but is generally given its own qualities beneath the encosmic realm. To be sure, there are more gods connected to the sub-lunar Demiurge, especially Hades and possibly Hermes, which is only natural as the hierarchy descends towards generation, but these two deities appear especially important to our demiurgic theology.

In *De Mysteriis*, Iamblichus mentions two Egyptian deities who take up the position of sub-lunar Demiurge: Ptah and Osiris.[422] He even identifies Ptah as the Greek Hephaistos, noting the Greek relationship between the two is based solely upon Hephaistos' technical skills as the divine blacksmith and the creator of humanity's physical form. For our purposes, Osiris is the more important figure.

Earlier in *De Mysteriis*, Iamblichus mentions part of the Osiris myth: the scattering of his parts by Typhon, the Greek equivalent of Set.[423] This is significant as it links the Osirian myth with that of Dionysos, lord of the Maenads, who in their divine frenzy tear all they came across to pieces, including Dionysos, his body scattered like the wine-making grapes sacred to him. In Roman tradition, the Maenads are called Bacchantes, which is also a title for theurgists. This suggests a possible connection between the daimons, especially personal daimons, which are ruled by the sub-lunar Demiurge, and the theurgists who commune with them.

Though Julian makes Dionysos an aspect of Helios, reigning with Helios as the giver of the Graces,[424] Sallustius rightly states the vine-god's paternity with Zeus, saying that Dionysos is "contained" within Zeus.[425] This suggests Dionysos' role as a lower aspect of the noeric Demiurge. Earlier, in section IV of the same work, Sallustius places Dionysos and Osiris in the sub-lunar realm.[426]

In his *Hymn*, Julian also connects the healer-god Asklepios with the noeric Helios. Again, this seems a little off, and may be contradicted by Julian himself, as he calls Asklepios "saviour of the whole world,"[427] *aretin edoke pan toian*, potentially suggesting the god operates on a lower level than the noeric. Sallustius views Asklepios as being "contained" within Apollo[428] much as Dionysos is within Zeus.

---

422 DM VIII.3, 311-3.
423 DM VI.5, 285.
424 Julian, *Hymn*, 407.
425 CGU, VI, 13.
426 *Ibid.*
427 *Hymn*, 419.
428 CGU, VI, 13.

This maintains the relationship between Asklepios and Helios, as Julian sees Apollo and Helios as the same god, but places Asklepios on a lower level.

Dionysos and Asklepios are an interesting pairing. Dionysos, like Osiris, represents the sub-lunar Demiurgic power of separation or division. As he is torn asunder by the Titans themselves, Proclus gives Dionysos the activity of dividing wholes into their constituent parts, separating the *logoi*, or manifestation of the Forms, from the bodies within which they are contained.[429] Asklepios is a god of healing, and the ill go to his sanctuaries to receive healing dreams.[430] Whereas Dionysos takes things apart, Asklepios restores them, putting the *logoi* appropriate to us in their proper order.

The notion that the role of the sub-lunar Demiurge is to separate, and possibly re-assemble, the *logoi* in the realm of generation is supported, at least in part, by Iamblichus. Though the sub-lunar Demiurge is absent from *De Mysteriis*, the single surviving fragment of his commentary on Plato's *Sophist*, illuminates the subject. The *Sophist*'s sophist is an imitator rather than a creator. According to Iamblichus, this dialogue is entirely about the sub-lunar Demiurge.[431] Here, the Demiurge is called "image-maker," *eidolopoios*, and "purifier of souls," *kathartis psychon*.[432] As souls descend into generation, this Demiurge removes from them *logoi* inappropriate to their nature, and attempts gives those souls a life appropriate to the *logoi* properly belonging to them, [433] displaying the activities of Dionysos and Asklepios respectively. In doing this the sub-lunar Demiurge also deeply binds the soul into the realm of generation.

Finally, there is some evidence Iamblichus, and possibly Porphyry, considers Hades or Pluto a form of this Demiurge.[434] Porphyry calls Hades *"the sun passing under the earth,"*[435] connecting Hades to solar Demiurgic symbolism. Iamblichus, although giving Hades the place between the sun and the moon, may have also meant for him to act as the sub-lunar Demiurge, which is in accordance with the Platonic interpretation of the Chaldean thought he revered.[436] Although Hades' position is higher than that of the moon, which is attributed to his wife Persephone, he can still act as sub-lunar Demiurge, just as Helios is a noeric god ruling the visible gods. The underworld associations shared by Osiris and Pluton are obvious, and the pre-Socratic philosopher Heraclitus says Hades and Dionysos

---

[429] In Julian, *Hymn*, 393, n1.
[430] DM III.3, 127.
[431] *In Soph.*, fr. I.
[432] *Ibid.*
[433] *Ibid.* However, each soul chooses its incarnate life, so there may be conflict between the Demiurge and a soul in this regard.
[434] Dillon, *Commentaries*, 246, also n2.
[435] "On Images," fr. 7.
[436] Dillon, commentary on *In Soph*, fr. 1, 246; Lewy, *Chaldean*, 279-82.

are the same god. As the sub-lunar Demiurge, Hades is the master daimon, *megistos daimon*,[437] especially over personal daimons.

In Jewish mysticism this Demiurge may take the name Adonai, as well as the form of the Shekhinah, the presence of God on Earth. Adonai is the divine name of the sefira Malkhut, the Kingdom. In Neoplatonic terms, Malkhut represents the Natural world below the psychic realm, which includes, but is not limited to, the physical world of generation.

Julian the Philosopher, in his anti-Christian writing, suggests an identity for the sub-lunar Demiurge in Christian thought. In *Against the Christians* and the *Hymn to King Helios*, Julian identifies Asklepios as the saviour of the world and son of Helios-Mithras, the noeric Demiurge.[438] Julian is possibly trying to present Asklepios as an alternative or rival to Christ. And similarities between Dionysos and his division by the Maenads, and Christ's symbolic division on the cross, further point to Christ, rather than Logos, as the sub-lunar Demiurge. A somewhat similar view is posited by the 13th century Kabbalist Abraham Abulafia, who sees Jesus as the messiah of the physical world, but not the spiritual.[439]

Three-in-One

So far, I have presented the Demiurges as three distinct entities. Or have I? You will note that as we have descended towards the realm of generation, the pagan Neoplatonists describe the Demiurge with reference to more and more gods. Each of these gods makes up a different aspect of the Demiurge in question. This has several important implications. One of these, at least in the case of Iamblichus, is that we are not necessarily dealing with "hard" polytheism, the view that each deity is absolutely distinct and individual, just like you or me, a perspective held by Proclus. Another is that this may hold true for the Demiurges as well.

At the beginning of this chapter we saw that the pre-essential Demiurge is Aion and Paradigm. But Aion and Paradigm are elements of the One-Being, meaning that in some manner that Demiurge is also some aspect of the One-Being, what we described as a "vertical extension" into the noetic realm. Julian describes all of the Demiurges as aspects of the sun, starting with Aion as the transcendent sun, then Helios as the celestial sun, and finally the physical sun, and we have found solar-symbolism for the sub-lunar Demiurge as well. Despite existing on separate levels, each Demiurge is still the sun. Further, the unparticipated Whole Soul, Nous, is an image of Aion. Given that the sun is one of the chief modes through which we tell time, it is not surprising to find Helios is

---

437 *Ibid.*

438 In Julian, *Hymn*, 419, n1.

439 Idel, *Studies*, 52-3.

identical to transcendent Time, and the later Neoplatonists also place the titan Kronos in the position the noeric Demiurge.[440]

What does it mean that the sub-lunar Demiurge is an image, or vertical extension, of the noeric Demiurge, who is in turn an image of the pre-essential Demiurge, who is a manifestation of the One-Being? This line of reasoning does not appear in the Neoplatonic texts, but it is clear there is, ultimately, but one Demiurge. This Demiurge, like the One, exists in three eternal moments. This perhaps serves as an explanation as to why the Neoplatonists usually only talk about "the Demiurge," rather than this or that Demiurge.

There is one further implication to this line of thought. That the Demiurge, as an extension of the One-Being, is ultimately subsumed into the One is an important piece of late Platonist cosmology. It suggests that the One manifests its monadic nature into multiplicity through the triadic Demiurge, and through them the gods. Because of this we are able to return to the One through theurgy, which is made possible by the Demiurge.

---

440 Clark, "Egyptian," 198.

Chapter Twelve

The Greater Kinds, the Gods, and Theology

As we've seen, the role of the Demiurge is of extreme importance. He is the orderer and organizer of the three realms beneath the One. Theurgy is only possible through the Demiurge, and we imitate the Demiurge in the carrying out of our god-working and demiurgy. But the spiritual universes are filled with more than just the Demiurge. In *De Mysteriis*, Iamblichus sets out a hierarchy of beings ranging from gods to incarnate souls.

These entities above us, above incarnate souls, are the gods and beings called the "greater kinds" or "superior class of beings," *kreittonon genon.* The gods and greater kinds are ontologically superior to humanity, which is in turn superior to non-human animals. Even the lowest, seemingly mindless daimon precedes us. The idea of something being ontologically superior or inferior has been brought up before. But how does it work? This is a question Porphyry poses in his letter to Anebo.

In this letter, Porphyry asks how the daimons, which are bodiless, are positioned below the visible gods, who have the planets as their bodies.[441] The problem is embodied entities are inferior and posterior to bodiless entities, and yet gods should be superior to daimons. Iamblichus' answer is although the visible gods have bodies, they are not identical to their bodies. Whereas incarnate human souls identify themselves as their bodies, as sometimes do daimons to their etheric vehicles,[442] the gods rule their bodies from outside and are unaffected by what happens to those bodies.[443] The gods remain superior to everything except their Demiurges and the One.

Porphyry's main concern here is ontological. Iamblichus' answer is that even though the visible or encosmic gods have bodies, their essence precedes that of bodies and that of daimons. This is how we can understand the hierarchy of the greater kinds, by looking at the roots from where their essences proceed. In the

441 DM I.8, 31.
442 See chapter seventeen.
443 DM I.8, 31-37.

Timaeus myth, Plato is explicit about the gods: they are the first beings to have their souls come out of the Demiurgic mixing bowl. We are the last.

But it's not that simple. The various genres of superior beings beneath the gods are also rooted in the gods. This means there is not a single genre of daimon or pure soul. There are many gods, which we can understand either as gods in a classical sense, or as the primary contents and makeup of the divine mind. Because there are many kinds of gods, it follows there are many varieties within the greater kinds, each corresponding to the essence, power and activity of their divine root. Though each kind may be sewn into the heavenly circuit of its divinity, its leader god to use Proclus' terminology, the order in which they come out of the Demiurgic mixing bowl, a Platonic metaphor for the order of creation, determines each genre of greater kind's position in the spiritual hierarchy.

But what does it mean to be ontologically prior to another class of being? This goes back to the idea of participation. A superior entity participates less in that which is above it in comparison to an inferior entity. Which seems strange. Shouldn't it participate more, being closer to its source? Participation occurs because of differences between a given being and its source. The closer an entity to its source, the less need it has of participation because it is already similar its source. This means it already has many of the qualities that stem from its superior and need not participate them. Something farther down the hierarchical chain contains fewer of the qualities of its superiors, requiring a great amount of participation in order for it to properly engage in, and revert to, that which came before. As we'll see, this idea is of great importance when it comes to the human soul.

The Divine Hierarchy

With one exception, the superior beings have their origins in the noetic realm, inclusive of the noeric. By origins I mean a particular entity's essence rather than Being, which always originates in the noetic realm. There is sometimes a confusion concerning the root of an entity and where it is active. Following Aristotle, we talk about a triad of essence, power, and activity, which is distinct from the intellectual triad discussed in chapter nine.

A being's essence is its truest nature. Essence is that which makes a particular being that particular kind of being. The essence of a god is not the same as the essence of a human soul, and although we can divinize ourselves, we can only do so "as far as possible." This does not reflect a change in our essence, but our activity. Essence is a tricky thing. Given the deep roots of any being's essence, given its divine quality and origin, how can we possibly know our own essence, let along that of one of the greater kinds? The answer is that we cannot, at least not directly.

Power is the second part of this triad, a median between essence and activity. Beings typically have only one essence, but their power is manifold. Power is potential activity; it is not what a being is doing, but the totality of what it is capable of doing. A being's power is determined by its essence and, in turn, power gives birth to activity. Though a being's essence cannot be accessed directly, its activities, and through them some of its powers, can. Through the observation of activity and power we can come to some understanding of their originating essence.[444]

What, then, is the divine hierarchy? We will look at two, one from Iamblichus, the other Dionysius. Considering the few hundred years separating the two, as well as the religious divide between Greek paganism and Monophysite Christianity, we may expect these two hierarchies to have little in common. On the surface this appears true:

Iamblichus	**Dionysius**
Hypercosmic Gods	Seraphim
Liberated Gods	Cherubim
Encosmic Gods/Celestial Archons	Thrones
Sub-lunar Gods/Archons	Dominions
Archangels	Powers
Angels	Authorities
Daimons	Principalities
Heroes	Archangels
Purified Souls	Angels

We might ask "Where are the similarities?" On the one hand there are entities from pagan religion, and on the other what is now a classical list of angelic choirs from Christianity. Dionysius created that list, pointing to his general importance within the history of Christianity. Even so, it is still a list of angels, not pagan daimons, archons, and gods. But that's the surface. When we dig deeper, some startling and important similarities appear, and we find Dionysius' hierarchy is,

---

[444] Cf. *In Alc*, fr. 4.

ultimately, based, by way of Proclus, on Iamblichus'.[445] This is a fact to which the Renaissance Neoplatonist Marsilio Ficino alluded when he wrote *"Certainly the gods, or as our theologians say, the angels, admire and love divine beauty."*[446] Of course, if Dionysius was a pagan Neoplatonist, working from Proclus' texts, the similarities, as well as others within the Dionysian corpus, are easily explained.

While we will cover the greater kinds in detail later, it is worth looking at an example of how this applies to them. We'll look at the gods as the highest rungs of the heavenly ladder. *De Mysteriis* describes four kinds of deities, hypercosmic, encosmic, a mean between them called the liberated gods, and sub-lunar gods, which are mentioned but not fully described. This excludes noetic, noetic-noeric, and noeric gods. While Iamblichus may have a full hierarchy of these gods nothing of the sort survives in writing.[447] In what remains of his writings, only descriptions of beings active in the phenomenal realm remain.

Of the phenomenal gods, the encosmic or material gods, also called "*kosmocratores*," world creators, and celestial archons, have the role of putting matter in its proper order,[448] an activity highlighted by purification in the form of division or tearing asunder. From the hypercosmic gods comes the perfecting principle of unity, received from the One through the Demiurge. In between these are the liberated gods, who know both the cosmic and hypercosmic realms, and can therefore act as a link between them.[449] It is these gods who, ultimately, lead us away from the material towards the spiritual realms.

Clarke, et. al., in a note to *De Mysteriis* II.3, say Iamblichus uses "*kosmocratores*" to mean a kind of being distinct from the celestial gods. However, their reasoning for this is unexplained and does not take into account how the term is used both before and after Iamblichus. Christopher Plaisance's work demonstrates the historical use of "*kosmocratores*," in relation to the celestial archons, makes them nothing less than the celestial gods.[450] Iamblichus' comparisons between the celestial archons and those ruling over matter suggest the latter are the sub-lunar gods, a subject upon which he does not elucidate in *De Mysteriis*.

To understand this better, we must first rearrange Iamblichus' hierarchy. As presented above, the greater kinds are ontologically arranged. What follows is an ordering based on their activity.

— Hypercosmic Gods

---

[445] Although Iamblichus' hierarchy is sensible rather that noetic, this refers to the activity of these beings, not their source. The only significant difference here is between the psychic purified souls, and the noetic angels.

[446] DAm I.2, 37. C.f. *Ibid.*, VI.3, 111.

[447] Proclus has nine unnamed noetic gods and nine noetic-noeric gods. The noeric gods are Kronos as pure Nous, Rhea as noeric life and Zeus as demiurgical Nous. Beneath these are the Couretes (Proclus, *Hymns*, 40).

[448] DM V.14, 249.

[449] Damascius in Shaw, *Theurgy*, 137.

[450] "Cosmocrators," 66-7.

— Liberated Gods
— Encosmic Gods/Celestial archons
— Archangels
— Angels
— Daimons
— Sub-lunar Gods/archons
— Heroes
— Purified Souls

This division allows us to properly divide the greater kind into triads, a common Neoplatonic structure, and one used extensively by Iamblichus and Dionysius. The triad is considered the source of harmony and unanimity and is concerned with the idea of "perfection" because it is the perfect sum of all that has come before it.[451]

This hierarchy consists of a triple triad, making the system an ennead. The ennead is considered the greatest of unique numbers: it is the last number not a repeating something from before. Divided this way, the hierarchy looks like this:

Iamblichus	Dionysius	Function
Hypercosmic Gods Liberated Gods Encosmic Gods	Seraphim Cherubim Thrones	Perfection Illumination Purification
Archangels Angels Daimons	Dominions Powers Authorities	Perfection Illumination Purification
Sub-lunar Gods Heroes Purified Souls	Principalities Archangels Angels	Perfection Illumination Purification

Each level of the triad has the triple function of purification, *katharsis*, illumination, *phôtismos*, and perfection, *teleiôsis*.[452] For a being to purify, illuminate, or perfect another means not only receiving the holy and transcendent fire, whose

[451] i.e. 1+2=3. Waterfield, *Theology*, 49.
[452] CH III.2.165C. Cf. EH VI.5.536D.

origin is in the One, but to also share it with those who rise to participate those beings.[453] In the *Celestial Hierarchy*, Dionysius discusses how each level of each triad has one of these functions, the highest perfects, the mean illuminates, and the lowest purifies.

These three activities also encompass the entire range of the soul's interaction with the greater kind and is accomplished through theurgy and hieratic prayer which *"enlarges our soul's receptivity to the Gods, reveals to men the life of the Gods, accustoms their eyes to the brightness of divine light, and gradually brings to perfection the capacity of our faculties for contact with the God.'*[454]

The division as found amongst the angels is the natural order in which Dionysius gives them. They are related to one another in a particular way. The position of the Seraphim is identical to that of the hypercosmic gods, whose main role is the establishment of the unity of the One in the phenomenal realm.[455] "Seraphim" means "fire-makers," which is reminiscent of the divine fire surrounding the gods. They are *"established immediately around God, and that the first-wrought Divine manifestations and perfections pass earlier to it, as being nearest.'*[456] Following the Seraphim are the Cherubim, whose name means "fullness of knowledge" or "outpouring of wisdom." They contain the power to *"know and see God.'*[457] Their knowledge of God allows those below them to experience that which is above, much like the liberated gods. The Thrones give us the most explicit similarity, as they have the power to transcend *"over every earthly defect.'*[458]

Though Iamblichus' and Dionysius' presentations are different, the activities of these beings suggest an identical essence. They are the same classes entities viewed from different religious lenses. The same can be said for the rest of the hierarchy, through which the triad of perfection, illumination, and purification is repeated.

The second division consists of a double tetrad. The tetrad signifies completion because when all the numbers up to the tetrad are added together, they equate to the decad.[459] This fulfillment of the divine hierarchy is the union of perfection and completion.[460] Divided this way, the hierarchy looks like this:

Dionysius' hierarchy is not here. Although Iamblichus' set of greater kinds readily fits an octad, Dionysius' does not. The reason for this is that Iamblichus'

---

[453] Cf. CH VII.3.209C and DM X.7.
[454] DM V.26, 277.
[455] Cf. DM I.19, 73.
[456] CH VII.1.205B.
[457] *Ibid.,* VII.1.205B,-C.
[458] *Ibid.,* VII.1.205D.
[459] i.e. 1+2+3+4=10.
[460] Waterfield, *Theology*, 61.

four kinds of gods can be collapsed into a single unit. Even though the genres of gods are technically distinct, they can be approached as a single essence because of their unifying nature as uniform, *monoiedes*:

Iamblichus	Function
Hypercosmic Gods Encosmic Gods Archangels Angels	Anagogic
Sub-lunar Gods Daimons Heroes Purified Souls	Genagogic

In the case of the gods, their order consists in the union of all, their primary and secondary classes and all the multitude which is generated around them constitute all together a totality in unity, and the totality is the unity, and their beginning and middle and end coexist in the very mode of unity; so that in respect of them, at any rate, there is no need to enquire whence unity comes upon them all; for whatever being may actually be in their case, it is this that constitutes their unity. The secondary remain on the same terms in the unity of the primary ones, and the primary ones give to their secondaries the unity proper to themselves, and all possess with each other a communion of indissoluble connection.[461]

However, there is still a distinct difference in the activities of the anagogic deities on the one hand, and the sub-lunar deities on the other. The hypercosmic gods; which includes the liberated gods; encosmic gods, and angels do not descend into generation, the sub-lunar gods, daimons, heroes and purified souls, do.[462] This is why even though the gods are uniform of essence, we may still place the hylic archons in the second tetrad.

Regarding to the dyadic tetrad itself, this represents the principles of Otherness and Sameness generated by the Simply One as repeated in the creation of the World Soul. Representing Otherness are the hylic gods, daimons, heroes and purified human souls. Their role is largely genagogic, aimed towards ensuring the proper running of the generative world, to inspire virtue in human souls and to draw them down into incarnation. The activities of hypercosmic and encosmic gods, archangels and angels is generally anagogic, working to organize the

---

461 DM I.19, 73-5.

462 Finamore, "Iamblichus," 119-132.

immaterial levels of the phenomenal realm, rain providence into the material level, and raise souls out of generation and to participation of the divine Intellect and the work of the Demiurge, even to union with the One, as far as possible. This is something of a generalization. The roles of the various kinds of daimons ere more complicated. The matter is made more complicated by the vague ways in which Iamblichus treats the daimons as either being anagogic or genagogic as the needs of *De Mysteriis* warrant, and on which of the three types of daimons Iamblichus has in mind.

The Sensible Gods

The offspring of noeric and sub-lunar Demiurges are the gods: hypercosmic, liberated, encosmic and sub-lunar, with each level acting as a vehicle for the one above. Iamblichus places the gods in the second Parmenidean hypothesis. This is contrary to Proclus' claim that Iamblichus, like Proclus, assigns them to the first.[463] Proclus' henadic gods are pre-essential, so the first hypothesis makes sense. However, this is not so for Iamblichus, who describes the gods as having being.[464] The second hypothesis deals with noetic beings, and that describes the gods in general, as they are of a single, intelligible form.

The hypercosmic gods are utterly transcendent and closest in activity to the noetic realm. Sallustius divides them into three orders.[465] Unfortunately he does not list the members of the orders, saying they are found in other treatises. He does say some create essence, some intelligence, and some souls.[466] This is somewhat similar to Proclus' four orders: creative,[467] life-making,[468] elevating, and immaculate.[469] Proclus does name these gods in relation to the above categorization: Zeus, within whom are assumed Poseidon and Pluto; Kore, within whom are Artemis, who is equated with Hekate, Persephone, and Athena; Apollo, who is equated with Helios; and the Corybantes.[470] These invisible gods are the ultimate source of liberation from the phenomenal realm for the descended soul.[471] However, because of their position, they are all but unknowable by the soul. Discursive reasoning, the rational soul's main mode of thinking, cannot grasp these transcendent beings. They are accessible only through gnosis via the liberated gods. This gnosis is like the knowing of the gods: complete and immediate.

---

463 *In Parm.* fr. 2.
464 DM I.5, 21.
465 *Ibid.*, VI.31.
466 *Ibid.*, VI.30-1.
467 Essence?
468 Souls?
469 Proclus, *Hymns*, 40-3.
470 *Ibid.*, 40.
471 DM VIII.8, 323.

The encosmic gods, whom Iamblichus alternatively calls visible and celestial, are the most accessible to the soul through theurgy. For Iamblichus, these are the leader gods in whose orbits our souls and etheric vehicles are sewn. All theurgists begin the hieratic arts with an aim to make contact with, and rise through, the visible gods to their own particular leader before assimilation with the sun, the body of the noeric Demiurge. The visible gods are in possession of bodies, the planets and stars. These bodies, being spherical in nature, are seen as perfect representations of divine activity, which is described as moving in a circle and so always returning perfectly to the place from which it begins. But the gods themselves are always incorporeal and intelligible.[472] Though acting in the natural realm, they are not of that realm, existing prior to it.

Due to their association with bodies we are capable of knowing the encosmic gods, or at least their activities and powers, better than those above them. On the most basic level, these gods are Kronos, Zeus, Ares, Helios, Aphrodite, Hermes, and Selene; the gods of the seven classical planets. But the visible gods are not limited to these seven. Sallustius lists four triads of what he calls "mundane" gods "*who make the universe.*"[473] Zeus, Poseidon, and Hephaistos create the world; Demeter, Hera, and Artemis animate it; Apollo, Aphrodite, and Hermes harmonize it; and Hestia, Athena, and Ares guard it.[474] Beyond these twelve, the visible gods encompass all of the visible heavenly spheres,[475] or all of the planets and fixed stars,[476] from the sphere of the moon up.[477] Further, the gods each have a sphere of influence. Hestia has earth, Poseidon water, Hera air, Hephaistos fire. Of the planetary spheres, Demeter is associated with Kronos, Artemis with Selene, and Athena is placed in the eighth sphere of fiery ether, which may contain the fixed stars, above the planets. In this way the twelve gods each have a specific heaven or sphere to occupy.[478]

This is, however, somewhat at odds with Iamblichus who also identifies the twelve Olympians as hypercosmic gods, placing twenty one encosmic gods beneath them, representing the powers of the seven planetary gods manifesting in the three elements, and forty-two sub-lunar gods below them. Also, there are thirty-six encosmic deacons, gods from the Chaldean mysteries, and seventy-two sub-lunar gods beneath them.[479] As at least some of the Olympians must be visible

---

472 DM I.19, 71.

473 CGU VI.32-3.

474 Proclus sees these as the hyper-encosmic gods, analogous to Iamblichus' liberated gods.

475 DM I.19, 71.

476 Julian, *Hymn*, 399-401.

477 The encosmic realm symbolically consists of a series of concentric circles or spheres. The first eight are those of the fixed stars and ether, and the planets from Saturn to the moon. The area "beneath" the moon, i.e. the sub-lunar realm, consists of the sub-lunar elemental spheres, water, air, and fire, with the physical universe and the element of earth in the centre of the entire series. There may also be super-lunar elements.

478 CGU VI.17-23.

479 *In Tim* fr. 79; Dillon, *Commentary*, 369-70.

gods, as they are the gods of the seven planets, it is necessary to distinguish between hypercosmic, hyper-encosmic, and encosmic levels of individual gods, which we see in Proclus. Given the fragmented nature of Iamblichus' writings, it may be impossible to readily solve this apparent problem.

The mean between the supercelestial and encosmic gods are the hyper-encosmic liberated gods. Existing in between the material and immaterial gods, the liberated gods connect the two. Although the hypercosmic gods are ultimately responsible for the liberation of souls, the unliberated soul cannot connect to their transcendent nature. The liberated gods are the lowest of the hypercosmic gods and the highest of the encosmic. Their Lives are double, being partially transcendent while somehow partially immanent.[480] If the liberated gods are not in the cosmos as well as above it, they have no way to lead souls to the hypercosmic gods, just as the visible gods lead us to the liberated. Unfortunately nothing of Iamblichus survives identifying these gods.

Theurgic Appearance

One of the chief concerns of later Neoplatonism is a direct experience of the greater kinds. Though hieratic invocation is discussed elsewhere, the descriptions of the superior beings provided by sources such as *De Mysteriis*[481] and the *Celestial Hierarchy*[482] are helpful in gaining a deeper understanding of these links in the chain of being between ourselves and the One.

Hypercosmic Gods, Including the Hyper-Encosmic Gods

Not surprisingly, the appearance of the hypercosmic gods is uniform, suggesting they do not appear through the guise of human imagination, but as themselves, without the overlay of symbols from their respective mythologies. Their appearance shines forth with a munificence stemming from their connection with the Good. This is in keeping with the idea that the gods are themselves completely good, incapable of evil, on purpose or by accident.[483] The uniformity of the hypercosmic gods' appearances extends to their size, shape, etc., in that they are entirely unchanging, reflecting the high level of reality the gods represent, and as such their divine appearance reflects the very nature of order and tranquility. Further, divine manifestations are unimaginably beautiful, causing sensations of joy in the beholding sage. The order they represent presents itself as an *"ineffable symmetry,"*[484] partaking of Beauty itself.

---

480 Damascius in Shaw, *Theurgy*, 137.
481 DM II.3-9, 87-107.
482 Encompassing the Seraphim, Cherubim and Thrones, CH 205B-D, 208D, 209C.
483 DM I.18, 67.
484 DM II.3, 89.

A distinct quality of the gods is their fire and pure light. This fire is inseparable from its source, and indescribable due to its purity. Partaking of the intelligible fire of the noetic realm, the deific flame fills the cosmos during divine manifestations. Their light is ineffable, a light beyond light, natural or supernatural. This brilliance extends to the manifesting images of the gods, which are brilliant and based solely in themselves. This brilliance is to such an extent physical eyes cannot bare it, nor can the lungs breathe it.

The hypercosmic gods' activities occur instantly. Their actions are inseparable from their originating thought, being completed even as they arise. Instantaneous in nature, divine activities are also motionless. When present to us, their divine power is absolutely perfecting, not simply raising our souls towards *theosis* and *henosis*, but causing us to attain those states. Their benevolent powers bring about health, virtue and purity in body, soul, and mind; raising every quality towards the Good from which it originates, purifying and illuminating us until our souls shine with their own purity. Finally, they free us from influence from the generative world, raising us to the state of purified souls.

The self-granted visions of the gods are seen *"more clearly than the truth itself,"*[485] and are filled with a light that differentiates them from everything else. The greatness of their presence is such that they blot out the whole of the heavens and the earth trembles at their approach. Such visions show the gods surrounded by encosmic gods, archangels and angels,. These holy epiphanies fill our souls with truth and power, aligning even our earthly activities with their own and granting us success in our endeavours and the blessing of Providence all the days of our lives.

Encosmic Gods

The encosmic or celestial gods, analogous to the Dionysian choir of thrones, have a purifying role in the cosmos. They have a very striking appearance and, like the appearances of hypercosmic gods, their appearances are stable and unchanging regardless of where they manifest.

The presence of these gods brings about an abiding steadfastness in those who view them and the space around them. Being a ruling class of entity, their beauty is self-derived and independent from matter, unlike the sub-lunar gods. Their fire is relatively pure and transparent, being free of material accretions. Being active in the generative realm, without descending into it, the appearance of the *kosmokratores* is not harmful, though they may be surrounded by powerful phantasms that may afflict the soul.

Engaged in time, archonic activities are powerful and extraordinary to behold. Illuminative beings, the visible gods have authority over the ordering of the cosmos, and can impart to the theurgist knowledge of cosmic cycles. That

---

[485] DM II.4, 93.

authority is reflected in their appearances. Their manifestations are accompanied by benevolence of a cosmic and celestial nature, filtering down to the material life as they may.

When appearing in a theurgic vision, the visible gods manifest clearly and with an air of undeniable authority. Unlike hypercosmic gods these archons are not accompanied by lesser beings, but instead gather around them the ordering of the cosmos. The contemplation of such beings brings about the movement of the soul into line with cosmic order.

Hylic or Sub-Lunar Gods

The sub-lunar gods rule over the material cosmos below the sphere of the moon and, unlike the encosmic gods, are surrounded by matter. Though sub-lunar, their role is perfecting, as they are the highest part of the sub-lunar realm. Their appearance is striking, like that of the cosmic archons, and brings with them as they do the chaos of the material world. The appearance of a sub-lunar god is unstable, changing in size and shape, and having many different forms due to its proximity to matter.

The presence of a material archon is chaotic. Though beautiful, their beauty is artificial, giving a sense of greatness not reflective of their material functions. Unlike cosmic archons, the fire of the hylic archons is mixed with the elements, dim and divided. As with their celestial cousins, the appearance of a material archon is not harmful, though they may also be surrounded by powerful, soul afflicting phantasms.

The activities of these gods appear extraordinary and powerful, but are not, in fulfillment, as great as they seem as those activities must manifest in matter. In general, these archons are characterized by boastfulness in deed and power. Their manifestations are accompanied by benevolence of a material nature, bringing with them the best aspects of the material life and attracting to themselves the chaos of the material world, leaving those souls in their presence more free from a turbulent life.

In a theurgic vision the hylic gods manifest dimly, surrounded by the accretions of matter, but with an air of undeniable authority. Like their celestial cousins, these archons are not accompanied by lesser beings, but instead gather around the hylic elements and their proper ordering. The contemplation of such beings brings about the movement of the soul into line with order of the material portion of the cosmos.

Towards a Monistic Panentheism

All this discussion of different kinds of gods is well and good if you happen to believe in multiple gods. But what if you do not? Certainly, monotheists can take a view of the gods similar to some modern Gnosticisms, and view the gods as lesser emanations of God,[486] maintaining their divine status while denying their godhood, or see them in Dionysius' and Ficino's terms as angels. In this, the gods can be understood as being similar to the Gnostic Aeons. Surely, the gods fit this description when taken in their Platonized form.

This speaks to the flexibility of Iamblichus' theology. Though ostensibly a polytheist, the surviving remnants of his writings, as well as works such as Julian's *Hymn to King Helios*, suggest a tendency towards monistic-like panentheism in Iamblichean theology through the *interpretatio Graeca*, the way the Hellenes interpreted the gods of other cultures as versions of their own gods. This is seen especially in three areas: the description of the gods as *monoeide*, the assumption of gods into their corresponding Demiurge, and the presentation of the Demiurges as forms of the sun.

Being of a single form the gods, though many, are also one. This, and that the gods have Being and do not exist pre-essentially, is perhaps the chief distinction of Iamblichus' divinities as opposed to later Neoplatonism as represented by Proclean thought.[487] While there are many essences amongst the gods, as well as many different powers and activities, at their root, the divine essences are one, or so close to one as to be indistinguishable. This is an important aspect of Iamblichean theology, as *monoeide* all the gods, regardless of rank as primary or secondary causes, immaterial or material, are connected at the highest level.

In Porphyry's letter to Anebo, he asks if the material gods, being in possession of bodies, are lower in the divine hierarchy than the daimons, who do not have bodies but should be subservient to the gods.[488] As discussed above, Iamblichus answers by saying the bodies of the gods are not connected to the gods but are actually perfect representatives of divine activity.[489] But the most important element of Iamblichus' overall description of the material gods is that they are of a single form with the immaterial gods.[490] As Iamblichus says, "*the gods of heaven are being homogeneous in all respects, entirely united among themselves, uniform and non-composite.*"[491] In other words, the gods are one, and Iamblichus' free use of the Egyptian counterparts of Greek gods supports this idea.

The nature of the gods as *monoeide* does not directly lead to any sort of panentheism or monism. The next link in the chain comes from Julian's *Hymn to King Helios*. In a number of places in the *Hymn*, Julian describes how the various gods, especially the celestial gods, are subsumed into their Demiurge, making them horizontal extensions of their Demiurge. For instance, Apollo is considered

---

486 Hoeller, "Catechism," #6, http://www.gnosis.org/ecclesia/catechism.htm#LESSON I.
487 See Clark, "Henads," 2010.
488 DM I.8, 31.
489 DM I.8, 31-3, I.17, 63-7.
490 For example, I.3, 13. Here the material gods are described as having a "unitary" (μονοειδὴς) connection to the immaterial gods.
491 DM I.17, 65.

to share an *"abiding sameness"* with Helios.[492] Admittedly, this is not much of a stretch, as both Helios and Apollo are solar gods. However, the goddess Athena is described as *"being contained within [Helios]"* and *"she is [Helios'] intelligence in perfect form."*[493] Moreover, Athena *"binds together the gods who are assembled about Helios and brings them without confusion into unity with Helios."*[494] Every activity of the gods stems from Helios, with whom they are one. Also, we have already seen how Zeus and Helios are considered identical, and how Dionysos and Asklepios are aspects of those gods.[495]

Further, Julian's Demiurgic theology describes these entities as three forms of the sun: pre-essential, noeric, and material and describes them, as does Iamblichus, in terms of various deities. Iamblichus, though using an Egyptian model, identifies one of these deities as Dionysos, who we may say is an "aspect" of the sub-lunar Demiurge. We have already seen how Julian includes Dionysos within Helios. Seen through such a lens, it appears that just as the gods are embraced within their Demiurges, so are lower Demiurges within higher ones.

But we need not stop there. That there are three levels of Demiurges, pre-essential, noeric, and material, is highly suggestive of the three "moments" of divine time. Just as the One, the noetic and the psychic realms are divided into three parts through this system, so is the Demiurge who, starting as an element of the One-Being, continues the process of Eternity into the sub-lunar realm.

The celestial and sub-lunar Demiurges are incorporated within Aion, representing the unparticipated Aion's moments of being participated and being in participation. In turn, Aion is not simply an emanation of the One-Being, but is the One-Being in another mode. This is what completes the panentheistic chain. The gods are one and are subsumed into their Demiurges. In turn, the sub-lunar Demiurge is embraced within the noeric, and the noeric within Eternity. Finally, Eternity, containing all the other Demiurges and gods as *monoeide*, is itself the last moment of the One, which is ultimately subsumed into the non-being of the ineffable One, the transcendent God.

This describes the essence of panentheism, with the divine being simultaneously transcendent and imminent. However, is this monism? Yes and no. From the point of view of the ineffable One we can speak only of that One, there is nothing else, and we cannot really speak of that One, either. However, from our perspective, there is multiplicity and emanation, and Iamblichus makes no claims as to the greater kinds being subsumed into their leaders. Still, this is an important point for Iamblichus. Iamblichus takes his hierarchies seriously, and the process of emanation, where an inferior being comes from a superior being, maintains the

---

[492] *Hymn*, 393.
[493] *Ibid.*, 407-9.
[494] *Ibid.*, 409.
[495] *Ibid.*, 395.

hierarchy. The posterior entity participates in its originator, but, having Being, is both distinct from and inferior to its originator.

This, in turn, creates a two-fold mechanism by which divine grace reaches the physical realm. Not only is there a hierarchy descending downwards towards generation, but the power of each entity descends as well, including from the hypercosmic gods who otherwise have no contact with generation. However, the descent of power has its limits. Though the invisible gods are superior to all other beings in the hierarchy, and therefore more powerful, as their grace descends it also weakens as it moves away from the source of Being. The effect is that a lower entity, though weaker, or having less Being, than the hypercosmic gods has more influence on the physical realm due to proximity.[496]

In the next chapters we finish discussing the greater kinds. There I show these other entities, up to and including purified and, by extension, human souls are products of the Demiurge, the gods or a combination of both. Through participating their sources these beings can experience a *gnosis* stemming from their sources, and may revert to them through *henosis*. As we'll see, for humanity, this takes place largely through the theurgic act of *theosis*, becoming god.

---

[496] DM V.22, 267

Chapter Thirteen

The Greater Kinds, Continued

The gods, the thoughts and mind of the One, are the first, and the greatest, of the greater kinds, and the governors of all existence.[497] Iamblichus associates the greater kind beneath the gods with the third Parmenidean hypothesis,[498] which other Neoplatonists take to mean the soul. Iamblichus does so because he sees the greater kinds as undergoing ascents and descents to and from generation, even if they are unaffected by generation,[499] corresponding to the Parmenides: *'For at one time [the subject of the third hypothesis] participates and at another it does not.'*[500] Also, although the gods are of a single essence, the beings they produce are multifarious in essences, powers, and activities. Each of these beings has, in turn, an identity appropriate to their place and function in the divine hierarchy.[501]

Everyone Comes From Somewhere - Divine Origins

Iamblichus is largely silent as to from where the rest of the greater kinds originate. The gods are created by the Demiurge, and humans are a product of both the Demiurge and the gods. What of the daimons and heroes? To make matters more complex, Iamblichus, like Porphyry, includes beings other than gods, daimons, heroes, and souls in his divine hierarchy. Added to this traditional set are, as we have seen, archangels and angels.

Iamblichus, in *De Mysteriis*, provides altogether too few clues as to the origin of the superior beings. In discussing the nature of daimons in relation to heroes and souls we find that daimons come from the last part of the emanations of the gods' powers before they are actualized as activities. Heroes, however, are produced not from the gods' essence/power/activity triad but from the Being/Life/Intellect triad, stemming specifically from the principles of Life.[502] As the source of a being determines its essence, powers, and activities, knowing that

---

497 DM I.20, 77.
498 *In Parm.* fr. 12. C.f. Dillon, "Henads;" Clark, "Henads."
499 Finamore, *Vehicle*, 112.
500 *Parm.* 155e.
501 C.f. DM I.20, 77: *". . . while those who have been assigned the type of administration proper to daemons [sic] extend their influence over certain restricted portions of the cosmos and administer these."*
502 DM II.1, 83.

source, as we do in the case of daimons and heroes, is advantageous to understanding the full complexity of that being. For instance, the essence of daimons, springing from power just before activity, makes them fitting generative powers whose purposes are, amongst others, to finish embodied natures and to oversee the human soul's incarnation. Heroes, stemming from divine Life, lead human souls towards a life of reason and virtue.[503]

Unfortunately, *De Mysteriis*, as well as the other extant portions of the Iamblichean corpus, are largely silent on this subject. While it is tempting to posit a division between beings coming from the intelligible triad or the essence/power/activity triad in a tidy arrangement, the lack of information precludes this. Instead of looking at where the greater kind stem, we may follow the *Timaeus* and conclude their souls were mixed by the Demiurge, in a process of emanation or creation, and that the souls first mixed, those of the gods, are more pure than those following.[504] Finally, there are some hints in *De Mysteriis* that allow us to posit the following associations between the gods and the greater kind:

> *"The archangels and angels are messengers for the hypercosmic and liberated gods, functioning above the level of matter. The good daimons serve as envoys of the visible gods, as, presumably, do the heroes, who are often described as demi-gods in classical myth. The evil and punishing daimons,[505] and those neutral ones governing the general functioning of the physical cosmos, serve the sub-lunar gods. Of these, the personal daimons are the most unique, as they serve the leader gods, but are led by the sub-lunar Demiurge so theurgists may properly invoke them. The greater kinds are attributed to the various genre of gods according to whether or not the greater kind in question is in possession of a pneumatic vehicle. Daimons and heroes are explicitly said to have such vehicles, the angels are not."*[506]

Archangels[507]

The first of the greater kinds beneath the gods are the archangels.[508] As the top of the median triad, discussed in the previous chapter, archangels have a perfecting function, though they do not descend into matter like daimons. Archangels may take over the duties of a personal daimon once its soul has passed on to worship the liberated gods. In general, the appearance, activity, and visions of the archangels are similar to those of the gods, but are always somewhat lesser.

---

503 DM II.1, 83; II.6, 99.
504 Dillon, *Commentary*, 379.
505 Iamblichus posits three kinds of daimons: those that help and govern incarnate souls, those that punish souls for evil activities and those that govern the basic functions of the physical world. Daimons I represents the first two or "essential" daimons.
506 DM II.3. 89-91.
507 The following descriptions are derived from DM II.3-9, 87-107 and CH 237B-261D.
508 Not to be confused with the Dionysian archangels, which are associated with Iamblichus' heroes. The archangels presently under consideration are analogous to the Dionysian choir of Dominions.

As servants of hypercosmic gods, archangels appear much like them, though always lesser in nature, emanating a solemn but gentle quality. Likewise, archangels reflect a mostly uniform shape, size, etc., but are not perfectly uniform, nor do they share in the singleness of essence of the gods. Again, tranquillity flows from the archangelic presence, but unlike the stable tranquillity of the supercelestial gods, theirs is associated with the sense of motionless activity.

Archangelic appearances are filled with beauty, though less than that of the gods, just as their light and fire is supernaturally bright, but not a brightness beyond brightness. Further, their fire is seen surrounding them, and their flames may sweep ahead or behind as they manifest. As secondary beings, the archangelic brilliance, as is the brilliance, or lack thereof, of all the other superior beings, seems based in something else, such as the glory of their god. And though powerful and unendurable to human breath, their holy fire and light is not as unbearable as that of the gods above them.

The activities in which the archangels are engaged, like the hypercosmic gods, are completed in the same instant they are conceived, but movement is now associated with those accomplishments. Their illuminating power is anagogic,[509] but does not accomplish the complete perfection of the soul. Though benevolent, and bringing about health, virtue, and purity, the powers of the archangels are such that these do not come about perfectly or completely.

Visions granted by archangels are true and perfect, setting parts of the world in concordant motion as a light goes forth announcing their presence. Like the gods, archangels appear surrounded by their heavenly hosts, consisting for them of angels orbiting around the same originating divinity. The epiphanies granted by archangels fill our souls with truth, but only the truths to which the archangel pertains, and not the whole of the truth encompassed by the gods. Each archangel presents its truth and power to us as befits the soul receiving it, and not fully and completely, thus granting us a portion of Providence while we are still subject to Fate.

Angels

The illuminating rank of angels[510] is the second member of the median triad of gods and greater kinds. Much as archangels are lesser in appearance, power, and activity to their gods, angels are less than archangels. Like archangels, angels have a solemn and gentle appearance, though milder than those of archangels. Overall, angels have a simple appearance, modeled on that of the god they orbit. They are lesser to the gods and archangels in every way, though still unchanging in regards to size, shape, and so forth.

---

[509] Compare CH VIII.1.237C and DM II.4, 95.

[510] Analogous to the Dionysian choir of Powers.

The appearance of angels brings with it a sense of calmness and order, but one signified by movement as opposed to the perfect quietude of the hypercosmic gods. Though bright, angelic beauty, as received from above, is only partial to that of archangels. The dimmed brilliance of angels means their presence is endurable to us, allowing the theurgist to engage with them in ways not possible with the suffocating presence of gods and archangels. Angelic fire is described as divided in nature, sometimes appearing with it, sometimes before and sometimes after, except when the angel appears in their most perfect forms.[511]

Because motion is their primary feature, angelic actions are not accomplished instantaneously. As illuminators, angels only help loosen the sway of the realm of generation through gnosis, but do not free us from it. However, that illuminating power, making the above visible to the below, brings within the soul the courage to fully imitate, and in doing so participate, the divine will of the gods and Demiurge.[512] Just as those beings above them, angelic benevolence brings about benefits to body, soul, and intellect. However, their lesser power only allows for benefits particular to their individual essences, and in manifestation those blessings are nowhere nearly as great as the illumination embracing them.

When appearing in a theurgic vision, angels are somewhat less than perfect, though their form is clearly discernible, as their light is not as blinding as that of an archangel. Angels are not accompanied by lesser beings, but instead their presence reveals those activities proper to them. The magnitude of epiphanies received by us when we invoke an angelic presence is less than that of an archangel, bringing about a *"rational wisdom, truth, pure virtue, a firm knowledge,"*[513] and an order proportional to the purity of soul and power of the invoked angel.

Daimons

Ostensibly the final rank of the median triad, the class of daimons[514] is remarkably different from those preceding it. First, daimonic activity is generally described in genagogic terms. That is, daimons do not seem to act to release incarnate souls from generation but bind them there. Second, though it is presumable that, for instance, angels come in a variety of powers and activities, there are explicitly three kinds of daimons. In this, daimons are the most complex of the superior beings, eclipsed only by human souls.

Iamblichus describes three daimonic genres. The first is the personal daimon, *oikeios daimon*. Such beings oversee every human soul fallen to generation. Second

511 DM II.4, 95.
512 CH VIII.3.237D-240A
513 DM II.9, 105.
514 Roughly analogous to the Dionysian choir of Authorities.

are the so-called "evil" daimons which oversee the judgment of impure souls,[515] as well as those daimons whose pneumatic vehicles have become encrusted with hylic matter, separating their occupants from their divinities and purpose. The third are those without reason who oversee the functioning of their particular portion of the physical world.[516] As described before, personal daimons belong to the visible gods, but act under the guidance of the sub-lunar Demiurge, and the other two kinds are ruled by the sub-lunar gods.

These three kinds of daimons appear to have nothing in common. How can daimons in charge of caring for the incarnate soul be anything like daimons without reason, overseeing the natural functions of all within the world? Moreover, how does the genagogic nature of personal daimons relate to the anagogic power of the visible gods they serve?

The main point of connection between these genres of daimons is their role associated with the realm of generation. All daimons serve to make the generative world the best it can be, not in relation to us, but its overall working. This function connects the purifying personal daimons to their gods while not separating the other daimons from theirs. This is because incarnation is seen as a necessary and important part of the fallen soul's process of purification. Without purification in generation, human souls cannot regain their position amongst the greater kind.

For these reasons, Iamblichus paints daimon-kind with a single stroke in those chapters of the second book of *De Mysteriis* concerned with describing the greater kinds. Though triadic in function, and of seemingly different natures, daimons are of a single genus, even if that genus contains different species or sub-species.

Unlike the other superior beings above them, daimons have varied and complex appearances. Further, they appear differently at different times, or in the same form but in different sizes. Whereas angels are mild and archangels stern, the daimonic countenance is fearsome to behold, especially for the impure.

All daimons are associated with matter in some way. Personal and punitive daimons oversee matter while the third class is immersed in it. Due to this association, the appearance of their pneumatic vehicles brings with it a tumultuous sense of disorder. The pneumatic bodies of daimons without reason, being surrounded by matter as they are, are said to take on a hylic vestment that is peeled off much as human bodies are set aside by the soul at death.[517] Though frightening to behold, daimons are nevertheless beautiful. That beauty is arranged in proportions, and distinct to each daimon as opposed to the general beauty possessed by their superiors. The brightness of a daimon is similar to that of an

---

515 This includes both incarnate and disincarnate souls, although the gods also have a role in the purification of the disincarnate.

516 DM IV.1, 203-5.

517 *Vehicle*, 57, n.28.

angel's, but more divided and not always of the same magnitude. Their fire, however, casts a smoldering glow rather than the brilliance of those before them.

Generally, daimonic activities appear faster than they really are, and their work is not accomplished at the moment of its conception. Their work is to distribute the divine impulses they receive to the world of generation in a *"harmonious and unconfused way."*[518] They bring about the binding of souls to bodies, causing our fallen souls to associate themselves with those bodies, binding us further to the *"chains of Fate."*[519]

Personal daimons associate with a particular soul before it descends into generation, possibly even when that soul is first sewn into the orbit of its leader god. That daimon *"stands over [its soul] as the fulfiller of the various levels of life of the soul,"*[520] ultimately binding the soul to its body and then watching over the human, the composite of rational soul and body, for as long as he or she lives.[521] Like the idea of the "guardian angel," an idea made popular amongst esotericists through the publication of the Sacred Magic of Abramelin, the personal daimon guides our lives and reasoning based on divine principles until, through theurgy, we become purified and transcend the need for daimonic guidance.[522] In this, the personal daimon is good in nature, always superior to the so-called "evil" daimons when it comes to the shepherding of their attended soul.[523] When they appear to us, they show their works and the goods which come of them.

The median class of daimon is less specific than the personal daimon, operating in a general judgmental fashion and not connected to a specific soul. However, punitive daimons are able to advise us on the proper course of moral action, viewing all such activities from a superior position outside of time, and so able to see the full ramifications of any and every action. They are understood to work against unjust human endeavours while cooperating with the just. Punitive daimons have the ability to harm, or even kill a human for their deeds if deemed necessary. They give visions of their terrible power when manifesting.

The final kind of daimon, sometimes called a "relational" daimon,[524] is without reason or intelligence as we normally understand it. Each of these daimons has a single function in the material world, having *"been allotted just one power, in the apportionment of tasks which has been prescribed for each entity in each of the parts*

---

518 CH VIII.1.240A.
519 DM II.6, 99.
520 DM IX.6, 335.
521 The personal daimon is also said to rule over all the other daimons associated with each individual human body. The idea of spirits ruling over the parts of the body can also be found in the Gnostic *Apocryphon of John* 15.29-19.32, though those spirits are evil Gnostic archons and not beneficial daimons.
522 DM IX.6, 335-7.
523 DM IX.7, 339.
524 As opposed to the "essential" daimons who are in attendance to the gods, such as personal daimons. *In Tim*, fr. 80.

(of the universe).'[525] These daimons can be likened to the terrestrial spirits sometimes called "elementals," though they are not necessarily described in association with the four classical elements.

The irrational nature of the relational daimons can be commanded by humans, both sorcerers and theurgists. This is because the human intellect, participating Nous, acts as an organizing force for these daimons, especially when that intellect is in concord with the ordering of the cosmos, but even when it has created an artificial order through sorcery.[526]

Heroes

The illuminating heroes, analogous to Dionysius' Archangels, make up the middle rank of third triad beneath the sub-lunar gods. Though not as complex as daimons, heroes have a seemingly anagogic function: to encourage humans to rise towards a virtuous life, which is a first step towards a theurgic life. This is reflected in the function of the Archangels, the chiefs of the divine messengers. However, though heroes are concerned with virtue, they lead, through those virtues, souls in generation towards a concern with the well-being of the physical world.[527]

In appearance, heroes are less frightening and gentler than daimons. Like daimons, they may appear differently at different times, and in various sizes. Their appearances are typified by movement and the urging on to great deeds. Heroes are always beautiful to behold, though not as beautiful as the ranks above them. Where daimonic beauty reflects the ordering of the cosmos, heroic beauty is courageous.

Being farther removed from primary causes, and working within the natural world, heroic fire is blended with pneumatic accretions, much like the sub-lunar gods. That fire is similar to that of daimon-kind, but not as grand or powerful, and appearing unstable at times. Being dimmer in brilliance than daimons, heroic presences are entirely bearable to theurgists, though exhibiting a greatness of presence, and their arrival can cause the earth to move and sounds to manifest.

The activities of heroes revolve around the arraying of souls in an orderly manner[528] due to their essential nature as vital beings, the natural leaders of human souls, and their life-giving and purifying power.[529] Their activities are magnificent to behold, but not as swift as a daimon's. Their manifestation can further bind our souls to bodies, but can also stir in us the desire to perform great and heroic deeds. When appearing in a theurgic vision, the images of heroes, like those of

---

525 DM IV.1, 205.
526 DM IV.1-2, 205-6. The former instance is an act of theurgy, the later sorcery.
527 DM II.5, 95.
528 DM II.2, 83.
529 DM II.1, 83.

daimons, are often obscured by the darkness of their fire. Heroes bring with them a desire for the realm of generation, but also zealousness for the perfection of the soul through the virtues.

Pure Souls

Pure souls, those that have either never fallen into generation or that have raised themselves above generation, are the last of the divine beings. These souls are analogous to the purifying choir of Angels. Beneath purified souls are only humans and irrational animal souls. As humans are a mixture of rational and irrational souls in a body, Iamblichus places the purified, rational soul under the fourth Parmenidean hypothesis, which deals with such a subject.

The appearance of a pure soul is somewhat like that of a hero, though not as grand or inspiring. They are also very changeable and smaller than those of a daimon or hero. These souls frequently have stamped upon them the dominating appearance of the god within whose train they are embedded. Their light is visible, but fitful and dim, and even when pure may have the remnants of their time in generation about them. Occupying the lowest of the divine ranks, pure souls appear unaccompanied. However, the most pure of these souls will manifest in a formless manner cognate with the Whole Soul.

The activities of pure souls are largely genagogic in nature. However, the most pure of these souls may have an anagogic affect, bringing to human souls an awareness of the spiritual world. And when these souls manifest in a theurgic vision, they bring with them goods that make human life more bearable in relation to the god to whom they are connected.

Understanding the Greater Kinds

The pagan Neoplatonists are polytheists and take the existence of various spiritual beings both seriously and literally. For Iamblichus and Proclus and those of their schools, the greater kinds are real, objective beings. So much so the basic existence of the gods and greater kinds is not only undeniable, but cannot even be affirmed, as this implies the possibility of denial. Instead, knowledge of the gods is innate with the human soul.[530] This is no less true for Dionysius's angelology and the Christianity from which it comes and will later inspire. Also, with the exception of the polytheistic view of the gods', common in varying ways to the pagan Neoplatonists, there is nothing in the idea of the superior beings necessarily antithetical to monotheistic belief. The belief in spiritual beings, such as faeries, is well attested for in Medieval and Renaissance Europe.

---

[530] DM I.3, 11-15

Today we enjoy a wide variety of beliefs about spirituality and spiritual entities. Our ideas about such subjects include various forms of theisms, from mono- to poly- to a-theism and everything in between. But modern spiritual beliefs are in no way limited to traditional forms of theology. Various forms of Freudian and Jungian interpretations of religion and myth are popular today, as is the rise of secular humanistic spirituality. To some, God or the gods might be real, but not necessarily Real.

Much of what Neoplatonism introduces to the Platonic corpus is mystical and theological. As such, the ways in which we understand the nature of the divine realm will influence our Neoplatonism as well. This is one of the primary powers of Neoplatonism as a hermeneutic. Even if you do not believe in the literal existence of the soul, what Iamblichus has to teach us about the nature of the soul, and thus about humanity, is still relevant. Though you may not believe in the efficacy of ritual, what *De Mysteriis* teaches us about theurgy still informs us about the interconnectivity of the whole world.

This is not to say Neoplatonism is a free-for-all. It does require certain things of us. Discipline, both mental and emotional, is high on that list, as is the ability to think critically. Above all else, however, Neoplatonists expect you to be open to experience what traditionally is understood as divine reality. Though we have a strong basis in theology and philosophy, theurgy is the crown of our discipline. And theurgy, though founded on knowledge, transcends knowledge to encompass the whole of the theurgist through experience. Without the willingness to experience what theurgy brings, including all of the greater kinds, it can find no useful place in your life. The greater kinds do not need to be accepted as presented in classical Neoplatonism, pagan or otherwise. They may be accepted in the form of psychological constructs or Jungian archetypes. None of this changes what they are, only how you perceive them. However they are accepted, accepted they must be. The chain of being is the heart of theurgy.

Chapter Fourteen

The Human Soul

Platonism defines a human being as a rational soul combined with a physical body. As such, Iamblichus places the human soul under the fifth Parmenidean hypothesis, which is concerned with irrational souls *"woven into"* rational souls.[531] Individual souls are the product of the Whole Soul via the World Soul. Iamblichus writes of the nature of the soul in his now fragmentary *Peri Psyche.* While Neoplatonists after Iamblichus, especially the Athenian school that produces Proclus, expand their understanding of the nature, powers, and activities of the soul, they stand upon Iamblichus' foundation. What we see after Iamblichus is largely refinement rather than refutation.

The Soul's Essence

All beings have essence, powers, and activities. The essence is a being's innermost or most fundamental self. Typically, an entity's essence is difficult to access, or even recognize. In humanity's case the difficulty is compounded, which is somewhat contradictory to how we might think. After all, we are humans. Shouldn't we be able to determine our own essences?

Iamblichus,[532] following Plato and the language of the *Chaldean Oracles*,[533] divides humanity into three different groups. In the case of the first two, the great herd of humanity and the beginning theurgist and philosopher, the soul is combined with a body and self-identifies as that body. Only the soul of the theurgic sage is fully and experientially aware of its ultimate separateness from the body which it inhabits.

The combined nature of the human soul, of humanity, is a unique trait of a unique kind of soul. Further, this view is set in opposition to the views of earlier Neoplatonists. Plotinus teaches soul is part of the noetic realm and that part of the soul remains undescended in that realm during incarnation, forever pure and untouched by the realm of generation. Through *theoria*, a philosopher reunites the

---

531 Hypotheses six through nine are: Forms-in-Matter, Matter, Body in the heavenly realm, and generated body in the sub-lunar realm (Dillon, "Paramenides," 24.)
532 DM V.18, 257
533 Shaw, *Theurgy*, 147, n. 9.

descended portion of the soul with the undescended. This ultimately allows us to exist in permanent contemplation of the movements of the gods in the noetic realm, never again to descend into the physical world. The entirety of this view is soundly rejected by the later Neoplatonists, based on principles of reason, cosmology, and on their need to reconcile texts such as the *Phaedrus* and the *Timaeus*.

Plotinus' treatment of the soul is seen by the later Neoplatonists as too elevated. His view also ignores the *Timaeus*' description of the soul's creation, drawing immortal elements from the Demiurge and mortal elements from the celestial gods. Correcting this opinion, Iamblichus says the soul comes after Nous. This soul is separate from all the greater kinds and is the mean between fully immaterial, indivisible beings and fully material, divisible ones.[534] Further, the soul descends completely into a body upon incarnation, with none of it remaining out of generation.

This view provides us with some significant knowledge about the nature of the soul. First, the soul depends from the level of Nous as it extends into the psychic realm. This makes the soul distinct from, inferior to, and dependent upon the rest of the greater kinds. Although the human soul is connected to Nous it also exists on its own, separated from Nous beneath the World Soul, and so must participate Nous in order to experience Intellect in its fullest. In this lower position human souls are the mediators between the divine and physical realms and their inhabitants. This recalls Julian's descriptions of Helios as noeric Demiurgos as a mean between the noetic and sensible realms, leading and uniting these two otherwise separate levels.[535] Just as the Demiurge leads the celestial realm, so too does the human soul participating Nous through demiurgic theurgy.

Part of the reason for Iamblichus' innovation is the need for a doctrine that is true to all of Plato's representations of the soul. This innovation must contain both pessimistic and optimistic elements, drawing from the *Phaedo* and *Phaedrus* on the one hand, and the *Timaeus* on the other. To understand this unique notion of the dual-essenced soul, it is necessary to be at least a little familiar with how it is described in these important texts.

It's a Trap! Body and Soul in the *Phaedo*

Plato's *Phaedo* presents Socrates' last discussion with his students before his death. Here he explains why he is unafraid of dying, and actually looks forward to it. While the dialogue's topic is the immortality of the soul,[536] we may say a main point of the *Phaedo* is to convey the idea that the soul is not only distinct from the body, but is so in every important way. The body is temporal, derived from a

[534] DA I.7, 31.

[535] Cf. Julian, *Hymn*, 377.

[536] *In Phaedrum* fr. 1.

mixing of elements, and therefore mortal and subject to dissolution. The soul exists outside of time, is an essence rather than a compound, and is utterly immortal. In the *Phaedo*, incarnation is a trap from which we should escape. The means to this end is philosophy, presented as a kind of psychic catharsis.

In the *Phaedo*, the soul's relationship to the body is decidedly negative. The incarnate human soul's ability to attain to truth is greatly diminished due to the fallible nature of the compound body. Sight, hearing, touch, taste, and all the other senses are inaccurate, never experiencing things as they actually are. These sensations are nothing more than distractions interfering with the soul's work.[537] As Socrates says: *'Then when is it that the soul attains to truth? When it tries to investigate anything with the help of the body, it is obviously led astray.'*[538]

How is the soul to acquire the truth of things, to experience the Forms in matter? When the soul is freed from the body and all that that goes with it:

> *"Surely the soul can best reflect when it is free of all distractions such as hearing or sight or pain or pleasure of any kind – that is, when it ignores the body and becomes as far as possible independent, avoiding all physical contacts and associations as much as it can, in its search for reality."*[539]

From the perspective of the *Phaedo*, the philosopher, and by extension theurgist, is not concerned with the body and directs their attention towards the soul. By doing this, the *"philosopher frees his soul from association with the body, so far as is possible.'*[540] The body is a trap that may be fully escaped only through a combination of philosophy, theurgy, and death.[541]

Falling Down on the Job: Body and Soul in the *Phaedrus*

Unlike the *Phaedo*, which focuses on the nature of the soul, the *Phaedrus* is about the Beautiful and the nature of Beauty and beauty.[542] Given Platonic views of the soul and its connection to Nous, a discussion of the nature of the soul in relation to Beauty is understandable. This is especially so in connection to the *Phaedrus'* secondary topic, love, which ultimately binds us to the Good.

The *Phaedrus* discusses the nature of the soul through a myth,[543] a technique also used in the *Timaeus*. In this myth, the soul's natural habitat is depicted as the realm of the gods in whose trains souls follow. All the divine beings, including pure souls, ride through the heavenly realm on personal chariots pulled by winged

---

537 *Phaedo* 65 a-b.

538 *Ibid.*, 65 b.

539 *Ibid.*, 65 c.

540 *Ibid.*, 64 e-65 a.

541 It is important to note that the *Phaedo* is strictly anti-suicide. The soul does not belong to the human but rather to its leader god. Just as we might be irritated with a possession that decides to destroy itself, so to the gods (*Ibid.*, 61 e-62c).

542 *In Phaedrum* fr. 1.

543 *Phaedr*, 246 a-249 e.

horses. Although the steeds of the gods are noble and tame, and are under the complete control of their divinities, the horses pulling the human souls' chariots are of a different breed. One of the chariot's pegasi is noble and obedient, the other is just the opposite, and these represent the dual natures of the human soul. The soul capable of controlling both animals may continue in the circuit of its leader god. If the soul loses control, the chariot falls, crashing into generation and incarnation, and the soul's own wings become bent and broken.

Although falling into generation is not a punishment it is still the soul's least desirable situation. Socrates explains to Phaedrus many lives must be lived in order to reestablish the soul's wings. Further, only through the life of philosophy, the spiritually highest of all possible lives, can this goal be accomplished. This is because the philosopher's soul,

> *"is ever near in memory to those things a god's nearness whereunto makes him truly god. Wherefore if a man makes right use of such means of remembrance, and ever approaches to the full vision of the perfect mysteries, he and he alone becomes truly perfect. Standing aside from the busy doings of mankind, and drawing nigh to the divine, he is rebuked by the multitude as being out of his wits, for they know not he is possessed by a deity".*[544]

The human realm, however, is unlike the divine. With each incarnation, a soul not dedicated to purification and philosophy moves farther away from its memories of the heavenly realm. Socrates goes so far to say human souls may even eventually fall into animal bodies once they have become so impure and irrational they cannot relate to a human body.

Body and Soul – Divine Creations: The Soul in the *Timaeus*

The *Timaeus*' myth of the soul[545] differs dramatically than that of the *Phaedrus* and the descriptions of the body in the *Phaedo*. In the *Timaeus* myth the noeric Demiurge is both responsible for the creation of the human soul, and, at least in part, the creation of the body via instruction to the celestial gods. Part of the Demiurge's instructions to the gods concerns the making of mortals, which are necessary for the universes' completion and perfection. As the soul is immortal[546] this can only refer to humans.

Human bodies, or the archetype for human bodies, are created by the gods in imitation of the divine image as dictated by the Demiurge. The matter, *hylē*, from which bodies are formed, is created by Aion, who then passes it on to Helios-Zeus for shaping.[547] None of this contradicts the previous two dialogues, except that those responsible for the soul and body, the gods, Aion, and the celestial

---

544 *Ibid.*, 249 c-d.
545 *Tim*, 41a-47 d.
546 Cf. *Phaedo* 71 d-72 b, 89b-102; *In Phaednm*, fr. 3, fr. 4.; *Phaedr*, 245 c-246a.
547 DM VIII.3, 313-4.

Demiurge, are incapable of any evil, even by accident. Therefore the body not only is good, but must be good.[548]

The human body is created by the gods and the soul by the Demiurge because of their goodness, but beyond this, the soul descends by the will of the gods. The reason is two-fold. First, in accord with the *Timaeus*, it is to complete creation in a uniform manner.[549] Second, it does so in order to manifest the life of the gods in creation. In either case, the will of the gods is carried out by the soul in generation.[550] By the Neoplatonic understanding of the nature of the gods as essentially good, the descent of the soul must likewise be good.

Reconciliation – A Matter of Perspective

On the one hand, the body is a prison for the soul, distorting its natural powers and blinding it to the greater truth of the super-lunar realms. The soul crashes into generation and is dragged into bodies by governing daimons, to stay there until the soul's divine wings are re-grown over innumerable lifetimes of purification. On the other hand, matter is holy and eternal, created by the pre-essential Demiurgos and handed over to the noeric Demiurgos and the gods for the creation of bodies, which are in turn formed in accordance with divine proportions.[551]

So, which is it? Is the body good or bad? For earlier Neoplatonists, as well as some Gnostics, matter is evil and the source of evil. But this is not the case for Iamblichus and later Neoplatonists. For Iamblichus, there is no contradiction in the Platonic dialogues, especially as they contain Pythagorean and theurgic truths. This means both views of the body and matter are correct. The key to this mystery is a matter of perspective. However, the perspective in question is not directly related to matter. Instead, it has to do with the soul's relationship with the higher realms and is connected to the ideas of Providence, *Pronoia*, and Fate, *Eimarmei.*

In his *Letter to Macedonius on Fate*, Iamblichus defines Fate as "*the one order that comprehends in itself all other orders.*'[552] Fate is the ordering principle of the sub-lunar realm, working like a clockwork mechanism, and necessary for the proper functioning of the natural cosmos. This ordering principle is based on all the higher ordering principles, such as the noetic moments and transcendent Time. Only humans and beings possessing only an irrational soul, non-human animals, are ruled by Fate.

---

548 DM I.18, 67.

549 Recall the Hermetic axiom "As above, so below."

550 DA VI.27, 55. The final sentence should be taken as Iamblichus' agreement with the positions of Heraclitus and Taurus (Finamore, *Vehicle*, 100).

551 C.f. Finamore, *Vehicle*, 91-2.

552 L8, fr. 1.

The difficulty here lies in the relationship between the human soul, which has free will, and its embodied and forgetful nature. Fate is beneficial for the natural world. However, the fallen soul forgets its place in the chain of being. Instead of viewing creation from the divine realm, we now view the divine from creation, and we do so in ignorance of the mechanisms which properly order all things. To us Fate is a burden, a shackle whose chains whip us back and forth in unpredictable ways.

But the soul is only governed by the world of generation, and by Fate, in as much as it inclines towards, and identifies with, that realm.[553] Or, in terms of the *Phaedrus* myth, the extent of control the soul has over its unruly steed. Above the natural world beings are not ruled by Fate but instead willingly engage with Providence, which flows from the Good. As we begin identifying ourselves with the divine realms rather than our bodies, we undergo a shift in perspective. This new life, made possible by philosophy and theurgy, allows the human soul to operate on its natural level, above the influence of Fate and aligned with Providence, even while still incarnate.

If all beings in the realm of generation, such as us, are ruled by Fate, how is this possible? The answer is that *"in reality Fate is Providence.*"[554] Whether we experience Fate or Providence is an index of our relationship with the greater kinds, especially our personal daimon, and the extent to which we are inclined towards the divine or physical realm. The only difference is in us, for there is no difference between Fate and Providence.[555] As we purify our soul, through philosophy, religion, and theurgy, we undergo a perspective shift. As we come to remember who and what we really are we gain the opportunity to participate in the unfolding of Providence rather than be enmeshed in the chains of Fate.

Our physical lives do not change, this is all but impossible as the process of incarnation stamps upon us an allotment derived from the universe in the form of our horoscope.[556] Once incarnate we can fall into the habits to which our star-impressed bodies have become used and be slaves to Fate. Or we can choose to incorporate our material natures into the supracosmic patterns, willfully participating the divine and ordering work of the Demiurge.[557] Once this form of embodiment is fully realized we cease to be slaves to Fate and instead, through demiurgy, become its masters. This is the goal of material theurgy.

---

[553] L8, fr 2, 21-3.
[554] L8, fr. 4, in Shaw, "Demiurgy," 50.
[555] Shaw, "Demiurgy", 50.
[556] L8, fr. 4. Presumably, a master theurgist could ritually change their horoscope.
[557] *Ibid.*, 51. C.f. L8, fr. 4: *"the originating cause of action in humans has indeed a concordance with both these originating causes in the universe; the origin of action in us is both independent of Nature and emancipated from the movement of the universe . . . For because it is not produced from Nature, nor produced from the movement of the universe, it is ranked above it as prior, and not dependent on the universe."*

The Soul's Descent

Although the *Phaedrus* myth gives an explanation for the original descent of the soul, the question remains as to why it continues to descend again and again, even after it is purified and no longer identifies as a physical body. Part of the mechanism of soul's descent is discussed in the *Timaeus*. According to Iamblichus' understanding of the *Timaeus* myth, after souls are created they are individually distributed to, and sewn into, the orbits of their leader god, the Dionysian choir of Thrones, and their train of daimons and heroes. From this position souls descend into generation.[558]

This sewing determines the general place from which souls descend, and also influences the soul's overall life, though it is not the only determining factor. Individual souls descend from different places depending on their leaders. However, each soul is connected to all of the greater kinds associated with its leader god, as well as those of the gods who the encosmic gods serve as vehicles. A freshly descended soul, or one fully engrossed with matter, is under the dominion of its personal daimon and enters generation under that entity's guidance. The fully purified soul of a theurgic sage is under the direct supervision of its leader god or possibly the angel of a hypercosmic god, as it works to come into contact with those higher gods. The theurgic sage willingly expresses the divine life as posited above.[559] The fully purified soul's descent is special, never inclining towards generation and remaining in connection with the noeric realm.[560] Such a soul, remaining free of sin, becomes much like a Bodhisattva, descending for the benefit of others.[561]

One reason the soul continues to descend is its lack of purity. The impure soul has not risen to its greatest heights and so must plunge back into the depths for further refinement. This is reflected in *Peri Psyche*, which says souls not perfectly pure and god-like descend either for the correction of their character or for punishment, depending on their level of impurity. Only the purified soul, descending *"for the salvation, purification, and perfection of this realm'*[562] does so by choice and is capable of entering a body without identifying itself with or as that body. Such a soul more fully participates Nous and never forgets itself.

When a soul does descend it also chooses a life. The best kind of life is involved with purification, elevation, and the perfection of the soul, the worst with the opposite of these activities.[563] How and when do we, or our souls, choose which life to live and learn which is the best kind to live? A life is chosen while the

---

558 DA III.26, 53.
559 C.f. Finamore, *Vehicle*, 102.
560 *In Phaed.*, fr. 5.
561 Dillon, "Introduction," in DA, 17.
562 DA, III.29, 57.
563 DA VII.35, 63. This is a common Neoplatonic theme, carried into Dionysius as purification, illumination and perfection.

soul is disincarnate, and is based on all of that soul's previous lives. This suggests the soul learns of the proper life while incarnate, and likely through the practice of philosophy and theurgy.[564]

A soul has free-will, and though it is sown into the circuit of its leader god, the soul does not have to follow that god in its choice of lives. This never occurs in the case of the purified soul, as although the soul's free-will remains, the pure soul voluntarily submits itself to the will of its superiors as this leads to its most appropriate lives. Less pure souls are mired in matter and have lost some of their connection to the will of the Good. Because of this, they may act to varying degrees in or out of keeping with divine will. Of this, Proclus writes:

> *"But what about the following: if souls dependent on the mantic power of the sun should project (προβάλλοιντο) a medical or telestic life, but other souls project a mercurial or lunar life? For the manner of variation is not the same for both."*[565]

This means any soul may or may not choose, or "project," a life corresponding to their leader. Renaissance Neoplatonist Marsilio Ficino presents some of the kinds of lives, which he calls gifts, associated with each planetary deity. Although his presentation is abbreviated, it is still a useful example:

> *"The gift of contemplation Saturn [Kronos] strengthens . . . . The power of governing and ruling Jupiter [Zeus] strengthens . . . . Greatness of soul, Mars [Ares] . . . . Clarity of the senses and of opinion (whence comes prophecy), the Sun [Apollo]. . . . Love, Venus [Aphrodite] . . . . Skills in speaking and interpretation, Mercury [Hermes] . . . . Finally, Luna [Selene] encourages the function of procreation . . . ."*[566]

Typically, a solar soul picks a solar life. An impure solar soul may, however, choose a mercurial, lunar or some other life, and incarnate accordingly. Further, a soul choosing a life appropriate to its nature need not be identical to all other such souls. A solar soul may pick a life of medicine, associated with Asklepios, or a telestic life associated with Apollo, both of which are solar in nature. The same soul, participating the life of its leader, may also choose to project a life that is in accord with another god.[567]

The point here is whether a soul will choose, or is capable of choosing, a life in line with its nature and the nature of its leader, which is the best life for that soul. Or will it choose some other life, which is not for the best. This is related to Iamblichus' notion of three different kinds of humans and three different modes of descent into bodies. The theurgic sage descends purely and chooses a life in keeping with its nature. The beginning philosopher and theurgist's descent is partially voluntary and partially involuntary. Such a soul chooses a more or less appropriate life in accord with the soul's level of purity. Those souls belonging to

---

564 *Ibid*, commentary VII.35, 175-6.

565 Proclus, *In Tim*, 279, 17-20, in Finamore, *Vehicle*, 69.

566 DAm VI.4, 112.

567 This doctrine is held both implicitly by Iamblichus and explicitly by Proclus. See Finamore, *Vehicle*, 67-72.

the great herd of humanity are typically dragged down into generation by their daimons and, being impure, typically choose inappropriate lives, again in keeping with their level of impurity.

The Soul's Powers

Power is an entity's potential expression of its essence. As with the superior beings, the easiest way to understand an entity's essence is through its powers and activities. Although the human soul eventually falls into generation and becomes identified with a physical body, the soul's power resides in the soul, not the body and soul together. Some powers are expressed when the soul exists away from the body while others are expressed only when soul and body are conjoined. Also, incarnation causes some of the soul's disincarnate powers to express differently while incarnate.[568] This is in line with the *Phaedo*'s view of the soul's ability to comprehend truth being lessened while incarnate.[569]

The soul is considered, when taken by itself, unitary and without distinct elements. However, when connected to the body Iamblichus, following Plato, says the soul is tripartite, divided into reason, spirit, and desire.[570] These parts relate to the three parts of the *Republic*'s just society.[571] The soul's first part allows us to learn, the second to feel strong emotions such as anger, and the third to desire physical things.[572] This division is not literal, but, as Iamblichus and Porphyry agree, used for the sake of understanding the virtues.[573] The soul's actual powers are different from the parts, and include: '*growth, imagination, perception, opinion, thought that moves the body, desire for good and evil and intellection,*'[574] as well as memory or the mental retention of images.[575]

Just as the soul has a life alone and a life with the body, some of the soul's powers are connected to one or the other of the soul's modes of existence. A distinction must be made here. Although the surviving fragments of *Peri Psyche* talk about a single soul, *De Mysteriis*, and Platonic thought in general, is clear there are two, one rational and one irrational.[576] The rational soul '*partak[es] of the power of the Demiurge while the other is contributed to us from the circuit of the heavenly bodies.*'[577] Through this second soul, our irrational powers become active, either stemming

---

[568] *Ibid.*, II.10, 35.
[569] 65 a-b.
[570] DA II.12, 37. C.f. Rep 436a-437d.
[571] *Rep* 441c-e.
[572] *Ibid.*, 436a-b.
[573] DA II.12, 35; commentary II.12, 113. See chapter four for more on the virtues.
[574] *Ibid.*, II.12, 35.
[575] *Ibid.*, II.14, 59.
[576] DM VIII.6, 319-21.
[577] *Ibid.* VIII.6, 321.

from irrational powers found in the rational soul itself[578] or originating in the irrational soul.

The Soul's Activities

A soul's activities, or power in expression, arise from the soul itself, from the passions of the body, or from the combination of the two. All activities come from the soul as their cause. We cannot attribute any activity to the body alone, even those that arise from bodily passions, because bodies are incapable of self-movement.

Iamblichus likens the One of the soul, the soul's principle of unity and Intellect, to a ship's helmsman, superior to the *Phaedrus'* charioteer. The helmsman controls the ship and sets its course, even if wind and other factors influence ship's response to the helmsman's command. Just as the ship has movements proper to it when controlled by the helmsman, so the helmsman, the One of the soul, has activities proper to it when separate from its ship. These include divine possession, immaterial thinking, and union with the divine.[579]

Unlike the activities of the gods and archangels, human activities, occurring only when soul and body are conjoined, are disconnected from the essence and life of the soul. Specifically, these activities include *"change, divisibility, corporeality dimensionality, and extension.'*[580] Such activities cannot belong to the immortal, unchanging, unextended or non-physical soul as it exists by itself.

The human soul, a fallen divinity, is, in its highest state, the last of the greater kind. The following section focuses on the summation of later Neoplatonism: *theourgia.* However, before theurgy is possible, the philosopher must engage in worship. Neoplatonic *cultus* is steeped in theurgic activity, and so serves as an introduction to divine activity.

---

578 DA commentary II.13, 117.

579 DA III.16, 43.

580 *Ibid.*

Chapter Fifteen

Cultus

Unlike in the Philosophia section, Theologia has had no exercises. The reason for this is due to the different natures of Neoplatonic philosophy and worship. While there is a kind of specifically theurgic ritual praxis that is at least semi-distinct from the practitioner's regular *cultus* or religious worship, Neoplatonism is also a tool by which the practitioner is able to interpret their religion along Neoplatonic and theurgic lines. This "theurgic worship" may be seen as a preliminary to theurgy beyond *cultus*.

Not surprisingly, the pagan Neoplatonists are concerned with polytheistic religious worship. This is the initial focus of the chapter. Regardless of the originating religious background of our sources on theurgic worship, we explore the concepts underlying these varied ideologies so they may be applied to a multitude of religious contexts.

Dietary Restrictions or I Drank What?

Both Judaism and Islam have specific, and similar, dietary restrictions placed on them by scripture. From the *Torah*, *kosher* laws are found in Judaism and the *Qur'an* holds rules for eating *halal* in Islam. Both Judaism and Islam also have holidays involving near total abstinence from food. Catholics also have certain dietary restrictions, although these are limited to a particular day of the week and Hindus have a completely different set of religious dietary restrictions. Ancient Hellenic religious beliefs also include different kinds of dietary laws.

Possibly the most well known Hellenic-related dietary practice is the one associated with Pythagoras of Samos and the Pythagorean Brotherhood. According to most of the stories surrounding his life, Pythagoras, as well as his followers, is a vegetarian. Socrates, as presented by Plato, possibly advocates vegetarianism as well, though it is not a necessity in the *Republic* or the *Laws*, where Plato sets out many of the requirements for living an ideal life.

Of the Neoplatonists, Plotinus and Porphyry are also vegetarians. Porphyry writes a treatise on the subject, *De Abstinentia*. This four-volume treatise is written to Firmus Castricius, Porphyry's friend and a fellow Plotinian disciple. Book one begins with Porphyry's claim of surprise at Firmus' rejection of *"a fleshless diet."*[581] He then deconstructs any criticism against not eating meat before laying out why a vegetarian diet is best. Especially important in this regard are the dietary restrictions associated with sacrificing to the gods.

This focus on diet and sacrifice is part of Porphyry's *Letter to Anebo*. Porphyry asks *"Why also do the interpreters of prophecies and oracles think it requisite that they should abstain from animals, lest the Gods should be polluted by the vapours arising from them; and yet the Gods are especially allured by the vapours of animals?"*[582] Porphyry is not questioning vegetarianism but a specific cultic practice, namely the dietary purity restrictions on the priesthood when performing sacrifices.

Iamblichus' answer pertains more to the nature of sacrifice but also highlights the importance of a specialized diet connected to cultic practice. Julian the Philosopher also takes up the issue of ritual diet. In his *Hymn to the Mother of the Gods*, Julian discusses dietary restrictions associated with the worship of the great Mother and her consort Attis or Gallus. Julian lists a number of foods prohibited during certain holidays. This includes at various times fruits, roots, pomegranates, and apples, but not almonds or meat.[583] On the surface, the reason as to why certain foods can be eaten and others not is symbolic. For instance, roots, which grow down in to the earth, may not be eaten because of Attis' upward moving focus towards the noeric great Mother, and his castration, which is an act of purification and movement away from generation. This dietary requirement *"enjoins that we turn our eyes towards the heavens, or rather above the heavens,"* the intellective realm.[584]

This prohibition is not, however, merely symbolic: it invites us to participate directly in the mystery of Attis. Through a correct understanding of the dietary restrictions they, when taken in their ritual context, have an anagogic effect, not simply raising our thoughts, but our souls as well. This is *De Mysteriis*' main theme: we ritually act in imitation of the divine in order to participate it.

Sacrifice or What Exactly Does God Need With a Dead Animal?

Animal sacrifice is an important element of pagan religious practice; it has existed for millennia and continues to do so in many modern paganisms. That it is advocated by some pagan Neoplatonists is not surprising. Later we take up the question as to whether or not animal sacrifice should or must be engaged in by modern Neoplatonists. For now, however, let us turn back to Porphyry's questioning of the Egyptian priest Anebo.

---

581 DAb, I.1

582 Porphyry, "Letter," 10, c.f. DM V.3, 229.

583 Julian, *Mother*, 174A-B.

584 *Ibid.*, 175C.

Porphyry's question is two-fold. First, if the essence of the gods is beyond all materiality, why make sacrifices at all? How are they good for the gods and how are they good for those who perform them? Second, if smells from sacrifices attract the gods, why should the priests avoid eating meat and its associated scents?[585]

The first question is simply answered, and points to Porphyry's lack of understanding of the nature of the gods in relation to bodies. The gods need nothing because they lack nothing. They certainly do not need our sacrifices, nor do sacrifices affect or persuade the gods. This is where Neoplatonic *cultus* differs from common interpretations of sacrifice. We cannot persuade, beg or coerce the gods into bestowing their blessings. This is impossible because the gods, like the Demiurges, are above all matter and cannot be affected materially. Moreover, their blessings are always raining down upon us. Of this, Proclus writes that "*[i]n virtue of their being, then, and in virtue of being excellences, the gods exercise providence towards all things, filling all with goodness which is prior to Intelligence.*"[586] We sacrifice for two reasons. First, the gods, or God, are worthy of sacrifice and inspire us to worship them.[587] Second, instead of the sacrifices having effect on the gods, they affect us.

Through theurgy, the proper sacrifices purify and unite us with the encosmic gods, and ultimately the celestial Demiurge within whom they are united.[588] Sacrifice should therefore be seen as anagogic rather than genagogic. While they raise us upwards towards the gods through participation, they are incapable of bringing the gods downwards. Nor is it necessary to do so. Also, while Iamblichus proscribes animal sacrifice, he does not do so for everyone. Each level of divinity, from the sub-lunar to the supercelestial, has an appropriate kind of sacrifice. Sacrifice of physical things is suitable for those gods who primarily interact with the generative world, the sub-lunar and visible gods.

An element of physical sacrifice is also fitting for the liberated gods. However, as these gods only have one foot in the material realm, animal sacrifice, with its close connection to the body and deep physicality, is inappropriate. Those souls advanced enough to worship the liberated gods employ what we may call "intermediate forms of sacrifice." This kind of sacrifice does not involve the slaughtering of animals. Instead, it employs a kind of materiality that is, nevertheless, less material than animals. This includes hieratic characters and symbols, possibly talismans, divine names and images, incantations and musical compositions.[589] All these depend on the physical world; names cannot be spoken without lips to utter them or air to vibrate them. However they are of a kind of materiality that is more refined than the sacrifice of bodies. The hypercosmic gods

---

585 DM V.1, 227.
586 ET §120, 107. C.f. DM V.22, 267.
587 C.f. Van Den Berg, *Hymns,* 18.
588 DM V.26, 277.
589 Shaw, *Theurgy*, 170; Shaw, "Geometry," 124.

are those to whom the famous "barbarous names of invocation" or *barbara onomata*, frequently come into play, those hieratic names with no human meaning, but are instead of divine origin and so have meaning only to the gods.[590]

Nothing of the physical world is an appropriate sacrifice to the fully hypercosmic gods, because they are entirely above the realm of generation and have nothing to do with it. Iamblichus does not tell us how the immaterial sacrifices of purified souls are performed, because those rare souls capable of performing them are *"superior to all legislation.'*[591] However, Gregory Shaw posits a Pythagorean approach to this kind of sacrifice. Given Iamblichus considers himself a Pythagorean, and he sees a direct connection between ritual worship and mathematical practices,[592] Shaw's idea is plausible. As we have seen, Iamblichus considers the Pythagorean decad as commiserate to the Forms. Hypercosmic sacrifices are made through numbers.[593] As each number represents a kind of Form,[594] which are connected to, and come from, the gods, sacrificing numbers raises the theurgist to the highest divine levels. How exactly these rites are performed is a mystery, but as Proclus relates them to Time and heavenly cycles, they possibly have an astrological component.[595]

All this, however, only serves to answer the first of Porphyry's questions. Sacrifice affects us, not the gods, but what about the question concerning the gods' attraction to the fumes of burning sacrifices while humans should avoid eating the same animals?[596] The logic behind the question is that if gods are attracted to the smells of such animals, why shouldn't priests eat them and so further attract the gods?

A partial answer to this question has already been alluded; gods are unaffected by sacrifices, which means they are in no way attracted to *"odours from living things.'*[597] Therefore we must look to the effect eating sacrificial animals has on humans rather than what they might do to the gods. In this case, pollution from the sacrificed animals may affect the purity of the priests performing the sacrifice.[598] Such pollutions are akin to those discussed in chapter fourteen and

---

590 See also Proclus, *Hymns*, 106, where Dillon postulates that the *barbara onomata* or hieratic names are, in Proclus' system, attributed to the liberated gods rather than the visible gods. The Greek magical papyri, however, association such names with all levels of divinity.

591 DM V.22, 265.

592 Shaw, "Geometry," 127. See VP XII.59, 83

593 Shaw, "Geometry," 126.

594 Or, according to Proclus, is beyond the Forms.

595 Shaw, "Geometry," 128. C.f. DM VII.4, 317. This works because the material gods act as vehicles for the immaterial gods. Otherwise the movements of the bodies of the material gods is irrelevant to the worship of the immaterial.

596 Note that in Iamblichus' *De vita pythagorica*, we are told only to eat animals that are sacrificed, as human souls never incarnate in those animals. VP XVIII.85, 109.

597 DM V.1, 227.

598 DM V.4, 233.

form accretions on the human soul's pneumatic vehicle, effectively blocking that soul from participating divine grace.

The Efficacy of Animal Sacrifice or Do I Really Need to Kill It?

The gods clearly do not need sacrifice, but do we? The simple answer is "yes." The Neoplatonists perform sacrifices as part of their worship, so we should, too. Neoplatonism develops as a hermeneutic for pagan religious practices before being brought into the Abrahamic religions. A number of cultural religiosities are represented by the Neoplatonists of antiquity, including not only Hellenic, but Egyptian, Assyrian, Mesopotamian and Levantine religions.[599] Animal sacrifice is common to all of these in their public forms. Emperor Julian seems to imply such a lens is appropriate for Jewish temple sacrifice as well,[600] and we can posit nearly any tradition of animal sacrifice might, and from a Platonist perspective should, be interpreted as discussed above, regardless as to how sacrifice might be popularly understood in those religions.

The hierarchy of sacrifice, with pure numbers or thoughts as the most sublime, and animal sacrifice as the least, is commonly accepted by the Neoplatonists, Neopythagoreans, and Hermeticists of the fourth and fifth centuries CE,[601] and we find a general decline in animal sacrifice within the Roman Empire during this time, despite Julian's efforts to revive the practice. Within Neoplatonism, blood sacrifice is rare, with incense, perfumes, herbs, sacred stones and invocations taking their place.[602]

Also, we must take into consideration the ultimate nature of Neoplatonic thought, which is not a religion in its own right, but a lens through which religions may be properly participated.[603] While it develops amongst polytheists, not all Neoplatonists are polytheists. Synesius, Bishop of Cyrene, is a student of Hypatia, for instance, and, of course, there is Pseudo-Dionysius and his practice of liturgical theurgy. Admittedly, these two examples are from Christianity, and Christianity does have a kind of sacrificial practice through the Eucharist. However Dionysius' theurgic liturgy is not limited to the Eucharist; all of the sacraments in the *Ecclesiastical Hierarchy* are described in terms of their theurgic efficacy. Beyond this, Neoplatonism spreads into Judaism, long after the destruction of the Temple, and Islam, especially into Kabbalah and Sufism, and still exists there to this day. By denying non-blood sacrificing religions access to

---

[599] *Ibid.*, 2.
[600] Julian, *Letter,* 313. This is not Julian's main point, however the surviving fragment of this letter deals with the importance of temple sacrifice, and I can see no reason why he would not apply this to Jewish sacrifice as well, despite what he sees as flaws in the religion.
[601] Bradbury, "Revival," 334.
[602] *Ibid.*
[603] C.f. Butler, "Offering," 1.

theurgic practice we are in the awkward position of claiming such religions are not "real religions" or that Neoplatonism is not a fully encompassing hermeneutic, neither of which are defensible.

If this is the case, we must conclude animal sacrifice is a non-integral aspect of Neoplatonic praxis, despite it having Iamblichus' and Julian's support. This leaves us with having to better understand the purpose and function of sacrifice so as to continue engaging in its function, without necessarily having to engage in animal sacrifice. As we have seen, the purpose of sacrifice is two-fold: it purifies us, and especially our pneumatic vehicle, and it illuminates us towards participating the divine. Other rituals, such as baptism, *wudu* and *ghsul* in Islam, and the Jewish *mikvah* or ritual bathing, almost everything involved in Pesach or Ramadan, and Hindu *puja*, amongst others, have a cathartic effect as well. As we have seen, the burning of incense, commonly practiced by pagan Neoplatonists, and found in the *Orphic Hymns*, and in the holy place of the Temple of Jerusalem, can take the place of animal sacrifice.

Theurgic Prayer and the *Barbara Onomata*

The *Chaldean Oracles* tell us *"Change not the Barbarous Names of Evocation, for these are names in every language which are given by God, which have in the Sacred Rites a power ineffable."*[604] This command is echoed by Iamblichus and, much later, the Edwardian magician Aleister Crowley. For the later Neoplatonists, this injunction relates directly to theurgic prayer, which involves what are commonly known as *barbara onomata* or *voces magicae.* The *onomata* are long strings of vowels and consonants understood as divine and ineffable names. These names are, in effect, "bodies" of the gods. To invoke a divine name is for the god to be present completely in its name and in the rite or hymn within which it is invoked.[605] By uttering the divine names we take the gods into ourselves, breathing them into our lungs and our minds. Exhaling the name does not expel the divine from us, but causes us to instead encounter the divine in another way, through their sound and vibration. So, to speak a divine name is to become permeated and surrounded by God. This can be understood as a theurgic interpretation of the third commandment, not taking God's name in vain.

Theurgic prayer functions as a support, completion, and perfection to the work performed in sacrifice and its correlates, having a purificatory effect.[606] According to Iamblichus:

> *"Extended practice of prayer nurtures our intellect, enlarges very greatly our soul's receptivity to the gods, reveals to mean the life of the gods, accustoms their eyes to the brightness of the divine light, and gradually brings to perfection the capacity of our*

---

604 CO 155, #150 as *"Do not change the nomina barbara;"* in Majercik.
605 Uždavinys, *Theurgy*, 91.
606 Van Den Berg, *Hymns*, 109.

> *faculties for contact with the gods, until it leads us up to the highest level of consciousness (of which we are capable); also, it elevates gently the disposition of our minds, and communicates to us those of the gods, stimulates persuasion and communion and indissoluble friendship, augments divine love, kindles the divine element in the soul, scours away all contrary tendencies within it, casts out from the aetherial and luminous vehicle surrounding the soul everything that tends to generation, brings to perfection good hope and faith concerning the light; and, in a word, it renders those who employ prayers, if we may so express it, the familiar consorts of the gods.'*[607]

Unsurprisingly, theurgic prayer has three levels. The first introduces us to the gods or God, or to whatever prayer is directed towards, the second connects us to the divine in demiurgy and intuitive knowing, realising the benefits from the divine through participation, and the third brings about *henosis* or divine union. Proclus adds to Iamblichus' third level, which is Proclus' fifth, not simply *henosis*, but a *henosis* connecting the One of the Soul to the One of the gods.[608] Prayer may occur before, during or after sacrifice but without it theurgic ritual is useless.[609]

Unfortunately, although Iamblichus spells out his theory of prayer, he does not describe its practice, nor does he provide any of the *barbara onomata*, or any examples of prayer at all. Proclus' theory of prayer extends the *barbara onomata* only to the hypercosmic gods and above, not to the visible and sub-lunar gods or even the hyper-encosmic gods.[610] It is impossible to know if Iamblichus' theory of prayer also reflected this. We do know the prayers of the PGM include *barbara onomata* of material gods. Because there is a difference between prayer as *cultus*, and prayer as *theourgia*, theurgic rites outside of religious worship might include *barbara onomata* encosmic and sub-lunar gods. Other forms of prayer, employing theurgic content other than *barbara onomata*, are also prescribed for the material forms of theurgy associated with the leader material gods.

At least five such prayers, hymns written by Proclus, survive. Other hymns, such as those by Synesius also qualify. None of Proclus' hymns contain *barbara onomata*.[611] Two of them are to Aphrodite, of whom Proclus is a close devotee. Despite Proclus' deep respect for the goddess, the prayers deal with her in her material form, rather than in her hypercosmic aspects, and so employ common titles and epitaphs rather than *barbara onomata*. The same is true of his prayers to Zeus, Rhea, Athena, and Hekate. Even though each of these deities has a higher aspect, that is not the focus of his prayers, and so no *barbara onomata* appear.

---

607 DM V.26, 277.

608 Dillon, "Iamblichu's Theory of Prayer," in Appendix A of the *Platonic Commentaries*, 410-11. Proclus' theory of prayer includes five stages: 1) knowledge of the divine hierarchy; 2) becoming like the gods through participation; 3) contact with the gods through the summit of our soul; 4) approaching the divine fire; 5) *henosis*. See, *Hymns*, 88-9.

609 DM V.26, 275-7.

610 Proclus', but not Iamblichus', leader gods. Van Den Berg, *Hymns*, 106.

611 Christian Neoplatonist hymns do not use the *barbara onomata*, and instead follow what will become Dionysius' theory of divine names.

Proclus' prayers, as do Synesius', contain theurgic symbols. These include the use of symbolic titles and names as well as references to the use of ritual objects. They also make use of innate symbols, such as the fact Proclus is a Lycian, which binds him to Aphrodite, the goddess of the Lycians, and that he was born in Byzantium, placing him in the series of Athena. They also make use of myths, or references to myths, as symbolic of the activities of the deity or deities to whom the hymns are directed.[612] These are common features to prayer practices found in many religions. That is, common prayer, when properly understood, becomes theurgic, at least to a level appropriate to the worship of the material gods or their equivalents, such as Christ manifest on earth.

This means prayers you may normally employ in your religious practice likely already contain the elements necessary for even the most basic form of theurgic prayer. However, there is something to be said for writing personalized hymns, as do Proclus and Synesius. If you wish to write your own prayers there is a common and replicable schema in Proclus' hymns. You may also find schema that fit your particular religious practice through a study of your religion's prayers.

In the case of the Proclean hymns, they, like Pseudo-Plato's Latin *Hymn to the Creator*, are modelled on the pattern of other ancient hymns and consist of three parts. First, they begin with an invocation declaring to whom the hymn is directed. Second is a biographical description of the qualities of the deity, and possibly other entities within the series or orbit of the deity, like the Erotes in Proclus' *hymn to Aphrodite.* This is not flattery; the gods cannot be flattered. Because thinking and Being are related, this has to do with our understanding of the divine, which helps us participate it. The descriptions of the deity often include cosmological functions that lead the hymn to the final part. This is the supplication or prayer, where the devotee states what they desire.[613]

Three things, diet, sacrifice, and hymnody, are the basic components of theurgic worship. Each serves a similar, cathartic and anagogic purpose, accomplishing those ends in distinct ways. Each observance is also engaged in differently, depending on the mode of worship appropriate to the practitioner: material, liminal, or immaterial. Though there are possible substitutes for these practices, that does not mean you should make changes without all due consideration. Prayer, the key component of all theurgic activity, begins with proper knowledge of the divine. Extend this ideology to all aspects of your worship, for we honour the divine when we begin with proper knowledge.

---

[612] *Ibid.*, 91-99, 101, 106-7.

[613] Van Der Berg, *Hymns*, 193 and Lewy, "Hymn," 245.

Hymns

What follows are five examples of hymns, the likes of which can be included in your personal religious life if you desire something as an adjunct to your regular religious practices, or if you do not belong to any organized religion but still wish to engage in this kind of praxis. The first is a simple prayer to Helios preserved by Macrobius, an early fifth century Roman Platonist. The second is a hymn to the goddess Aphrodite as one of the leader gods, in the style of hymns discussed above.[614] The third example is a prayer to the celestial Demiurgos in the style of the PGM. The fourth example is a hymn to the manifest Christ modeled after the hymns of Synesius. The fifth example is a prayer to Athena, goddess of wisdom.

To Helios [615]

Hêlie pantokrator,	All-ruling Sun,
Kosmou pneuma,	Spirit of the World,
Kosmou dunamis,	Power of the World,
Kosmou phôs.	Light of the World.

According to Macrobius this is how the sun is invoked in the mystery religions. The word "helios" is both the name of the Titan of the sun and the word for the sun itself, and so can be used as a brief invocation to the noeric Demiurgos.

Gemistus Plethon, in the 15th century CE, advocates a "neo-pagan" calendar reform. In this pagan liturgical calendar, Plethon includes three daily prayer cycles for morning, afternoon and evening.[616] This prayer to the sun is easily adapted to such a cycle, and helps align the practitioner to the sun and the movements of the Demiurgos.

---

[614] However, hexameter, common to "Homeric" hymns, does not work well in English. Instead, meters common to English language hymns are used.

[615] Macrob. Sat. lib. i. c. 23, in Cory, *Fragments*, 355.

[616] This is comparable to Proclus' worship of the sun at dusk, noon and dawn. More on this is found in the following section of this chapter.

To Aphrodite

8.6.8.6 [617]

<u>Incense:</u> Myrrh

I erect a statue to you
with my hymn, O sea born
Aphrodite. Heavenly one,
supreme bliss and true sworn.

Mother of Charities, queen of
elevated love, and
sage of the Form of Beauty. Sea
foam one, whose love is grand.

O averter of unlawful
desires, nude Beauty
beyond all earthly beauty, you
of sacred duty.

From you flows the harmony of
the middle term, and it

is you who sooths Ares' wrath
by Zeus' sacred writ.

Lady of noeric union,
heavenly beauty of
the great mother, hear this my prayer
and grant me holy love.

---

[617] The numbers after the hymn's title designate the hymns' meter. 8.6.8.6 means line of eight syllables, followed by one of six, then one of eight, and then one of six, with the last word of the six syllable lines rhyming. This is the same meter in which "Amazing Grace" is written.

To the Celestial Demiurgos

8.7.8.7D [618]

Incense: Pounded Frankincense and essence of Heliotrope.

Face the rising sun, adorn your brow with frankincense scented oil, sacrifice incense in great abundance, and repeat the prayer seven times.

Hearken, great celestial and
noeric lord, king of kings
and leader of the leader gods.
rejoice in my heart, who springs
forth the east wind. Oh masterful
image of holy Aion,
universal Agathodaimon,
hear this your sacred paean.

Crown of the universe within
whom youth and old age are made
naught. Hear these words in your honour:

BRINTANTĒNŌPhRI BRISSKYLMAS AROYRZORBOROBA
MESINTRIPhI NIPTOYMI ChMOYMMAŌPhI.

Purify all that is faulty
in me, oh you director
of angels and men. Free me from
of the Moirai's straight vector.
Rain upon me being, life, and
intellect. Grant me triumph
over impure forces, raise my
soul to your omniscience

Let the eye of justice reside
in my mind. Yes, great lord:

ABLANAThANALBA
AKRAMMAChAMARI
PEPhNA PhŌZA PNEBENNOYNI
NAAChThIP OUNORBA

I pray in your name EYE YIA EEI AO EIAY IYA IEO!

---

618 8.7.8.7D is a meter of alternating lines of eight and seven syllables, with each stanza containing this set twice. Here, the first two seven syllable lines have one ending rhyme and the second another.

To the Christos

8.7.8.7D

Incense: Frankincense and Storax

I lift my voice up to you, with
ivory-laid lyre and love,
O Blessed Immortal Christos,
illustrious offspring of
the Virgin Mary, Son of God,
Saviour of the whole world. Hear
my prayer. Save me, a descended
soul, from this my fleshly bier.

Iesous Christos Soter, hear my
prayer, raise me with your light
divine, and purify my soul
with your holy Word and sight.
Accord me, in your Name, O great
Divine image, a sweet life,
blesséd and pure. Hear my prayer
Lord, that I may rest from strife.

To Athene

8.7.8.7

Incense: olive leaves and aromatic herbs

Hail, aegis-bearing daughter of
Zeus, child of paternal
Mind, spear-holding virgin warrior,
Helios' deep kernel.

Hearken to my hymn with kind thought,
you who dispense wisdom to
the seven spheres. O Athena,
splitter of Giants in two.

Grey-eyed goddess, who gives
madness to the wicked and
of prudence to those with virtue, I
give my soul to your remand.

Your fierce strength is foe to Giantes,
you bare Gorgo's awful head.
Mother of learning, you who lead
people to knowledge's bed.

You who won Athens, you who slew
foul Typhoeus. Great, divine
noeric intelligence, fine
lady of the sacred shrine.

Hail, victory laden goddess,
hear my hymn and grant to me
your consecrated wisdom. O
goddess, please hear this my plea.

Praxis

If you already have a regular religious practice within which to work then there is no need to immediately alter that practice. Neoplatonic cultus at the material level works within your regular worship. You can now aim to readjust your understanding and experience of your worship. What follows is a kind of daily cultic prayer practice based loosely on Gemistus Plethon's calendar reform.[619] This sort of practice, designed by a Renaissance Neoplatonist with both an Orthodox Christian and "neo-pagan" background, may be employed by anyone, either as an observance in its own right or as an adjunct to any other kind of worship with which you may already be engaged.

Plethon's liturgical calendar is a luni-solar cycle. Most of its feast days are in accordance with the phases of the moon, although some, like the celebration of Helios, are solar based. Having a lunar basis, the calendar has thirteen months, each of which is associated with a particular Greek deity. Each moon-phase-based feast has an attendant vigil and each feast is, in turn, associated with a particular deity or religious practice such as purification. While all of this is both interesting and important for understanding the completeness and complexity of Plethon's thought, it is also beyond the scope of this book. Instead, we will look at a single facet of Plethon's praxis: daily prayer.

Plethon divides each day into three segments, morning, afternoon and evening. These segments are loosely comparable in ideology to the numerous Offices of the day in Christianity, the three times of prayer within Judaism, and *salat* in Islam, though is not likely historically connected to them. Each prayer session is devoted to different deities, which could be expanded to saints or angels, with specific prayers said at different times of the day, depending on the day and month. The liturgy is designed for group worship and is lead by a *hierokerux*, or sacred herald, a priest or someone chosen by a priest, or a respected lay person, and can be adapted for a single person. Instead of focusing on the specific prayers, what follows is the general outline of daily worship, the specifics of which can be tailored to your needs. Each cycle of prayer, morning, afternoon and evening, follows a similar pattern.

There are five daily prayers. The first prayer is said at morning, anytime after rising and before breakfast or beginning the work day. The afternoon, or any time before dinner, has three prayers, with a hymn sung in between each prayer. Evening prayer occurs any time after dinner and before going to bed. On fast days the evening prayer is said after sunset.

Each prayer session begins with a call to prayer:

---

[619] See both Anastos, "Pletho," 1948 and Gandz, "Calendar-Reform," 1950. The following description is derived from Anastos' analysis of the liturgy.

> *Worshippers of the gods, give ear. This is the hour for the morning (or the afternoon, or the evening) prayer to the gods. Let us invoke all the gods and Zeus, who reigns over them, with all our mind, and all our reason, and all our soul.*[620]

This announcement is made once on regular days, twice on holidays and three times on the new moon, which begins the each lunar month. Those assembled then kneel on both their knees, look up, raise their hands with palms up and say *"O gods, be propitious."* This is repeated once for the Olympians while touching the floor with the right hand while lifting one knee. The extra-Olympic gods are honoured with the same prayer with the left hand on the floor. Then Zeus is prayed to following the same formula, but invoking Zeus by name and as king, with both knees and hands touching the floor. The honouring of Zeus is repeated three times. On holidays the entire formula is repeated three times at each prayer session.[621] While everyone remains on their knees, someone is selected to recite the prayer of the hour. In the case of the afternoon prayer, three people are chosen to recite the prayers and the whole company sings the intervening hymns. After prayer a philosophical tract is expounded upon. This possibly involves reading from Plato or the various commentaries such as by Iamblichus or Proclus.

The individual components of Plethon's prayer service are derived from a number of sources, both pagan and Orthodox Christian. Many religions already have symbolic gestures as part of prayer, and learning their meanings is an important aspect of theurgic worship. For instance, worshiping with the right or left hand relates to Plato's *Laws*. The Olympians are associated with the right hand and odd numbers, which is related to the circle of sameness and the idea of limitation, making it, and them, ontologically superior to the other gods who are worshiped with the left hand, representing even numbers, the circle of difference and the infinite. Touching the ground may refer to the worship of the gods of the underworld.[622]

Any and all of these gestures can be adapted to your cultic praxis. The more you are able to find out about whom you worship the better you can participate them. As part of a group setting, the whole of Plethon's liturgy works well with different types of groups, such as monastics. There is a great deal to explore in Plethon's system and, indeed, a whole book could be devoted to the subject. Hopefully, this small amount gives you enough with which to work.

---

620 Anastos, "Pletho," 255.
621 *Ibid.*
622 *Ibid.*, 259.

Theourgia

Chapter Sixteen

On Theurgy

From the *Theaetetus* we learn the chief human good is *"becoming like the divine so far as we can."*[623] Every element of Platonic thought is geared towards this goal. This is why we study philosophy, become virtuous, and seek the best for all people. Philosophy is the first area of study for the later Platonists, and is considered not just philosophical but spiritual. However, philosophical practice takes us only so far. This is not a denigration of philosophy. Without philosophy no initial advancement is possible; it is the foundation of the spiritual work of later Platonism. It is simply not enough to know the gods so far as we can.

The primary mode of Neoplatonic religious engagement is sacrifice and prayer. By "religious engagement" I mean the way through which the practitioner most commonly encounters and engages with, or in, divinity, be they saints, daimons, angels, gods, or God. Philosophical and religious practices support one another. Together, they purify the philosopher and begin raising him or her towards the divine. Unlike the popular ideology of "spiritual but not religious," later Platonism is spiritual and religious, as well as highly intellectual. Through these combined practices it is possible to rise on the scale of virtues from political to purificatory. This marks a shift from the height of human virtuosity to the admittedly lowest level of divine virtues. As "low" as are the purificatory virtues, they are still divine. Unlike the mortal political virtues, purificatory virtues, being divine, are eternal. This is a radical, difficult, and essential step towards divinity and divinization.

By themselves, philosophy, sacrifice, and prayer are not enough to theurgically participate the gods. A philosopher is not a theurgist. The common person, engaged in common worship, is not a theurgist. Yet the engagement of philosophy and the popular religious practices become theurgy. A philosopher and religious practitioner is not a theurgist, but a theurgist is always a philosopher and practitioner of religion.

---

[623] *Theat*, 176b.

Theoria – Pure Human Thought

Throughout the *Philosophia* section I presented you with a number of meditations. These take the form of thought exercises, contemplative readings, and visualizations. All of these fall under the category of *theoria* or contemplation. There are other kinds of *theoria*, such as Thomas Keating's centring prayer, poetry, and *zazen*, the seated meditational practice of Zen Buddhism. All forms of *theoria* engage, or disengage, the mind to access realms ontologically prior to ourselves. All the well known philosophical traditions of ancient Greece, the Platonists, the Stoics, the Epicureans, and so on, engage in some kind of contemplative practice.[624]

Contemplation holds a mixed position in Neoplatonic thought. For Plotinus and Porphyry and their schools, contemplation is all that is necessary to ascend to the highest ontological realms, where one rests eternally in the vision of the One and the gods. This view is connected to Plotinus' idea of the undescended soul. Beginning with Iamblichus, the later Neoplatonists take a somewhat dimmer view of *theoria.*

Iamblichus writes, *"it is not pure thought that unites theurgists to the gods.'*[625] Contemplation ceases effectiveness above the level of the Mind. Beyond this level are the Intelligibles beyond discursive thought. Our minds cannot carry us to this place because *theoria*, unlike theurgy, is essentially a human endeavour, and no purely human endeavour brings about divine works.

Despite the inherent limitations of contemplation, contemplative practices are a part of the later Neoplatonic curriculum. The inability of contemplation to advance the mind beyond the level of Nous is no reason to abandon it. Iamblichus' connection to Pythagoreanism's strong contemplative history likely involves at least mediating on the *Golden Verses* of pseudo-Pythagoras. Therefore, we must conclude *theoria*, which has cathartic effects, is both useful and necessary as a foundation upon which other exercises are built.

What does Neoplatonic *theoria* entail? This is impossible to know as none survive in writing. I have already provided you some modern contemplative practices viewed through a Neoplatonic lens. I heartily recommend exploring the contemplative practices of your own religious background whenever possible, and doing the same. Beyond this, the new Christian tradition of Centring Prayer, the Stoic writings of Marcus Aurelius, Jewish *hitbodedut*,[626] and meditating on the *Golden Verses* of pseudo-Pythagoras are all examples of contemplative practices

---

[624] For a deeper examination of contemplative practices from Greek philosophical schools see especially Hadot's *Philosophy as a Way of Life.*

[625] DM II.11, 115.

[626] For example, see Kupperman, "Hitbodedut," http://www.jwmt.org/v2n20/hitbodedut.html.

you may wish to explore. The appendix contains an apophatic *theoria* based on Dionysian thought.

Once begun, contemplation is never dropped from one's array of spiritual exercises. However, eventually the emphasis shifts from *theoria* to *theourgia*. This occurs initially through the medium of exoteric worship re-experienced through the Neoplatonic lens. In order to engage in this, it is necessary to understand the nature of theurgic practice and what makes it work. While theurgy is not knowledge, and especially not dialectical knowledge, knowledge is pre-requisite to theurgy.[627]

Theourgia – Divine Activity

The word theurgy, *theourgia*, is derived from the Greek words *theos*, god, and *ergon*, activity or work. *Theourgia* is ritualized divine activity, God working. On the surface this may appear to mean the work or activity in which God is engaged. For the pagan Neoplatonists, theurgy is not only the activity of the gods, it is also human activity participating the divine. Theurgy is our engagement in the work of God, as far as possible. The word itself is but one of several used by the later Neoplatonists to describe this kind of ritual action. Others include sacred rites, *hierougia*;[628] initiated mysteries, *mustagogia*; liturgy, *hieratike*; sacred art, *hieratike techne*; divine wisdom, *theosophia*; and others, almost all of which are rendered "theurgy" by scholars.[629]

The word *theourgia* is coined by a father and his son during the reign of Marcus Aurelius, in the second century CE. These two men, known as Julian the Chaldean and Julian the Theurgist, are responsible for writing the *Chaldean Oracles*, which greatly influences much of later Neoplatonism, especially Iamblichus, who writes a now lost thirty-volume commentary on the subject. While the Julians first use the word and develop its general use, it is not until over a century later theurgy is taken fully into Platonic practice. While no Neoplatonic theurgic rituals survive in writing we still know a great deal about how theurgy works, thanks largely to Iamblichus' *De Mysteriis*.

Theurgy is not magic, a charge levelled at it by Porphyry as well as many modern scholars of the subject. Iamblichus is at great pains to distinguish theurgy from other ritual practices, especially sorcery or *goeteia*.[630] Although theurgy involves physical techniques similar in appearance to magic and sorcery, theurgy is neither simply a technique nor a technology. These are purely human machinations. Rather, when properly understood, theurgy:

---

627 DM II.11, 115.

628 Like Damascius, Dionysius called this *hierougia*. This term is applied by Dionysius to the liturgy.

629 Uždavinys, *Theurgy*, 81.

630 This is the root word of *goetia*, often translated as "howling." This is made popular with the first book of the *Lesser Key of Solomon*, better known as the *Goetia*.

> *"presents a double aspect. On the one hand, it is performed by men, and as such observes our natural rank in the universe; but on the other, it controls divine symbols, and in virtue of them is raised up to union with the higher powers, and directs itself harmoniously in accordance with their dispensation, which enables it quite properly to assume the mantle of the gods. It is in virtue of this distinction, then, that the art both naturally invokes the powers from the universe as superiors, inasmuch as the invoker is a man, and yet on the other hand gives them orders, since it invests itself, by virtue of the ineffable symbols, with the hieratic role of the gods."*[631]

Theurgy is part human and part divine. Without the divine aspects, theurgy becomes no more than magic or sorcery. From the theurgist's perspective, magic and sorcery are merely techniques for controlling the physical world and some of the lower spiritual beings mired in matter. Such practices create artificial patterns that mimic the divine. This control is seen as artificial and, though not necessarily illicit, part of the world of generation. Theurgy engages directly with the divine patterns inherent to the generative world as well as the realms above. In this theurgy is the opposite of sorcery.

When discussing the nature of the human soul and its relationship to Fate and Providence I said that to the advanced theurgist they are the same. Fate does not somehow become Providence. Instead, the theurgist, through an act of free will, and due to an increasingly deep experience of divine reality, chooses to give him or herself willingly to the cycles and patterns of divine reality as they are made manifest in the cosmos.

Of Signs and Signatures – *Symbola* and *Synthemata*

The divine symbols Iamblichus writes of are all around us in the generative realm. They are what make sacrifice effective. They are at the heart of hieratic prayer and theurgic ritual. These symbols are typically referred to as symbols, *symbola*, signatures or tokens, *synthemata*, and signs, *semeia*. *Synthemata* are described in the *Chaldean Oracles* as the *"thoughts of the Father"*[632] and are analogous to the noeric Forms in manifestation. These tokens are inherent in the entire physical world as well as our souls, placed there by the noeric Demiurge. Theurgy is made possible through recourse to the signs and tokens of the Demiurge and gods.

Tokens are anagogic and intimately involved our remembering the divine realm. By remembering the *"pure, paternal token"* the soul is able to *"emerge from forgetfulness"* to Nous.[633] In Platonic thought all learning is recollection, *anamnesis*. Specifically, learning is the remembrance of the soul's experiences in the divine realm. The tokens are key to that *anamnesis*. However, if the signs and tokens remain in the noeric realm, they remain invisible to us and useless.

---

631 DM IV.2, 207.
632 CO 108.
633 CO 109.

Fortunately, this is not the case. The tokens, created by the Demiurge and the gods, are produced in nature and not just the noeric realm. Further, there is a connection between *synthemata* at the particular and universal levels.[634] The *Emerald Tablet of Hermes* describes this succinctly: *"What is below is like what is above, and what is above is like what is below, to accomplish the wonders of the one thing."*[635] To engage with *synthemata* found in nature is to go beyond mere sympathy. Sympathy exists in physical things, not their source, the gods, and so sympathy cannot affect the presence of the gods in any way.[636] Instead, *"friendship and affinity"*[637] are how the divine signatures connect us to higher realities. The signatures, which stem from the gods, but are not parts of the gods, attach us to the gods through their love for us and our corresponding love for them, as we begin to remember our origins.[638]

The physical signs and tokens make sacrifice effective. We are, in effect, sacrificing a possession of the gods to the gods from which they came. In doing this, we activate the corresponding symbol in our own souls, which in turn lead to our recollection of the gods. These divine symbols are the gods' *energia*, their activity, and through sacrifice we begin to participate that activity.

Sacrifice, however, is only the beginning of theurgy. All theurgic ritual employs *synthemata* and *symbola.* In pagan Neoplatonism this often involves ritual objects taken from nature, such as the initiatory *thyrsus*, a fennel staff tipped with a pine cone dripping with honey, all tokens of Dionysos. To these natural symbols, Dionysius adds human-made ritual objects derived from scripture. Dionysius sees scripture as a kind of divine signature, an idea already found in Sallustus' *Concerning the Gods and the Universe,* and so anything described in scripture, and by extension the stories of the gods, is potentially a *synthema.*

Sallustus' work also suggests the use of other kinds of symbols in theurgic practice, such as those found in chapter fifteen's hymns. So, we find the common names of the gods, along with their titles, functioning as signatures and symbols. Such titles are an element of non-narrative myth, making sense only in the greater context of their stories. The *Cratylus*, for instance, discusses the symbolic meaning of the gods' mundane names, Athena and Kronos for example. Such a discussion can be extended to all divine names. However, such names are of the lowest sort; they stem from human language and human understanding. The theurgic names, the *barbara onomata*, are divine names coming from the gods themselves and so contain their signatures, regardless as to whether any human understands them.

Every element of theurgic ritual draws upon divine signatures, signs or symbols. This allows the theurgist to be *"raised up to union with the higher powers,"* and

---

[634] DM III.15, 157.
[635] ETH 2.
[636] DM V.7-8, 237-9.
[637] V.9, 239. Clarke, et al. mistake this idea for a kind of "supracosmic sympathy," which rather puts words in Iamblichus' mouth.
[638] C.f. Sorabji, *Philosophy*, 370.

in doing so allows him or her to act *"harmoniously in accordance with their [the gods'] dispensation"* and so *"to assume the mantle of the gods."*[639] Without fully engaging in the *synthemata*, the ritual act is at best an act of magic, at worst, sorcery: an attempt to play at being god rather than at actually being god. Where theurgy focuses on aligning the will of the theurgist with that of the divine, sorcery attempts to place the *goēs* in the centre of his or her own system. Instead of raising the rational soul to the divine spheres, the sorcery inflates their irrational soul, in the end potentially convincing themselves they are gods. Given the nature of the soul, and that of our personal daimons, such illusions, while perhaps glorious while they last, are as doomed to mortality as everything to which they are connected.

Besides the handling and sacrificing of physical objects, and the invocation of divine names, *synthemata* and *symbola* are further engaged with through imagination. As we have seen, true imagination is a function of the rational soul. Through noeric imagination the eternal gods may be viewed, though they have no forms. The imagination acts as a bridge between the physical and intellectual realms, allowing the soul to project externally what exists internally,[640] such as the *synthemata* of the hypercosmic gods. As imagination is an activity of the soul, we may see this projective function in light of the allegory of the cave. Whereas the cave's screen receives mere shadows and falsehood from a mortal light source the soul receives true images projected by divine fire. The soul, imaginally projecting true divine images upon its internal screen, is a corrective to the false shadows of Plato's cave. Because of this, you will find visualizations accompanying some of the theurgic rites presented in the next chapters.

Theourgia and Divinization

The primary role of theurgy is divinization, *theosis*, or becoming *"as much as possible like and in union with God."*[641] As we've seen, theurgy is a divinely inspired ritual practice, or set of such practices. But theurgists are more specific than this. Theurgic, telestic, and hieratic rites are not simply divinely inspired, they bring about divinization. Theurgists hold a wide variety of rites as authentically theurgic, from the invocation of gods and daimons "into" icons or statues to the rites of union of an individual theurgist to their leader god and beyond, the term theurgy always refers to various kinds of ritual practices. Even so, divinizing activities go beyond cultic and ritual practice if the primary component of theurgy is not ritual but the divine origins and aid in relation to a given practice, be it sacrifice and liturgy or visualization and contemplation. So long as the greater kinds are anagogically involved, we may describe such activities as theurgic.[642]

---

639 DM IV.2, 207.
640 Uždavinys, *Theurgy*, 88-9.
641 EH I.3.376A.
642 Uždavinys, *Theurgy*, 83

Just as "theurgy" represents a wide variety of practices, "divinization" also refers to a wide variety of phenomena. This includes worship and sacrifice, the invocation of gods into statues, talismancy, purificatory rituals, medical practices, divination, and the invocation of the personal daimon. This last is perhaps the most important of these practices, as it is only through the personal daimon that higher modes of theurgy are attained.

These are examples of material theurgy, most appropriate for the intermediate soul who is just moving from exoteric to esoteric worship. These kinds of rituals are the focus of the remaining chapters of this book. In this, we explore theurgic practices from different periods ranging from rites similar to the *PGM*, to Dionysian liturgy, to the astrological talismancy of Marsilio Ficino. This discussion culminates with a ritual to invoke the personal daimon.[643]

Read the above list again. Spells from the PGM and renaissance talismancy are included as theurgic rites, or at least potential theurgic rites. How does this fit with the idea of divinization? I have employed anagogic or uplifting language throughout this book. Theurgy raises the practitioner to the divine. What does something like animating statues, divinatory spells or the creation of talismans have to do with that? What is spiritual or uplifting about these practices?

Potentially, nothing. A great deal of modern ideology presents such operations as genagogic. Spirits are invoked into the statues or talismans, the gods are invoked to grant some kind of divinatory aid, and so on. In other words, powers are called down here; the plane of activity is that of generation, not the divine. Further, such practices appear entirely practical rather than religious or spiritual. They seem to use other entities as means to our ends. That is about as far away as possible from how we have discussed theurgy. So, why discuss them now? The simple answer is that theurgy is practical. Manifesting the divine, whether as daimons, archons or God, in the realm of generation is both theurgy and demiurgy.

Further, while the genagogic ideology surrounding practical magic is perhaps valid, it need not be the only ideology. As theurgists, we argue that the popular ideology of magic is false. As Iamblichus says, invocation does not bring the gods down to us; it raises us to the gods. The same can be said for consecrating a talisman or engaging in divination. These practices are theurgically successful exactly because they are anagogic. Talismans are effective because they act as bodies and pneumatic vehicles for non-physical entities. This is possible because the talisman is raised upwards from a merely physical object to a spiritually enlivened being in the series or orbit of a particular divinity. True divination, theurgically speaking, occurs because of divine possession, which again requires the theurgist to become so god-like that the higher power naturally overwhelms

[643] Beyond this are anagogic rites connecting the theurgist to their leader god, and then to the celestial Demiurge, which are beyond the scope of this book.

the practitioner. As theurgy is not only "divine action" but demiurgy, it must not only have a spiritualizing or theoretical element; it must also be efficacious in the physical world.

Purification

Although theurgic rites take many different forms, dependent upon time, place, religious background, and so forth, at least one element is common to all of them: catharsis. Catharsis, or purification, is in some ways the primary subject of this book. We have already seen how the practice of philosophy and *theoria* has a purificatory function. This way of life is the mark of souls choosing a life in keeping with the leader of their divine series[644] and is preliminary to any and all theurgic workings, which are also punctuated by cathartic rites. These rites often take the form of lustrations before the principal mystery or central act of the ritual, but may even include public and private purifications, such as bathing in sea water.[645] The lustrations conjoin with the ascetic or contemplative philosophical life for a deeper purification of body and soul, which is enhanced through the hieratic rituals that raise us to our leader god, the monad of the series to which our souls belong.[646]

The purpose of ritual purification is manifold. Iamblichus divides the effects of purification into greater and lesser benefits. The lesser benefits focus on the separation of the soul from the decay of the body and generation. While the individual certainly profits from this, such profits are particular rather than universal. The greater benefits of purification are universal rather than particular and focus on reversion to one's essence.

While reversion to one's essence appears to be a particular, rather than universal, benefit, the opposite is true. In Proclus' Iamblichean-based theology, reversion to one's source partakes of the movements of remaining, *monê*; procession, *prohödos;* and reversion, *epistrophê.*[647] This circular motion is the movement of all universal things. Souls associated with the body move in straight lines, away from their source and representative of generation and the falling away from Nous. Purified souls, and other all divine beings, move in circles, which simultaneously encompass their beginning and end,[648] and, through the movement of the leader gods, to the liminal and hypercosmic divinities beyond.

As purification leads to universal freedoms, it is not surprising to find water as the near universal means of ritual catharsis. In Hellenic tradition, lustral water comes from springs and must be running, alternatively sea water may be used. The

---

644 DA VII.35, 63.

645 Lewy, *Chaldean*, 44-5, 237.

646 *Ibid.*, 276.

647 ET §35.

648 Shaw, *Theurgy*, 89-90, c.f. DM I.9, 39-41.

container for lustral water is historically gold for state or group rituals while private rites use silver, copper or bronze. If working alone, dip your hands into the vessel to ritually cleanse yourself, or if you have an assistant, they may pour the water onto your hands. Sprinkling is again done by hand or a sprig of laurel, myrtle or olive, in Christian tradition an aspergillum, and is used to purify others present and the space within which you work. This acts to mark the boundaries of the sacred space, which the impure cannot access.[649] Personal sprinklings and ablutions always take place before entering the temple or ritual space, and may be equivalent to the public purifications mentioned by Olympiodorus in his discussion of Chaldean theurgy.[650] Once inside, more lustrations may also take place.

The above tradition is most closely paralleled in the Christian tradition of sprinkling with holy water, which typically also comes from a natural source rather than the faucet. Similar practices are found in medieval and Renaissance grimoires, frequently with the addition of hymns or the reciting of certain Psalms. The so-called *Fourth Book of Occult Philosophy* by pseudo-Agrippa, possibly one of Agrippa's students, outlines this kind of practice. For consecrations with water the practitioner should remember the separation of the watery firmament in the divine act of creation, and the destruction of the Nephilim by the flood, the drowning the Pharaoh's army in the Red Sea, and other similar Biblical stories.[651] This is reminiscent of Sallustius' and Proclus' discussions of myths and their use in theurgy. I have already mentioned the Jewish *mikvah* and Muslim *wudu*. These are immersion rituals and apply only to the practitioner engaged in the rite, not the place where the ritual is performed. However, that does not make them any less effective as theurgic purification rituals within their religious contexts.

Water is the most common ritual purifying agent, but it is not the only one. Along with lustrations, fumigations are also commonplace. Fumigation is the use of smoke for the purpose of purification. Hellenic tradition testifies to the use of sulphur and bitumen[652] and the *Orphic hymns* mention fumigations by frankincense, storax, torches, saffron, myrrh, and other substances which might also be used as sacrifices. The incense is circled around the object to be purified and "Χερνίπτομαι!" or "Be purified!" may be exclaimed in the east as well. Once again, Christian tradition has the most similar practices, and the use of incense for purification and consecration is well attested in numerous Western esoteric traditions, where the sacred smoke is wafted over the object or person to be purified.

One thing we may expect to find in a discussion of ritual purification is the practice of banishing rituals. Those familiar with modern esoteric practices are

---

649 Hellenismo, "On purifications- some details…"
650 See Lewy, *Chaldean*, 237.
651 Pseudo-Agrippa, *Fourth Book*, 16.
652 Hellenismo, "On purifications- some details…"

aware of rituals such as the "banishing ritual of the pentagram," "supreme ritual of the hexagram," the "setting of the wards of adamant," or the "sapphire star," to name but a few. Such rites are meant to banish planetary, zodiacal or elemental energies and spirits, or unwanted magical energies in general. They are also missing from traditional theurgic practice. While these rituals may be performed within an overall context of lustration and fumigation, they are meant to have their own special effect in a ceremony. In Golden Dawn or Aurum Solis ritual work fumigation and lustration never stand on their own.

Traditional hieratic rites do not employ such rituals, nor are they necessary in theurgy. Or, we might say lustration and fumigation are theurgy's banishing rituals. Rituals such as the lesser banishing ritual of the pentagram employ various divine names and symbols in order to effect their goal. Theurgic ritual is a kind of divine *mimesis*. In engaging in divine activity, *theourgia*, the divine names echo throughout the rite, even if no names are uttered. The inclusion of hymns, psalms or mythic readings further engages the theurgist with divine *symbola* and *synthemata* so, in effect, divinity itself prevents impure things from entering the sacred space.

The purificatory effects of lustration and fumigation work through a sympathetic and synthematic connection to the pre-essential, celestial, and sub-lunar Demiurges. This connection is found in the *Chaldean Oracles*. These three rulers purify through the virtues connected to them: Love, Truth, and Faith respectively. The *Oracles* say everything exists through, and are governed by, these virtues[653] and through this triad we communicate with the divine levels.[654]

Of these virtues, Love is associated with the pre-essential Demiurge, identified by both the *Oracles* and Iamblichean theology as Aion. Love is the foremost quality of the "substance" of the noetic realm. Through Love, Aion conducts the *"wings of fire,"*[655] the soul's wings in the *Phaedrus*, which are shed and must be re-grown to rise into the heavenly realms. This, however, is in the realm of immaterial theurgy. Material theurgy is concerned, to varying degrees, with the two lower Demiurges and their faculties.

Truth is associated with the sun. The connections between Truth, *aletheia*, which at its root means to reveal, the Christian Logos, and the concepts of *emet*, truth, and Tiferet, beauty, in Kabbalah, are well attested, and are also symbolically connected to the sun. This Demiurge is the *"ruler of the soul"*[656] who consecrates all within its realm through Truth.

The virtue of Faith, *pistis*, which has nothing to do with blind belief, is associated with the sub-lunar Demiurge. In the *Oracles*, this is represented by Hekate, Hades, and possibly Dionysos. Faith is represented by the rays of the

653 CO 48.

654 Lewy, *Chaldean*, 144.

655 CO. 85.

656 *Ibid.*, 86.

visible sun in Iamblichean theology, and the crucified Christ in Christianity. Proclus sees it as the sole theurgic power through which union with the One occurs. Together, the Demiurges are the *"Teletarchs of the mysteries,"* and are engaged in the most important parts of theurgic rites.[657]

A Note on Changing Rituals

Iamblichus is emphatic that, as divine things, theurgic rituals cannot be altered. This is, of course, true. But theurgic rituals are also human things, and while it is romantic to think of a ritual as being fully divine in origin, an examination of any such claims always shows cultural influences. With perhaps the exception of fully immaterial theurgy, all rituals exist within a cultural milieu. As such, they may be altered or tailored to fit those coming from different cultural or religious backgrounds.

This is true of any of the rituals found in this book, and purposefully so. Neoplatonism touches, and is engaged by, people of numerous religious and cultural backgrounds over a period of some 1,800 years. To assume only ancient Hellenic theurgic ritual is "true" theurgy is to miss the point, and to engage in a host of logical fallacies. Each kind of theurgic practice represents a manifestation of Neoplatonic theurgy throughout time and place. By studying the different expressions of theurgy we learn about what is essential to theurgic rites and what is not.

Not all of the following practices will suite you. Some of them are pagan, some are Abrahamic, some are astrological, and so forth. You are, of course, free to not practice some rite you find offensive, or to not engage in any of them. You are also free to alter elements of the rites. That said, before changing any of the ritual elements, fully understand what you have decided to change. While it is true there are aspects of theurgy that are human in origin, it is equally true that some are not. One of these is as mortal and changeable as their source, the other is as immortal and unchangeable is theirs. Only experience teaches the difference.

---

[657] Lewy, *Chaldean*, 144-149; Majerck, *Oracles*, 11-12.

Chapter Seventeen

Medicine, Talismancy, and the Pneumatic Vehicle

Material theurgy is the first hieratic practice undertaken by every new *theourgos*. As such, our first topic relates to the body. Many traditions see a correlation between the purity and health of the body and the soul.[658] So we begin with medicine. This is not modern medical science, which, in its western form, is largely reactionary in nature, and often as toxic as it is purifying. Instead, we look to the Renaissance esoteric medicine of the Neoplatonic magus, Marsilio Ficino, and his last masterpiece *De vita libri tres*, the *Three Books on Life*.[659]

The Medicine of *De Vita*

Published ten years before his death, *De vita libri tres* is a masterpiece of esoteric medicinal practice. *De vita* is also the first book to claim to instruct its reader on how to be an intellectual while retaining one's health. This is an important proposition given that Ficino believes intellectuals are plagued by *melancholia* and its related discomforts. The book, as the name implies, is divided into three sections. Book One focuses on having a healthy life, Book Two on a long life, and Book Three is *"On Obtaining Life from the Heavens."*

At first, a treatise on health for intellectuals seems oddly specific. What about the rest of us? While health for those of us who live in our heads is Ficino's stated purpose, this is an outer explanation, and *De vita* goes beyond it. This is apparent by the fourth chapter of the first book, where three reasons for melancholy are given: celestial, natural, and human. The primary cause for melancholy is celestial, or astrological. Ficino writes:

---

[658] For instance, on the subject of John the Baptist and baptism, the 1st century CE Jewish historian Josephus wrote: *"and commanded the Jews to exercise virtue, both as to righteousness towards one another, and piety towards God, and so to come to baptism; for that the washing [with water] would be acceptable to him, if they made use of it, not in order to the putting away [or the remission] of some sins [only], but for the purification of the body; supposing still that the soul was thoroughly purified beforehand by righteousness"* (*Antiquities*, 18.5:2).

[659] While not necessarily as reactionary as modern medicine, many of the treatments found in books on medical astrology are equally as toxic.

> *"Because both Mercury … and Saturn … are said by astronomers to be somewhat cold and dry (or if it should happen to be true that Mercury is not cold, he is nonetheless often very dry by virtue of his nearness to the Sun), just like the melancholic nature, according to physicians. And this same nature Mercury and Saturn impart from birth to their followers, learned people, and preserve and augment it day by day."*[660]

The above paragraphs' final sentence reflects the idea of the Neoplatonic leader gods, cast in astrological language. While natural and human explanations for melancholy are given, *De vita* focuses almost exclusively on medicinal astrology. Indeed, a number of recipes for curatives to various ailments are given which require either knowledge of planetary hours and days or the ability to erect natal or electional horoscopes.

Traditional astrology is not theurgy. Traditional medical astrology, iatromathematics, is somewhat different. Iatromathematics relies on reading natal horoscopes, and assigns body parts somewhat subjectively to planetary and zodiacal rulership. There is also an element of medical astrology that goes beyond human-originated crafts and techniques, *technê*. This resides not in the correlations between body parts and stars but in the ingredients used to cure various afflictions.

While *De vita* includes some formal astrological medicines, this is clearly not its focus. For instance, a speech given by Mercury presents a medicine from Jupiter. This consists of four ounces *chebulie myrobalans*, three ounces of rose-sugar, and either an ounce or a half-ounce of preserved ginger, depending on whether it is winter or summer. These are cooked over low heat in emblic honey and the resulting mixture is coated with seven leaves of gold. A "morsel" of this is taken on an empty stomach four hours before dinner for at least a year. Doing so shall restore your youth.[661] This recipe has nothing to do with traditional astrology. No planetary hours or days are involved, the concoction does not need to be brewed at a certain conjunction of planets, and there is nothing else we might normally associate with astrological processes. Yet this cure is said to have come from Jupiter himself.

Certainly, we can dismiss the idea that Jupiter, or Zeus, personally gave this curative to Ficino. However, we should remember that Ficino takes his astrology, as well as his metaphysics and theology, seriously. By the time he writes *De vita*, Ficino has translated the *Hermetica* and Plato, as well as Plotinus, Iamblichus, Proclus, and pseudo-Dionysius. While he may not use the terms *synthemata*, *symbolon*, or *seima* in his writing, Ficino is certainly aware of them takes them, along with the rest of Platonism, as seriously as his theology. The ideas, if not the terminology, are vital to Ficino's Platonic theology and theurgy, even if that theurgy is hidden in the language of astrology.

---

660 *De vita*, I.4, 113. Emphasis added.

661 Ficino, *De vita*, II.15, 215.

During Ficino's time writing about certain kinds of astrology, especially the horoscopes of kings and popes, places the author on theologically shaky ground. Even Ficino defends himself against the Inquisition for his astrological texts. Therefore, it comes as no surprise that he is reticent to write directly on the more pagan and magical concepts of *De Mysteriis*.

While Zeus may not have given this recipe directly to Ficino, we are sure all the ingredients are Jovial in nature. From the Neoplatonic perspective on *symbola* and *synthemata*, Zeus might as well have given the medical instructions, as without Jupiter, and the metaphysical power behind it, nothing is Jovial and there is no remedy. Given the connection between Ficino's medical astrology and his knowledge of Neoplatonic signatures and tokens, *De vita libri tres* is not simply a book of medical astrology for the overly intellectual or aged, but a compendium of planetary *synthemata*. *De vita* is an encyclopedia of *synthemata* related directly to the leader gods.

While astrology may not be theurgic, herbal medicines or concoctions, *pharmaka,* can be. Such "concoctions" are mentioned specifically in relation to theurgic rituals by Iamblichus, and are a common component of the so-called animated statues of Egypt and later Neoplatonism. While various concoctions may possess chemical qualities rendering them useful as medicines, theurgists understand that their efficacy lies in their synthematic nature. These tokens, inherent to the ingredients as they are, are what render them useful for theurgy.

Practice – Don't Try This At Home

Unlike almost everything else in we've discussed, I do not recommend practicing medicinal astrology. Today we know many of the ingredients in astrological remedies are highly toxic. Also, some books, such as the *Picatrix*, contain errors or blinds, so only the truly knowledgeable can use their information safely. If you have a medical background, or one in herbalism, it *may* be safe to experiment with the cures given in *Picatrix* or *De vita*, but that does not mean I recommend doing so. In all instances, be sure to consult someone knowledgeable in the medical field before ingesting anything recommended in books such as these.

The various concoctions proposed by Ficino and others can be used in non-medicinal ways. This includes anointing oils for talismans and *pharmaka* placed inside sacred statues for the purpose of their "animation." These, talismancy and animated statues, are discussed in the next section and chapter eighteen.

Talismancy – Drawing Life from the Heavens

De vita is not just a book on synthematically derived medicine. Book Three, *On Obtaining Life from the Heavens*, relies heavily on the anonymous *Picatrix*, Thabit Ibn Qurra's *De imaginibus* and Al-Kindi's *De Radiis Stellicis*, well known books on astrological talismancy. In Neoplatonic technical language, talismancy is a form of the telestic art, *telestikê technê*. Talismans are hardly original or unique to Neoplatonism. They do, however, gain a particular place in Neoplatonism, especially during the Middle Ages and Renaissance.

A talisman is an object consecrated towards a specific end.[662] The English word is derived from the Greek *telesma*, which in turn comes from *telin*, meaning to initiate, to consecrate, and to complete.[663] Today, with the prevalence of magic based on the Order of the Golden Dawn and the Rosæ Rubæ et Auræ Crucis, the word talisman may bring to mind pieces of cardboard or construction paper, marked with Hebrew divine names and geometric shapes in complimentary colours. This conception is based largely on a combining of the pentacles from the *Key of Solomon* with elements of Henry Cornelius Agrippa's *Three Books of Occult Philosophy* and the RR et AC's colour theory. While something vaguely similar to this may have existed by Ficino's time, the driving force here, Agrippa's *De occulta de philosophia*, isn't written until 1509, ten years after Ficino's death. The talismans found in *De vita*, as well as *De vita*'s sources, are something quite different.

The talismans Ficino describes in *On Obtaining Life from the Heavens* are astrological or "astral" talismans. In this instance, "astral" is understood in its literal sense of "starry," as opposed to the modern, Theosophically-derived sense of a plane of existence, i.e. the "astral plane," which is directly related to human emotions and mundane imagination. We must instead connect Ficino's astral talismans to the visible gods. As a form of astral magic, Ficino's talismans, and traditional Arabic-derived medieval talismancy in general, combine particular images associated with the planets, constellations, and fixed stars with precise astrological timing.

What form do traditional talismans take? Thabit Ibn Qurra's 9th century *De Imaginibus* gives us a hint in its final chapter. Chapter nine instructs us to carve the necessary images into two soft stones that have been fitted together through grinding. At the appropriate time, the stones are joined together and you *"cast the image you wish to make in that same hour under the proper conditions."*[664] Ibn Qurra is not explicit, but he is talking about casting a talisman in metal. The previous chapters suggest he is not talking about decorative disks with images on them, such as we might normally think. Instead, Ibn Qurra describes the creation of small talismanic statues. But what is Ficino talking about when he writes about talismans?

---

[662] We can artificially distinguish between a "talisman" as an artificially created object and an "amulet" as a natural object. We can see the third pentacle of Venus from the *Key of Solomon* as a talisman and a "lucky" rabbit's foot as an amulet. A natural object, such as gems, that have images or words carved upon them are talismans. See Kiekckhefer, *Magic in the Middle Ages*, 75-80. Ficino holds a comprehensive discussion on synthematic amulets in book three of *De vita*.

[663] Uždavinys, *Theurgy*, 152.

[664] Ibn Qurra, *De Imaginibus*, IX.I, 62.

Ficino describes some classical accounts of talismancy, such as the image of a scorpion impressed in frankincense that is then given as a drink to treat a scorpion sting, and of a useful image of a serpent being made as the moon enters the sign of Draco. He even mentions the famous "animated" statues of ancient Egypt.[665] Beyond this, cast or carved images are the form Ficino's talismans take. He specifically rejects images carved in wood as insufficient to receive and hold "cosmic life," while noting metals and gems are much better.[666]

While Ficino is more impressed with synthematic amulets, finding the astrological component superior in attracting celestial vigour to any figure inscribed on stone or cast in metal, like a true Neoplatonist he does not discount or discredit the use of images. In what may be an allusion to the *Timaeus*, Ficino says talismanic images, especially those related to number and heavenly figures, are related to the noeric Forms and the World Soul, and therefore have within them a *"distinctive force,'*'[667] a force somehow different from other kinds of synthematic amulets. Such images are the "faces" of the heavens, which Ficino uses to describe the "faces," ten degree subdivisions of the zodiac, or decans, attributed to the planets. Each planet has three faces, and an image is associated with each face. There are also many other astrological images beyond these.

By themselves, celestially derived images contain the Form upon which they are based, and so are synthematic. However, when their creation is coupled with astrological timing, their ability to attract and hold life from the heavens is greatly increased. This is because the image is a reflection of a particular astrological time or power, or the activities of the gods at that time. For example, the Sun in the 16th degree of Aries is not only in, but rules over, the second face of Aries. Just as the strings of one lute vibrate when another, identically tuned, is played near it, so there is a reinforcing of the power of an image when it is created at the time it reflects in the first place.[668]

How does all this work? Drawing on Plotinus' *Enneads*, Ficino writes:

> *'In addition, the World Soul possesses by divine power precisely as many seminal reasons of things as there are Ideas in the Divine Mind. By these seminal reasons she fashions the same number of species in matter. That is why every single species corresponds through its own seminal reason to its own Idea and oftentimes through this reason it can easily receive something from the Idea since indeed it was made through the reason from the Idea. This is why, if at any time the species degenerates from its proper form, it can be formed again with the reason as the proximate intermediary and, through the Idea as intermediary, can then be easily reformed. And if in the proper manner you bring to bear on a species, or on some individual in it, many things which are dispersed but which conform to the same*

---

665 Ficino, *De vita*, III.8, 307.

666 *Ibid*, III.8, 308.

667 *Ibid*, III.17, 331.

668 Ficino, *De vita*, III.17, 331.

Idea, into this material thus suitably adapted you will soon draw a particular gift from the Idea, through the seminal reason of the soul.'[669]

Ficino cites a specific connection between the Forms, or Ideas, and everything existing under the auspices of the World Soul. This connection is not sympathetic but a shared, or at least descended, essence, power or activity. That is, everything in the series of Mercury is descended from some Mercurial element. When that element is perfected, there is no difference between Mercury and its descendant.[670] Therefore, if we carve upon an emerald the image of an old man leaning on a staff while Mercury is in the 25th degree of Virgo, we will create a strong Mercurial talisman. This is because the emerald is a mercurial stone, made famous by the *Emerald Tablet of Hermes Trismegistus*, and the image is that of the third face of Virgo, which is ruled by Mercury, while simultaneously being the sign in which Mercury is both exalted and rules.

Although an emerald is in harmony with Mercury, it is also in harmony with Venus and the moon.[671] However, the compounded elements present in the Mercury talisman are far more harmonious to Mercury than Venus or Luna. Also, while the stone's carving is, strictly speaking, part of human artifice, the image itself can be understood as divinely inspired from the Forms. If we add a hymn and the burning of frankincense, perhaps carve an ineffable name of Hermes on the stone, we have the makings of a theurgic ritual.

Talismans are compound images symbolically, through *symbola* and *synthemata*, representing or reflecting some element of the cosmos, and can be considered a kind of image or statue, *agalma*. While *agalma* literally means "statue," it can also mean "shrine." This is one of the senses used by Plato in the *Timaeus*, when the Demiurge sees the created cosmos as *"a shrine brought into being for the everlasting gods.'*[672] Even if we use the more normative "statue" or "image" in place of "shrine" in the *Timaeus* quotation, there is still a close correlation to the kind of talismans found in *De Imaginibus* and *Picatrix*.

Theurgic *agalmata* are created in the character or image of some greater reality, a Form, a saint, a god, etc. They contain names, which contain the gods themselves, and are filled with *symbola* and *synthemata*. This is precisely how Proclus describes the Demiurge's creation of the cosmos. Proclus further likens the consecration of *agalmata* to the act of naming, with the divine words and names containing the *logoi* of the gods, and acting as divine images or *eikones*, all of which proceed from Nous.[673]

But how is this connected to astrological images? We can see how an image acts as a divine token, but how does this relate to an image being created or

---

669 *Ibid*, III.1, 243.

670 C.f. Ficino, *De vita*, III.8, 307.

671 *Ibid.*, III.16, 327.

672 *Tim* 37c, in Uždavinys, *Theurgy*, 279.

673 Uždavinys, *Theurgy*, 133.

consecrated at a particular, astronomically calculated time? Iamblichus affirms the truth of the science of astrology, citing countless observations and prognostications made by the Chaldeans and Egyptians. Specifically, he refers to the finding of conjunctions, eclipses and the like, and the ability to predict such things.

Iamblichus does not, however, affirm astrology's predictive ability when it comes to horoscopes, which is a matter of *technê* rather than theurgy. Such technical predictions, even if sometimes accurate, have nothing to do with theurgy because the divine has no direct role in its performance.[674] While theurgic astrology, which Iamblichus does not elucidate upon, is a perfectly valid form of divination, astrology based on technique is only barely so.

The only thing saving technical astrology from complete damnation is its basis on the movement of the planets. As the planets are the bodies of the material gods, their movements naturally reflect divine activity, and so their observation can possibly tell us something about the movements of Fate as it affects the physical world. By relying only on the movement of the planets, an element of the divine is brought into the creation of talismans, without astrology's technical, predictive aspect.

The distinction between technical and theurgic forms of divination is important. *Technê* is human in origin. Anything created solely as a human technique is not theurgic. Iamblichus soundly condemns the art of image making, *eidôlopoiêtikê technê* for this. He writes *"that the image-maker does not use the astral revolutions or the powers inherent in them, or the powers found naturally around them, nor is he at all able to control them; rather he operates with those emanating last from nature in the visible (realm) about the extreme part of the universe, and does so purely by technical skill, and not by theurgic skill.'*"[675] Further, such things rely on matter and, as he writes in an earlier passage of the same chapter, *"What good, then would arise as springing up from matter and things material?'*"[676]

This is a fairly damning condemnation of the subject at hand, so what are we to make of it in relation to talismancy, or the next subject, animated statues? Iamblichus' proclamation is difficult for a number of reasons. First, as Shaw points out, it contradicts other things Iamblichus writes concerning the nature of matter, both in *The Theology of Numbers* and *On General Mathematical Science*,[677] two of his Pythagorean works, and in his various commentaries on the Platonic dialogues. As we've seen, while matter certainly has its problems, Iamblichus is also aware of the good within matter.

---

674 DM IX.4, 333.

675 DM III.28, 191.

676 DM III.28, 189.

677 Shaw, *Theurgy*, 39.

Second, it is contradictory to the Neoplatonic aesthetic. As early as Plotinus, and continued through Proclus, we find art, which is a form of *technê*, being saved by the artist's transcending the physicality of their subject to the Forms beyond it. Given that Iamblichus includes the use of symbols as part of theurgic rituals, this transcending of the mundane for the Form is especially true in the case of theurgic talismancy.

Third, as Shaw points out, this entire section of *De Mysteriis* is a defense of theurgy against the material manipulation of the gods.[678] Outside of this context Iamblichus' view on the matter is different. For instance, as the visible gods preside over their physical bodies, the planets and stars, and are not controlled or contained by them, can this not also be true of talismans and idols? Just as the Demiurge creates *agalma* can we not, engaging in demiurgy, do the same?[679] Instead of condemning all kinds of talismancy or idol making, we may conclude Iamblichus' argument is against a particular kind of practice, one focusing on purely material practices.

What Materials Should I Use? or That Sounds Expensive

Ficino spares no expense in his talismancy. He describes using plates of silver, emeralds, gold, sapphires, and a multitude of difficult to obtain, or impossible to afford, substances. Why does he do this, and do we need to follow suit? The first answer is simple: Ficino is using the *synthemata* associated with the planetary powers with which he is dealing. Emerald is appropriate to Mercury, so use emeralds in your Mercurial talismans. Lapis lazuli is appropriate to Jupiter and Sol combined, so use that when invoking those powers. Ficino is also writing as a relatively wealthy individual, or at least someone with a wealthy patron.

Whether or not we must use the same materials is also simply answered. If we can afford such things, we certainly may use them, but it is not absolutely necessary. Each planet, for instance, has many *synthemata* and *symbola* depending from it, so there are always alternatives. You cannot afford a plate of gold? Golden yellow is the colour associated with the sun, paint your talisman instead, or use gold leaf. You cannot obtain a large emerald for the centrepiece of your talisman? Perhaps look into synthetic gems, or use the colours and symbols associated with Mercury and Hermes. In the same way we may substitute incense and herbs for animal sacrifice, different tokens may be used in the case of any talisman and, by extension, animated statue or anything else involving the use of divine symbols. However, be sure to use appropriate symbols. Both a lion and a rooster are solar in nature, but a lion is not a rooster.

---

678 Shaw, *Theurgy*, 39.

679 Proclus, *In Parm*, IV847, in Burns, "Proclus," 6.

The Pneumatic Vehicle – How to Get From Here to There

All of the above helps us understand what goes into the construction of a talisman, but not how a talisman works. Talismans function through the Forms, but how? How does consecrating a talisman connect the physical object to the non-physical world? This question is linked to another, obliquely related, topic: the soul and its connection to a body. The answer to both questions, while not identical, is closely related to the pneumatic vehicle, *ochema-pneuma*, or the vehicle of the soul.

Modern Western occultism derives its theories of the vehicle of the soul largely from Hinduism and esoteric Buddhism as seen through the eyes of the 19th century Theosophical Society. There are several robust sets of such theories concerning the vehicle, or "bodies" as they are often called. The number of such bodies varies from two or three to upwards of seven, the most well-known being the astral or emotional body. Given the Neoplatonic origins of much of modern Western esotericism, the non-Theosophical *ochema-pneuma* is a true part of the West's esoteric inheritance.[680]

According to Iamblichus, the pneumatic vehicle is described in the *Timaeus* as being created directly from the ether by the Demiurge. This description is in opposition to Porphyry, who believes the vehicle is an accretion around the soul drawn from the spheres of the seven planets as it descends into generation. If Porphyry is correct the vehicle is changeable and subject to dissolution. Instead, according to Iamblichus and the later Neoplatonists, the pneumatic or etheric[681] vehicle is immortal, surviving its separation from the rational soul as that soul ascends towards its source.[682] Plotinus and Porphyry believe the vehicle is mortal, dissolving back into its constituent parts upon separation from the soul. Although it contradicts the *Timaeus* this makes sense for Plotinus' school, as it believes the purified soul never returns to generation. Iamblichus, as we've seen, believes the soul always returns to generation, regardless of its state of purity. With an immortal vehicle, the soul is able to return again and again to its chariot of choice, especially the purified soul which *"administer[s] the universe together with the gods."*[683] This is only possible with a vehicle that is not composed of anything but itself, as described by Proclus.[684]

---

680 It is by no means the only theory, as Jewish Kabbalah also deals with certain kinds of bodies associated with the various levels of the soul. Here I use "West" and "East" as ideological constructs, rather than geographical locals.

681 Do not mistake this for Theosophical etheric body, which is said to be made up of a kind of matter not apparent to the immediate physical senses. The physical body is supposed to be based on the etheric body, and all physical things have etheric bodies.

682 Finamore, *Vehicle*, 11, 15-16.

683 DA VIII.53, 75. C.f. *Ascepius* 8, 71: *"Thus god shapes mankind from the nature of soul and of body, from the eternal and the mortal, ..., so that the living being so shaped can prove adequate to both its beginnings, wondering at heavenly beings and worshipping them, tending earthly beings and governing them."*

684 *Ibid.*, 11, 17-18.

Humans are not the only beings with pneumatic vehicles, heroes and daimons, and the material and sub-lunar gods, possess them as well. The hypercosmic and liberated gods do not, nor do their angelic servants. This makes sense as the material and sub-lunar gods, and their daimonic and heroic servants, are directly involved in the realm of generation. The pneumatic vehicle connects them to the physical world. Without their etheric vehicle, the material gods and their daimons could not affect the realm of generation, nor could we rise to them through theurgy. All of the greater kinds who possess a vehicle are also distinct from it, and it may be these vehicles that Iamblichus refers to as "bodies" when he says the material gods *"envelop bodies."*[685] This is radically different from the impure human soul's relationship to its vehicle, which is caused by the soul's lower ontological position in relation to the greater kind. The function of the vehicles is different for the greater kinds as well, reflecting the rank and nature of its possessor.

Although Iamblichus establishes the immortality and unchanging nature of the pneumatic vehicle,[686] the question of purification remains. If the vehicle is unchangeable by any external, material cause, how does it become impure, and what effect can purification via material theurgy have? The pneumatic vehicle is unalterable by outside influences; nothing can make the vehicle anything other than what it is. That does not mean it cannot be affected, it simply cannot be changed. When there is an improper relationship between the soul and its vehicle contamination occurs, and chitinous hylic and pneumatic accretions accumulate around the vehicle. These accretions serve to further sever the soul's ability to participate Intellect and the One. As the soul descends, these accretions become the human body, with which the soul then mistakenly identifies.[687] Pure souls also take on bodies, but do so in a matter that does not cause the soul to associate or submit itself to the body and generation. The pure soul remains pure even in incarnation, being in the world, but not of it.

The descent of the soul begins with the sowing of souls, by the Demiurge, into the orbits of the leader gods. In Proclean terms, this establishes the "series" to which every being belongs, and is encosmic in nature, placing human souls under the sway of Fate so they may be saved by their leaders.[688] Monotheists do not need to take the idea of leader gods in a polytheistic sense, and the corresponding hierarchy of angelic choirs is only one example of this ideology outside of polytheism.

What does the pneumatic vehicle have to do with talismancy or animated statues? The topics appear quite distinct, given the temporal nature of the products of generation and the eternal nature of the vehicle are not just different,

---

685 DM I.17, 65, c.f. Finamore, *Soul*, 34-5.
686 DM V.4, 231, *In Tim* IV, fr. 81.
687 Finamore, *Soul*, 51.
688 *Ibid.*, 63.

but in opposition. Yet this opposition exists in every incarnated soul. With one foot in the psychic realm, the other in generation and the head in the clouds of Nous, human beings are simultaneously mortal and immortal.[689]

A similar relationship between the souls of the greater kinds and the bodies of talismans exists as it does between those of humans. The relationship is similar, but not identical, because of the nature of the greater kinds in relation to that of human souls. The greater kinds rule over their pneumatic bodies and do not identify with them. The key difference is that while life is given to the lifeless, the greater kinds, being entirely above the realm of matter, maintain their immortality whereas human souls, in incarnating, are both entirely immortal and entirely mortal. Also, whereas the gods, according to the *Timaeus*, model human bodies after their own, humans model talismans and animated statues after divine images.

A final difference is that the human theurgist does not, even in their demiurgy, create an immortal pneumatic vehicle for whatever entity is invoked "into" the talisman or statue. And this, the enlivening of talismans and statues by the greater kind, is exactly what happens when a talisman is consecrated. Of this, Henry Cornelius Agrippa writes: *"But know this, that such images work nothing, unless they be so vivified that either a natural, or celestial, or heroical, or animastical, or demoniacal, or angelical virtue be in them, or assistant to them."*[690] He continues by saying no human can give a soul to an image. The theurgist does not create a pneumatic vehicle, the invoked entity already has one. Instead, through use of divine symbols, tokens, and invocations the theurgist creates sympathy between the image and the invoked being. Once so identified, the being is present, via its etheric vehicle, through the image. Because the greater kind and their vehicles exist above the level of generation and the soul, above mundane and transcendent Time, they are able to "attach" their vehicles to multiple bodies at once.

This also means the way a talisman is disposed of when no longer needed should be carefully taken into consideration. A talisman is, in effect, a shrine to, or perhaps even the equivalent to sacred scripture of, a particular entity or series of entities. While destroying a talisman will not harm these entities that doesn't mean they will not take offence at having their shrine destroyed without so much as a by your leave. Before any action is taken to destroy the body of a talisman, be sure to properly and ritually thank the powers it enshrines, or to "de-consecrate" it. After this, the talisman should be respectfully destroyed in a way appropriate to its status.[691]

---

[689] Shaw, *Theurgy*, 104.

[690] Agrippa, *De occulta*, II.50, 404. C.f. *Picatrix*, I.2, 27.

[691] This may vary in different religious settings. For instance Islam destroys marred *Qur'ans* by fire while Judaism buries *Torah* scrolls.

Exercises

The following two exercises in talismancy are derived primarily from Marsilio Ficino's *De vita libri tres*. Both employ a variety of synthematic and symbolic components, and variations on these are possible. A general outline for consecrating talismans may be derived from these. The first talisman is a talisman of the cosmos, the second of Mercury and Hermes.

A Talisman in the Image of the Cosmos

This talisman is based on Book Three, chapter nineteen of *De vita*, *"How to Construct a Figure of the Universe."* What is the purpose of such a talisman? Typically, when I think of talismans, I think of them as performing some particular, usually practical, thing, such as procuring a job, wealth, love, the death of an enemy, better memory, and so forth. These talismans might fall under the category of sorcery, but may also be thaumaturgy or "wonder working." Such things are not necessarily out of the realm of theurgic talismancy, demonstrating the close relationship of these categories. This is one of the advantages to medieval and Renaissance talismancy. Because talismans are created according to the movement of the planets, or, if you prefer, gods, they may be created for personal, even practical reasons without involving sorcery as understood by late Neoplatonism.[692]

However, a talisman of the cosmos falls far outside the prevue of that kind of talismancy. The purpose of this talisman, especially if taken to Ficino's extremes,[693] is to align oneself with the movements of the universe itself. Why do this? After all, Fate is found in the movement of the stars. Won't aligning oneself to the movements of the universe be tantamount to binding oneself to Fate and generation? Possibly. However, Fate is identical to Providence, the difference being the observer's vantage. Further, the physical cosmos is the body of the World Soul.[694] The World Soul is the source of individual souls, and it is through the World Soul the individual participates Nous.

There is, therefore, a two-fold benefit to a cosmic talisman. First, by creating the talisman in the image of the universe at its most propitious, we are able to benefit from that omni-benevolence, both physically and spiritually. This is because both our bodies and souls exist under the sway of the World Soul. Second, such a talisman, by aligning us to the World Soul, brings us into closer participation of Nous, one of the primary goals of theurgy.

---

692 Iamblichus' view of sorcery is a theological distinction. However, its political dimension, as a way to separate "us" from "them," cannot be ignored.

693 Ficino recommends an entire room be designed after the figure of the universe. The room should include a movable model of the celestial spheres as well as a bed so that one may sleep surrounded by the perfected cosmos.

694 C.f. *In Tim.* III, fr. 49.

Ficino's description of the "figure of the universe" is a classical image of the solar system. The image contains concentric spheres or rings, because the motion of the heavens is circular. Each ring represents one of the "spheres of the planets," with the universe being divided into eight of these, representing the seven classical planets and the ether. The sphere of the fixed stars may be beyond this or the same as the ether.

In Ficino's description, the sphere of the fixed stars depicts stars in gold, and the planets are in the "Chaldean" order: Saturn, Jupiter, Mars, Sol, Venus, Mercury, and Luna, from outermost in. This leaves a central circle representing the earth or the sub-lunar realm. This circle contains an anthropomorphized image of the World Soul, whom Ficino describes as Vesta or Ceres, Hestia and Demeter in Greek tradition, clothed in green. This kind of image is actually fairly common, and sometimes includes the spheres of the elements before the central circle of the World Soul. Some include several outer circles of fire[695] representing the empyrean between the primum mobile and the divine realm, and sometimes the ether comes right before the planets.

The image is in green, gold and sapphire-blue. Green represents of the moisture of Venus and the Moon. Gold is the colour of the Sun and is also related to Jupiter and Venus. Sapphire-blue is especially related to Jupiter. Together, these three colours "capture the gifts of the celestial graces."[696] The spheres or rings are blue.

Create the figure at the beginning of the celestial year, when the Sun enters the first degree of sign of Aries. This is the spring equinox in the Northern hemisphere, the autumnal equinox in the Southern. This represents the cosmos' birthday, as it were, so the figure of the universe is a figure representing the horoscope of the cosmos.[697] Also, the image should not be created on the Sabbath, the day of Saturn, Saturday. Instead it should be created, if possible, on the day or hour of the Sun, which rules the planets and is the visible form of the Demiurge. The timing of the image's creation is more beneficial if Jupiter and Venus are in positive astrological aspects as well. If possible, engrave the image on bronze and print it on a "thin gilded plate of silver"[698] at the proper time. The moment the image is stamped onto the silver is the moment of the image's birth.

What kind of image is this? Ficino is somewhat vague as to the specifics. The following image is my interpretation of his instructions.

---

695 Aether or ether is something placed outside the zodiac or fixed stars to represent the heavenly fire of the noetic realm.
696 Ficino, *De vita*, III.19, 345-7.
697 *Ibid.*, III.19, 145.
698 *Ibid.*

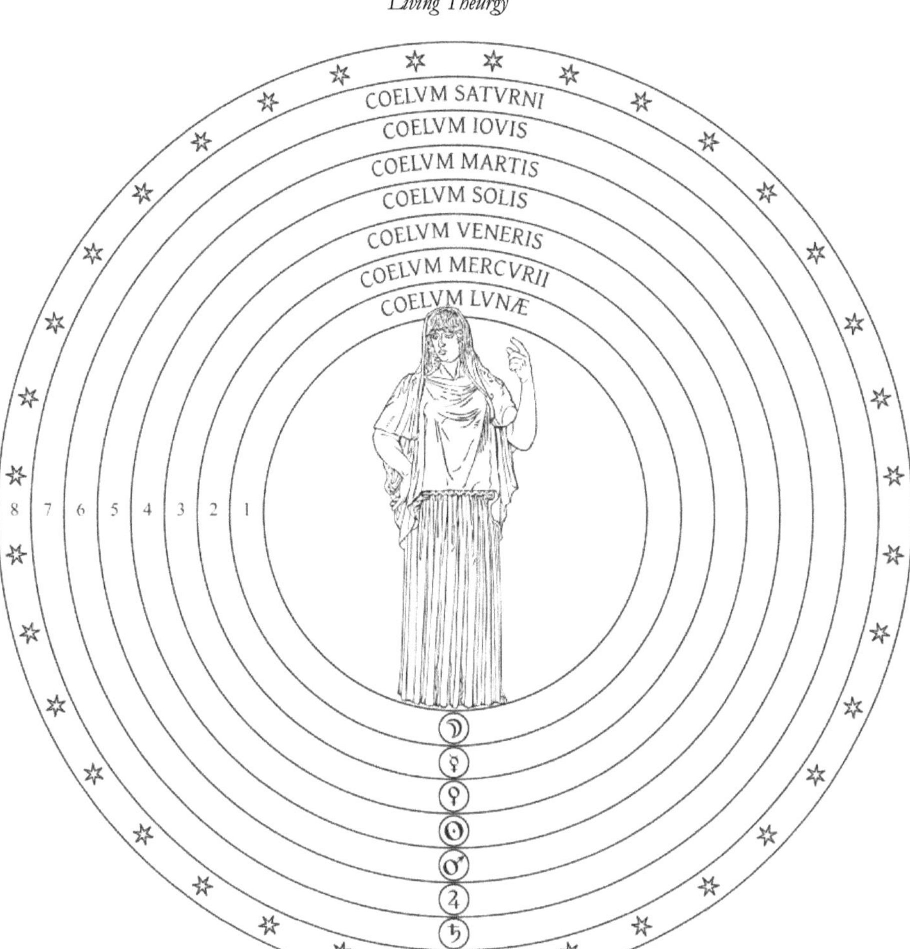

The above figure is based on Ficino's plan. The circles represent the seven planets and the ring of the fixed stars. At the center is the goddess Hestia. There are many possible sources for magical images of the planets, such as chapter eighteen of *De vita*, which has close parallels in Agrippa's *De occulta philosophia*, book three, chapters thirty-eight through forty-four. However, here I have simply used the standard astrological symbols.

Ficino's insistence on a brass or bronze stamp to make the image on silver is not necessarily important, though the use of silver puts the impression of the image on a lunar substance. This suggests the place of the talisman's action represents the culmination of power through the planetary spheres, ending with that of the moon. Given the price of silver, the use of white paper or cardboard, white being the colour of the moon given in medieval grimoires, is a useful substitute. In this case, print the image on paper, rather than stamp it onto metal. If metal is used, the appropriate colours should be painted on the silver plate, preferably during the time allotted for the figure's birth.

This is, of course, only one possibility for a figure of the cosmos. If you are more familiar with astrology, the images of the faces and other astrological images, can be found in the *Three Books of Occult Philosophy*. Religious symbolism, such as the figure of the Gnostic Sophia or Kabbalah's Shekhinah, both of whom have been interpreted as the woman clothed in the sun with the moon at her feet from the Biblical *Book of Revelation*, can replace the image of Hestia or Demeter.

After establishing your figure of the cosmos, perform a ritual of consecration in conjunction with its creation. Begin with purification as discussed in chapter fifteen. It is as important to purify the object to be consecrated before the beginning of the operation as it is to purify yourself and anyone else present. Neither Ficino nor Iamblichus provide any examples of their ritual practices. In this case we will borrow from the *PGM*. Our consecration ritual consists of an invocation of the World Soul and celestial Demiurge. The invocation, or hymn, works under the same principles as discussed in chapter sixteen, including the use of hieratic names. This is perhaps the simplest form of ritual from the *PGM*. Others involve animal sacrifices, obscure items, such as water from a shipwreck or the iron ring of a leg shackle, various writing implements and papyri to write on, and so forth.

The following ritual assumes the talisman will be born at the appropriate timing; when the sun enters the first degree of Aries. A casting of the talisman could take the place of the engraving stamp with little modification to the ritual. If the talisman is created in some other fashion, especially one that takes more than an instant or two to produce the completed talisman, the ritual may need modification to take the timing into consideration. Ritual instructions are in italics, spoken parts in regular type.

Ritual of Consecration of the Figure of the Cosmos

Calculate the moment Sol enters 0° of Aries. Burn frankincense and myrrh in copious amounts as the sun enters Aries. Purify yourself and the *agalmata*. Birth the Figure of the Cosmos either when Sol enters Aries or, if the sun remains in the 0° of Aries when the hour of the sun beings, birth the figure then. After the Figure is born, take it and face the sun, raising the Figure on high. Say or sing the following prayer:

Holy Soul of the whole Cosmos
O you who encircles all
with the divided cross and the
seven wanderers. You call
us to manifestation and
this fleshy grave and you
raise us to the heights of the great
Father. Death I shall not rue!

O Queen, fashioned by the Craftsman
before all worldly bodies
and mother of all souls, through you
I conquer death. The aeries
divine I will mount until I
rise to my series. Fill me
with your grace that I may know you
and may rest upon your knee.

As you say this, see the two circles of the World Soul encompass the Figure. The circle of Sameness, containing the bodies of the celestial gods, glows brilliantly.

Place the Figure at your feet. Kneel on both knees, raise your hands upwards and look up and say:

O divine ones, be propitious.

Touch the ground with your right hand and raising the left knee. Say:

O divine ones, be propitious.

Lower the left knee and rise the right while lifting the right and touching the ground with the left. Say:

O divine ones, be propitious.

Touch both knees and hands to the ground. Say:

O God, be propitious. O God, be propitious. O God, be propitious.

Pick up the Figure, rise to face the direction of the sun, holding the Figure out in welcome and reception to it..

Hail and hearken O glorious
Father of amber hewed tears.
O divine chariot driver,
Whose heavenly circuit cheers
All who follow in your series.
Lord of seasons and hours
and attendant to the mixing
cup. Hear this prayer of ours.

Hear me, you who in the first hour
is PhROYER![699] *Hear me, you who*
in the second hour is great
BAZĒTŌPhŌTh! O do
hear me AKKAMMAChAMAKEI
of the third hour. In the hour
fourth DAMNAMENEYS hearken!
Great Lord, grant me your power!

PhŌKENGEPSEYARETAThOYMIS
ONIKT! In the sixth hour, hear
my prayer ELAY AKRI LYX! In
the seventh hour, great seer
ABLANAThANALBA! Now, great
one of the eighth hour, Lord
PEPh ThA PhŌ ZA PhNEB ENN OY NI,[700]
hear me and make me your ward.

In the ninth hour is ABRASAX[701]
mighty Demiurgos. The
lord of the tenth IAŌ[702]
I call to you with this plea
and hymn. In the eleventh I
call upon SABAŌTh,[703] *great*
king. And in the twelfth, ADŌNAI![704]
You twelve, free me from all Fate!

With each divine name, see the Figure absorb the solar rays, even if the sun is still beneath the horizon. By the time you invoke the last name the Figure should be nearly too brilliant to look upon. Slowly this light will fade, but its power remains

---

699 "Pre the Great" in Egyptian (PGM III. 494-611, 31 n. 97).
700 Egyptian for "He is Ptah the healthy, the lord of the Abyss" (PGM XXXVI. 69-101, 270 n. 2)
701 From the system of the Gnostic Basilides. The seven letters represent the seven planets over which Abrasax rules as Demiurgos.
702 A common name in the Greek magical papyri, and equivalent to the Hebrew YHVH or "Tetragrammaton."
703 Or Tzbaot, "Hosts" or "Armies" in Hebrew.
704 Hebrew for "Lord."

Holy Craftsman, divine Mind and
Soul of All, let me be raised
to the Mother of psyche through
this token. She shall be praised
through this Demiurgy, and by
this hieratic rite I
rise to the Father from Mother's
place by this sign I do ply.

When finished, placed the Figure in a place where you may regularly contemplate its mysteries.

A Talisman of Chthonic Hermes

In Greek tradition, the god Hermes, the son of Zeus and the nymph Maia, is the only god who freely comes and goes from the realm of Hades. Hades, a form of the sub-lunar Demiurge, commands the personal daimons. While chapter nineteen focuses on the invocation of the personal daimon, this talisman begins that process by making contact with the psychopomp, *psychopompos*, the soul's guide in the afterlife, represented variously by Hermes, Anubis,[705] and the angel Michael, all of whom are associated with the planet Mercury.

Instead of designing a complex image, the Mercury talisman consists of a caduceus. This can be a pin or pendant or anything else that is easily carried. While the talisman's body is simple to procure, the consecration timing is somewhat more complex. Ideally, the consecration takes place when Mercury is rising in the sign of the sun as found in your natal horoscope. This means Mercury rising above the ascendant in your sun sign. Because of this the ritual is performed around your birthday. Mercury should have no negative aspects, such as being in opposition to Saturn or combust, being too close to the sun. If Mercury holds a favourable aspect with one of the benefics, Jupiter or Venus, so much the better, but it is not necessary. The moon should also be unafflicted. In this rite, planetary days and hours are unimportant.

Caduceus

[705] Anubis, the Egyptian god who oversees embalming, may not be directed related to Mercury. However, the god is often combined with Hermes as Hermanubis, and is so linked to Mercury.

Ritual of Consecration of the Token of the Psychopompos

Purify yourself and the Token. Burn copious amounts of incense of storax, strawberry and/or crocus. Hold the talisman in your right hand and kneel on your right knee, touching the ground with your left hand while looking upwards. Say:

O divine ones, be propitious.

Rise and turn to face the place of Mercury. Raise your arms in welcome, holding the talisman towards the source of its series.

Holy Psychopompos, you who
travels freely between here
and the daimons' realm, I call you
to be present and endear
me to your orbit. O you who
fears not Tartarus' gloom
or the realm of generation
hearken to this song in bloom.

Through this token I would know you
O great son of God. Your hand
shall be upon my shoulder, your
blade shall guard my back. Your brand
gives wings to my soul that I
may travel the darkened road
to find there my guide allotted
from the immortal abode.

O you who are like God. O you
who interprets. O you way
finder. You speaker. You silence.
O you great god of the day
and royal child of heaven
and earth, put upon this sign
your essence, your power, and your
motion that they may be mine.

O messenger and guide, all you
promise those on the hoary
path of chthonic dusk is the

hope of eternal glory
in the ambit of our god's train.
Bring me close to your orbit
that I may find my charged guide
in whose sum I am sorbate.

Lower the talisman and place it upon your body. When not worn, keep the talisman on an altar or shrine and wrapped in white or orange silk or linen.

These two rituals of theurgic talismancy are only brief examples of what is possible. As you practice more of the hieratic rites, and especially after you have made contact with your daimon, other such talismans will occur to you. Also, while I have used a ritual form based loosely on the *PGM*, that is not the only possible source of ritual practice. According to Iamblichus, and echoed in the theurgic *Sacred Magic of Abramelin*, your daimon or guardian angel will guide you to appropriate forms of worship and theurgy. While we may wish this to take the form of a magnificent epiphany, it is just as likely to appear to you as a book falling into your lap at the right time. Once you are familiar with your daimon you will better recognize its promptings. The two talismans in this chapter will help you move towards that contact.

Chapter Eighteen

Animated Statues & Divine Possession

Statue animation is one of the highlights of the telestic art, far outstripping talismancy in importance. This is because talismancy invokes the powers of a daimon or perhaps even a god for a particular purpose but an animated statue embodies the god itself. Perhaps the only higher form of the telestic art is the purification, illumination and perfection of souls, *telestikê* meaning "completion" and "perfection."[706] That the same term is used to describe the animating of divine statues and the purifying or completing of human souls suggests a strong connection between the nature of such statues and souls. This is explored below.

Animated Statues – Archaic Androids or Vehicles of the Gods?

As we have seen, Iamblichus appears to be against the creation and use of so-called "animated statues." I have suggested it is not animated statues in general he argues against, but the production methods connected to certain kinds of statutes. The section of *De Mysteriis* in which Iamblichus' argument appears focuses on Porphyry's belief that theurgy compels the immaterial gods and daimons by material means. This is, of course, incorrect. First, the greater kinds cannot be compelled and, second, theurgy is not merely a physical, but metaphysical, art. Also, Iamblichus elsewhere mentions the *"consecration of statues"* positively in connection to theurgic rites.[707]

In relation to this, talismans or animated statues, as mere physical objects, even if created at the correct astrological time, cannot have a strong connection to the divine. What about theurgically consecrated statues? Iamblichus answers positively. Also, the production of animated statues is not only prevalent in the Hermetic texts Iamblichus reveres, but is also important to the Neoplatonists after Iamblichus. Ultimately, Iamblichus is not attacking *hê telestikê technê*, the telestic art, but *eidôlopoiêtikê technê*, the art of image making, where the sculptor is not trying to

[706] Johnston, "Animating Statues," 453.
[707] DM V.23, 269.

make a statue of a god but is trying to make a god. Such images or idols are created by humans, not the gods, from matter, not intelligible substances.[708] Presumably, such matter, although ostensibly holding divine tokens, is not put together in such a way as to invoke a deity, instead containing a mish-mash of the tokens of different deities or Forms, rendering their efficacy void.[709] Where image makers attempt to create a god by forming their statue at the correct astrological moment, the telestic priest animates a statue through the use of *symbola*, *synthemata*, and hieratic rituals.

What is an "animated statue"? The term conjures to mind anything from golem-like giants to the animatronics at Disneyland. The Latin word "anima," from which the English "animated" is derived, can be translated as breath, life, soul or spirit. Anima animates, or gives life. The Greek word *pneuma*, also means spirit. An animated statue is not necessarily one that moves, but one that is enspirited or is connected to the pneumatic vehicle of one of the greater kinds.

In short, an animated statue is a kind of talisman, an *agalma* in the literal sense of the word. However, the statues of the gods are not mere talismans. A talisman is created for a specific purpose and fulfills that particular application. That is, a talisman is at the command of the theurgist in their demiurgy. An animated statue is at the command of the god who fills it with *pneuma*. The statue is ensouled, and called by the theurgists *agalma empsychon*, an ensouled shrine.

Why make an ensouled statue? Cannot the greater kind manifest themselves to us in other ways? As we've seen in the section on theology, yes. However, such appearances can be violent, even life threatening, or require a specialized form of the telestic art in order to induce divine possession. Divine possession is typically used for divinatory or oracular purposes, which may not coincide with what the theurgist wishes to accomplish. Also, Julian the Philosopher adds that even the material gods cannot be properly worshiped in their natural, transcendent state, nor can their divine images, the seven planets. Therefore another kind of body is created on earth.[710] Ensouled statues are more than simply valuable tools; for those practicing material theurgy they are necessary means of connecting ourselves to the divine.

The ability to go beyond the creation of a mere image to that of an ensouled statue relies on an argument similar to that used to save art from Plato's critique in the *Republic*. While the technical art of image making is merely the creation of an inanimate idol, we cannot deny the telestic theurgist's ability to capture the essence of what is depicted by the idol. Just as the skilled painter captures the divine Form of his or her subject, sculpted cult statues can contain the *eikon* of a

---

708 DM III.28, 189.

709 C.f. Krulak, "Animated Statue," 135.

710 Julian, *Frag. Epist.* 293b-c, in Johnston, "Animated Statues," 464.

higher reality,[711] becoming its visible representation. This, in turn, becomes a kind of demiurgy, for just as the Demiurge creates the universe as an *agalma* for the everlasting gods,[712] so the theurgist creates an ensouled statue for a particular god or goddess.[713]

Simply sculpting a statute to look like a particular god, daimon, angle, etc., is not enough, though it is a beginning. Such an image is a mere reflection, *eidolon*, and there is little purpose in revering an *eidolon*, or mistaking it for true divinity. By including the correct symbols and tokens, whether sculpted into the statue or included as *pharmaka*, amulets and/or talismans inside the statue, and through purifications, fumigations, and invocations, the reflection becomes a true image, an *eikon*, of the divine, fully invested with its reason-principles.

There is, of course, a difference between the Forms represented in paintings and regular artwork and the images of the gods or any other entity with its source above the noeric realm. This is because the Forms are noeric, but the essence of the gods is noetic and utterly ineffable. Although in Iamblichean theology the gods are not before Being, as they are in Proclean theology, but at the top of the chain of Being, they are still beyond even the reaches of the soul's imaginative mirror.

Why, then, are the statues of the gods anthropomorphic? The same can be asked about the images of any spiritual entity, none of which are naturally defined by a humanoid appearance. According to the *Timaeus*, living beings are the most beautiful things, and human bodies are created by the visible gods to be like their own, that is, consisting of spheres.[714] We see here the closest embodied thing to the gods is the human form. However, not all statues are in human form. There is some suggestion in Iamblichus' Pythagorean material, and his lost *On Statues*, of an egg, spherical or dodecahedron-shaped *agalma* connected to the World Soul. The World Soul also plays a role in the consecration of statues and their preparation to receive the divine influx of purifying light.[715]

According to the Alexandrian Neoplatonist Olympiodorus, the statues themselves are not considered divine, nor do they literally house a god or other being.[716] Theurgy raises things up; it does not bring the divine down. The statue becomes connected to the invoked being and its pneumatic vehicle through its tokens, effectively making it a body for the divinity, ruled from without rather than within.

Further, as theurgists, we use statues to remind ourselves of the divine realm, by filling them with signs, symbols and tokens. This, in combination with theurgic

---

711 Siorvanes, "Personification," 92, Krulak, "Animated Statue," 111-2.
712 *Tim*, 37c-d.
713 Uždavinys, *Rebirth*, 219, 223.
714 *Tim* 44d.
715 Krulak, "Animated Statue," 91-95.
716 C.f. Krulak, "Animated Statue," 112-4.

worship, awakens in our souls the *sumthemata* placed there by the Demiurge, ultimately lifting us to the heavenly realm and our leader god.[717] Of all this Proclus summarizes:

> *"The ensouled statue, for example, participates by way of impression in the art which turns it on the lathe or polishes it and shapes it in such and such a fashion, while from the universe it has received reflections of vitality which even cause us to say it is ensouled; and as a whole it has been made like the god whose statue it is. For a telestic priest who sets up a statue as a likeness of a certain divine order perfects the symbola of its identity with reference to that order, acting as does the craftsman when he makes a likeness by looking to its proper model."*[718]

Icon as Eikon

We need not limit our sacred images to statues. I have already argued that Orthodox Christian iconography is directly descended from Neoplatonic aesthetic theory. An icon is not simply an *eidolon*. By containing sacred symbols, the *synthema* and *symbolon* of a particular saint, or of Christ, an icon is a true *eikon*.

How is it images are permissible in Christianity, which comes from a religious tradition of iconoclasm in Judaism? There are still iconoclastic forms of Christianity, but clearly Catholicism, with a rich history of paintings and statuary, and the various form of Orthodox Christianity and iconography, are not part of this movement. The theology behind this movement away from Jewish and Muslim iconoclasm[719] says the incarnation of Christ as Jesus is the ultimate icon, the divine manifesting in a physical image. This, in turn, allows for the human creation of icons in celebration of the divine within Christ, the Virgin Mary, the saints, prophets, and angels.

Christianity is not the only otherwise iconoclastic Abrahamic faith to embrace some form of iconography. While Judaism prohibits the creation of humanoid images, *Torah* describe the statues of the Kerubim on the lid of the Ark of the Covenant as well as on the veil before the Holy of Holies. Each of the twelve tribes also has an associated image, represented on their banners, that can be used for ancestor veneration because as every Jew is connected to a tribe, which in turn can be seen as part of their series, leading up to the angel that governs the Jewish people, Mikhael, and above that, God. Also, while no form of representational religious artwork is allowed in Islam, there is a rich tradition of sacred calligraphic art, also found in Judaism. Such artwork consists of various divine names, titles and scriptural passages, and is therefore just as theurgic in nature as iconography and statuary.

---

[717] Uždavinys, *Theurgy*, 156-7.
[718] *In Parm.* 847.19-29, in Johnston, "Animating Statues," 454.
[719] Hardon, *Dictionary*, "Iconoclasm," 263.

Exercises: Making an Ensouled *Eikon*

An *agalma empsychon* consists of a mixture of components, because no single *symbolon* or *synthema* is enough to fully embody one of the greater kind,[720] regardless as to whether you see them in terms of gods and daimons or choirs of angels. In order to create an appropriate receptacle, *hypodochai*, for god or angel, *"the theurgic art in many cases links together stones, plants, animals, aromatic substances, and other such things that are sacred, perfect and godlike, and then from all these composes an integrated and pure receptacle."*[721] Each of these *"sacred, perfect and godlike"* things is a *symbolon* or *synthema* appropriate to the entity to be invoked. These are put together to create the image. They may be part of the actual body of the statue or receptacle. They may be placed around or beneath the receptacle, such as we might see with a sacred character.[722] They may go inside or be attached to the statue, as we see in some descriptions of a statue of Hekate in the *Chaldean Oracles*.[723] What symbols you employ in the creation of your sacred eikon depends entirely on what you want to embody. We will look at two examples: first, an *agalma* of the goddess Aphrodite, then an icon of Christ.

A Hypodochai of Aphrodite

There are a number of basic images we can employ for Aphrodite, taken either from classical mythology, medieval magical images or Renaissance artwork. From mythology there is Aphrodite Erikine holding the world egg from which Phanes Protagonos is born, and the now classical image of the birth of Aphrodite Ourania. The most famous version of the latter is perhaps Botticelli's *"The Birth of Venus,"* which shows a nude Venus or Aphrodite standing upon a clamshell, surrounded by other figures. Marsilio Ficino describes a magical image of Aphrodite holding apples and flowers and dressed in yellow and white. This image is especially associated with *"gaiety and strength of body."*[724] Other images drawn from the myths of Aphrodite or Venus are also appropriate.

If possible, it is best to sculpt your own statue. This has the advantage of getting precisely what you want in the statue and even the ability to make one with openings to insert tokens or *pharmaka*. If this is not possible, try having one made to your specifications. Failing that, an unpainted statue you can decorate yourself will allow you to add at least a level of personal touch and your own impressions of the immaterial image of Aphrodite. This is not necessary, although it does add a level of psychological connection to the process. What is most important, however, is the use of the correct symbols and tokens.

---

720 Proclus, *On the Hieratic Art*, 70, in Copenhaver, "Hermes," 105.
721 DM V.23, 296.
722 Johnston, "Animated," 454, n. 11.
723 Lewy, *Chaldean*, 88.
724 Ficino, *De vita* III.18, 337.

As for tokens, many are associated with Aphrodite. The colours green and gold,[725] yellow and white are appropriate, especially if you are going to paint the statue. Additionally, the statue can be placed on silken cloths of those colours. Although silk is not necessarily a token of Aphrodite, anything that is sensuous and voluptuous is in her domain. Coral, connected to Aphrodite's sea-birth, is always associated with her, and may be sculpted into the *agalma* and real coral may be placed in the statue or on the statue's shrine.

Roses are closely associated with Aphrodite, as are myrtle and sandal. Turtle doves, pigeons, and wagtails are also within her series. While the cult statues of antiquity had parts of actual birds in the statues, this is unnecessary. The inclusion of feathers, or painting the sacred animals on the clothing or scenery, or even including them in the sculpture, is also appropriate. The same is true for the various stones in her series, such a carnelian, sapphire, and lapis lazuli, the last of which she shares with Zeus and Apollo. Brass is also associated with her, as are any multicoloured gems or flowers and pleasant tastes and odours in general.

Before designing your statue, or composing the statue's setting if you are purchasing one, take time to read the stories of Aphrodite. This is where you will find many of her symbols and tokens. Afterwards, let your imagination go to work, for it is a mirror of the heavenly realms. Also, unlike the other exercises, I am not giving any concrete examples. There is no one particular statue of Aphrodite, or any other deity, hero or saint that must be made in a particular way. Although it is important to include as many appropriate symbols and tokens as you can, how you do so is up to you and your imagination. However, remember that as you are making a humanoid statue, the *agalma* is connected to both the divinity it portrays but also to the Form of Beauty, so incorporating a design aesthetic, making the image beautiful, is as important as making it complete.

An Eikon of the Logos

The Christian iconic tradition, especially in Greek Orthodox and related Christianities, is a longstanding pictorial practice. Although deriving from Neoplatonic aesthetic theory, Orthodox iconography has developed along its own lines, combining a rich symbol set with a series of loosely traditional imaging observations. In practice, this means the kinds of symbols included in a formal icon of a saint, angel, prophet, the Virgin Mary or of Christ are well established, as are the general, and sometimes specific, ways in which those figures are depicted. Simultaneously, Orthodox iconography allows for a personal, or inspired, touch and aesthetic to each icon. No two icons of the same figure must be portrayed in

---

[725] All the tokens of Aphrodite in this section are derived from Ficino's *De vita* and by no means represent the fullness of her iconography.

exactly the same manner. While icons of a single person are often similar to one another, they are rarely identical.

It is possible to portray any given iconic figure differently, even within the same symbol and traditional pose sets. The most important images are often figured differently depending on which of their aspects is emphasized. Taking Christ as our example, there are at least six different iconic portrayals of Christ, from Christ Pantocrator, to the crucifixion, transfiguration, and so forth. Each aspect of Christ has its own traditional poses and symbol sets setting it apart from other Christly aspects. For our example, we will use the oldest known Christian icon, Christ Pantocrator, Ruler of All, which is a fitting representation of Christ as noeric Demiurge.

The icon of Christ Pantocrator first appears in the sixth century, the oldest example of which was kept in a monastery in the Sinai desert. This depicts Christ from the waist up, though some icons show him fully enthroned over the universe. The image typically shows Jesus looking directly at the viewer. He holds the *Bible* in one hand, his other hand is held in a sign of benediction. His tunic is red, representing his human blood, and his outer robe is blue, signifying the mystery of his divinity.

There are two different poses in which he holds his hand in blessing. The older way has the ring finger, thumb and pinkie bent together. Like the colours of Christ's clothing, this signifies his divine and human natures. The forefinger and slightly bent middle finger are slightly raised. The newer way, coming after 1667, has his hand making the letters IC XC, for Iesous Khristos. Here, the index figure is straight, for the letter "I," the middle finger and pinkie are curved to form the two "C"s, and the thumb and ring fingers cross for the "X."

All icons of Christ depict him with a glory. Unlike those of lesser figures, Christ Pantocrator's icon bares a stylized, open faced cross. The three visible arms of the cross bear the Greek letters ο, ω, and ν. The last letter is always on the right arm of the cross while the first two letters are often seen interchanged on the left and top arms. The bottom arm is hidden behind Christ's head. These letters spell "*ho on*" or "who am," which comes from the name God gives Moses in *Exodus 3:14*. The background of the icon always contains the letters IC XC.

There is also a traditional way to depict Jesus' face. Although his skin tone varies between icons, he otherwise has a long, slender nose; a high forehead; wide, open eyes; a small, closed mouth; and long curling hair. These represent Christ's nobility and wisdom, his ability to look into everyone's soul, his silent contemplation and his participation in eternity.[726]

---

[726] All of the above information on the symbolism of the Christ Pantocrator icon comes from The Printery House, "Christ Pantocrator."

Despite all the very specific imagery found in this and other icons, there is still a wide variety of Christ Pantocrator icons. Some depict the outer robe as covering both shoulders while some have it covering only half his body, with the other half covered by the red tunic, representing Christ's equally human and divine elements. Some pick out the glory in blue, others in red. Some show designs in the halo, others paint different portions of it different colours. Hair colour; skin tone; the arms held open or closed; what page, if any, to which the *Bible* is open; the specific background; the way he is enthroned, or not enthroned, and what the throne looks like, all vary and carry different symbolism. Just as paintings of the Birth of Venus always depict Aphrodite on a shell on the sea shore, her nudity semi-covered, but each artist showing her according to their inspiration and aesthetic, there is still room to depict the Christ Pantocrator, or any other icon, in a personalized way.

I should add that there is no particular reason why a pagan deity cannot be represented by an icon as seen in Christianity. After all, the ideology behind Orthodox Christian iconography comes from pagan Neoplatonism. Similarly, there is no reason why a full *agalma* of Christ, the Virgin or any other figure from scripture[727] cannot be created. The creation of pagan icons can allow for a full development of synthematic symbol sets for representation in a stylized and highly symbolic way. There is, of course, a long history of statues in Christianity, especially Latin Christianity, but it is one that does not partake fully of the nature of an *agalma empsychon*. A theurgic devotee of Christ can easily remedy this.

A Rite of Ensouling – The Hypodochai of Aphrodite

What follows are two rituals for animating eikones. Despite the elevated nature and role of the *agalma empsychon*, there is little evidence suggesting one should be consecrated, and thus ensouled, in a manner overly different from that involved in talismancy. However, due to the significantly higher nature of the being invoked, a god rather than a daimon, we can expect such rituals to be more formal, containing an element of worship and hieratic hymn, and more complex, with multiple purifications of the *agalma* as well as its shrine and the theurgist.

The idea is to invoke the deity by every means possible. The titles and *barbara onomata* used to invoke the goddess are drawn from the magical papyri. These are combined with purifications related to the goddess, in this case an invocation of Tethys and the fiery heavens, both of which are related to the story of foam-born Aphrodite, and offerings connected to her stories. With the tokens and symbols already present in the *agalma*, the invocations function to raise our awareness of

[727] This is specifically in relation to Christianity. As we have already noted, both Judaism and Islam are largely iconoclastic.

their activity and her presence as the hylic matter is stripped away to reveal the goddess's true image.

The outline for this ritual is relatively simple, and is given here more fully than with the talismanic consecrations. An announcement is made that the ritual is starting and the door to the shrine area is closed against the profane or unconsecrated world. Following this, the theurgist purifies and fumigates themselves and the room and finally the goddess' shrine. Next is an invocation to the World Soul because the World Soul, along with the sub-lunar Demiurgos, distributes the divine *logoi* into matter. After this invocation, the goddess herself is called upon, using some of her ineffable names. The statue is sprinkled and fumigated, and brought to its shrine and once again invoked. Another sprinkling and fumigation occurs followed by another prayer of invocation. The feet, abdomen and head of the *agalma* are touched and different aspects of Aphrodite are called upon to ensoul the statue. An offering of roses and apples is made before the final invocation and the closing of the ceremony.

The ritual rubric is relatively short, not quite 1600 words. The ritual itself, however, is to be paced slowly, building up through the invocations and brought back down into stillness for periods of contemplation and devotion. Do not rush at any point, and do not force any aspect of the ritual; each section should flow naturally. Be sure to read the entire ritual before performing it. Also be sure to say the ritual out loud a few times before performing it. All this helps ensure a smooth, unhurried rite when put into practice.

Be aware that theurgy is not guaranteed to produces the desired results every time. Much of the success of any theurgic operation is dependent upon the ritual purity of the theurgist and their already existing alignment to whatever work is being performed. Ritual is the last step in the process, not the first. Before attempting this, or any other ritual presented in this book, spend time contemplating the object of the ritual, in this case the goddess Aphrodite. Make offerings to the goddess, read her stories, pray to her. The same holds true regardless of what deity is invoked. Aphrodite, Christ, Odin, it does not matter; you must put in the work ahead of time in order to receive a response. The world may be full of gods, but they do not come just because you call. Also, this is not a one time performance. While the gods are always present wherever their signs and tokens are gathered, we are not always open to that presence. To maintain the connection between yourself and the goddess, she should be invoked and sacrificed to often.

Once the statue is made, appropriately decorated and adorned, set up its shrine in whichever room the statue will live. It is preferable this be a place especially dedicated to religious and theurgic work, but should at least not be a place where refuse collects. Decorate the altar with the signs and colours of Aphrodite. Have on hand an incense burner and some apples and roses to offer the goddess.

The statue should not be enshrined yet. For now it is merely a statue, not an *agalma empsychon*. If possible, the statue's consecration should take place on the day and hour of Venus, or on a festival sacred to the goddess. Prepare the statue by resting it on a green, white, yellow, pink or violet cushion so that it may be properly carried to its shrine. Place the statue by the entrance to the room, preferably on a table, covered with white, rather than the ground. Sprinkle and fumigate it before bringing it into the shrine room. A version of the temple consecration ritual from the next chapter can be performed ahead of time if desired. Know the location of Venus in the sky for the time of the ritual. A banner or sign in green and gold bearing a triangle in a square[728] may be placed to mark the position of the planet. Place a small table in that part of the room, covered with a white cloth. Before entering the room, purify and fumigate yourself.

At the appropriate time, begin the ceremony with the following words, attributed to Orpheus:

> *I speak to those who lawfully may hear:*
> *Depart all ye profane, and close the doors.*

Follow this with a loud shaking of a sistrum, an important instrument in the cult of Hathor, whom the Hellenes associate with Aphrodite, or a single clap of the hands. Close the room's door.

Purify yourself with lustral water while reciting this fragment from the *Chaldean Oracles*:

> *So therefore first the Priest who governeth the works of Fire, must sprinkle with the Water of the loud-resounding Sea.*[729]

Fumigate yourself. The incense for fumigation may be any of those associated with Aphrodite. Ficino lists rose and sandalwood, but anything pleasantly aromatic and not too strong is appropriate. As you feel the water on your skin and inhale the incense, see a heavy shell around your body. With each sprinkle and fumigation the shell cracks and pieces fall away, dimly revealing a luminous sphere around you. Once you have purified and fumigated yourself, proceed to do the same to your ritual space and altar. See these actions as illuminating the room. This may also be accompanied by the shaking of the sistrum, or any other joyous musical instrument, the sound of which further adds brilliance to the space.

---

[728] This is after the idealized Sabbean or Neoplatonic-Hermetic Venereal temple. (Warnock, "The Sabians of Harran & Thabit Ibn Qurra," in *De imaginibus*, 7). In modern hermetism the seven pointed star is attributed to Venus, but this is quite against the symbolism of the heptad , which is named "virgin," which Iamblichus would have been familiar. The triad, however, is known as "harmonia," which is one of Aphrodite's activities. A pentagram, meaning wedding and marriage, is also appropriate.

[729] CO 133. Of course, "Priestess" can be substituted for "Priest."

When the room and altar have been purified and fumigated, set the lustral water and incense on a side altar. Move to the part of the room closest to the direction of the planet Venus, face the centre of the room. Raise your arms in a gesture of welcome, palms held towards the sky:

Holy and encompassing soul
of the universe, hear this
hymn sung to your glory! O great
encompassing one of bliss,
whose rings of same and difference
form the holy letter, wrapped
in Nous' cycle, and hung with
gods, let this, my prayer, be apt.

Psyche kosmou, who fill all things
with the logoi of the gods,
I call upon your divine and
sacred power that the odds
of Fate are overcome and that
Providence sets me on high
with the bright star Aphrodite,
towards whom all people do vie.

Great image of eternal Time,
formed in the divine season,
your power spans the whole cosmos.
Rain upon me the reason-
principles of holy Venus,
daughter of heaven, lady
of harmony and queen of love.
Bring her in sacred aurae.

As you pray, visualize the World Soul in the form of a sphere embraced by two rings. The outer ring slowly turns horizontally to the right, the inner diagonally down and to the left. The diagonal ring holds seven stars. As the image of the World Soul solidifies in your mind, see rays from one of the stars, shining brilliant green and gold, wash over the room and especially the statue.

With sistrum or other instrument in hand, proceed to the statue on its cushion, playing the instrument as you go. If you have no instrument, clap rhythmically. Carry the statue to the part of the room closet to Venus, and face the direction of that holy planet. Raise the statue on high and say or sing:

Hearken, great mother and mistress
of nymphs and charities, fair
one and ally, harmonizer
of opposites and whose heir
brings contraries together. Come,
daughter of heaven, fulfill
my prayer and be present to me
do not leave yearning chill.

I call upon you, the mother
of erotes I call you
ILAOYCh OBRI Ē LOYCh TLOR; come
in, holy light, and give due
answer, showing your lovely shape.
Bring forth the pneuma of your
chariot that this shrine may be
filled up with your holy aer.

As you pray, see the face of the goddess, beautiful and symmetrical, far away in your mind's eye. Visualize the graces and erotes, beings of her series, streaming from her. As you pray, see the goddess becoming more present to your awareness. Set the statue on the table before the banner of Aphrodite. Retrieve the lustral water and sprinkle the statue. Say:

Tethys, with cerulean eyes,
I call you. Let this pure clean
water lash the hylic matter
that weighs this eikon careen
away towards Hades' gloom that it
may radiate with the signs
and tokens of your daughter, oh
hearken to my prayer's lines.

As you sprinkle the statue, visualize around the statue Aphrodite's pneumatic vehicle in the form of a chariot drawn by doves. With each splash of water the statue's physical form lessens and the etheric vehicle becomes more established. Now fumigate around the statue, saying or singing:

Raging and purifying fire,
ruled by mighty Zeus, and whose
sweet smell and vivid blasts of heat

inspire life. Disabuse
this hylic form of its earthly
mire and tame its impure
nature that Aphrodite's flame
may illuminate the pure.

Again visualize the goddess' vehicle. Even though the statue may be small, the surrounding vehicle is of a grand, divine size while simultaneously no larger than the physical representation. As the statue is fumigated fully establish the pneumatic vehicle in your mind's eye. Having purified and fumigated the statue, take it from the table, leaving behind the cushion, and place it on the altar in its proper place. Say or sing:

Laughter-loving Aphrodite,
Daughter of heaven, foam-born,
Sacred Alitta, great goddess
ruling love and beauty, sworn
to harmonize the cosmos and
raise all to noeric love.
You who gave birth the graces
and Eros, and rules above.

By your secret name ILAOYCh
I call to you, delightful
queen, by your holy name, hidden
NEPhERIĒRI, rightful
daughter of Zeus, the beautiful eye
and queen of Hephaistos and
Ares alike. Oh soul raiser
come and lift me with your hand.

I adjure you, queen Kythere
NOYMILLON BIOMBILLON
AKTIŌ ERESChIGAL and
NEBOYTOSOYALĒTh and
PhROYRĒIXA and holy
ThERMIDOChĒ BAREŌ!
Come forth, holy one, beautiful
one, sacred Aphrodite!

See the goddess becoming more present to you throughout the prayer until she is seated in her chariot and surrounded by her series. Although contained in the statue, the goddess also transcends the physical limitations of the room, with her head in the heavens and the chariot's wheels on earth. Sprinkle and fumigate the statue. Kneel on both knees before the altar and say three times:

> *This is the hour for the morning (or the afternoon, or the evening) prayer to the goddess. Let us invoke heavenly Aphrodite, with all our mind, and all our reason, and all our soul.*

Look upwards while kneeling and raise your hands to the goddess. Raise your left knee and touch your right hand to the ground and three times say:

> *O goddess, be propitious.*

Put both knees on the ground and raise your arms in invocation, saying:

I have shaped this image of you,
Apotrophia, and made
it holy and true to your Form.
Give it life that does not fade.

OBRIĒTYCh KERDYNOYChILĒPSIN
NIOY NAYNIN IOYThOY ThRIGX
TATIOYTh GEKTIATh GERGERIS
GERGERIĒ ThEIThI.

OISIA EI EI AŌ ĒY
AAŌ IŌIAIAIŌ
SŌThOY BERBROI AKTEROBORE
GERIE IBOYA

Bring me light and your lovely Form
and you, shining with fire
all around, lift me to your realm,
to the heights I may aspire.

IŌ IŌ PhAThAIĒ ThOYThOI PhAEPhI

Pause to contemplate the goddess before you as you await her response. When you receive this touch a rose to the statue's feet, seeing the goddess' star shining brilliantly there, and invoke:

Aphrodite of the fair shape,

I invoke you by the name
ILAOYCh, who treads the orbit
of love. Goddess whom none tame.

Touch the statue's abdomen, seeing Aphrodite's star shining brilliantly there, and say:

Mother of uplifting Eros,
By the name ELGINAL I
call you. Fill your grace giving womb
with light that none may deny.

Touch the statue's head, seeing the goddess' star shining with a blinding, noeric brilliance, and say:

Ourania, fill your image
with essence, power, motion.
AChMAGE RARPEPSI be here,
present to my devotion!

Place the roses on the altar. Say:

Oh you of the heavenly garden, great
Aphrodite, accept this
first offering, whose scent rises
to your realm of sacred bliss.
Holy ILAOYCh, the Zeus-sprung
Phusis of all things, two-formed,
foam-beautiful Aphrodite,
with you here let me be warmed.

Offer the apples to Aphrodite, saying:

Queen of Unions, daughter of the
Good, accept this second gift
to the most beautiful, that your
Form may give a sacred lift
to my soul as I travel in
your orbit. Great ILAOYCh,
your grace, let it now being!

Pause to contemplate the goddess, awaiting her response. When you receive it sprinkle and fumigate the *agalma empsychon*, saying:

In purity of love you are
welcome, Aphrodite of
Victory. Now let your image
beckon to the gods above.

That you may be forever present
Oh ILAOYCh, I call
upon your ineffable names
that you are present to all.

I invoke thee, giver of life-
breathing fire, ELGINAL
the sacred and pure womb of the
heavens and all life's canal.

ILAOYCh Aphrodite ILAOYCh Aphrodite!

See Aphrodite fully established in her shrine, present to it but not of it. Sprinkle and fumigate, this time including the whole room and ending with yourself. Afterwards, stand before the altar and say:

Hail thou, Aphrodite, O my
goddess, be true author
lift me to the heavenly Mind
of your source and Father.

The rite is finished. Spend time in contemplation or prayer before the living Aphrodite. Leave on a light when you leave the room so as not to rudely leave the goddess in darkness.

A Rite of Ensouling – The Eikon of the Logos

It is unlikely Pseudo-Dionysius engages in animating statues or icons. However, the language of his extant writings, especially the *Ecclesiastical Hierarchy*, connects the sacralizing activity of statue animation with the work of the Hierarch or Bishop. In both instances, some form of the word *telestikē* is employed.[730] Through this, we may connect the ritual by which a Hierarch is consecrated with the rite by which the Hierarch blesses oil. Both of these rites are sacralising and perfecting, which is the root meaning of *telestikē*, and have been used here to form a ritual of icon ensoulment.

The ritual begins with a prayer at the altar, followed by fumigation, the reading of psalms and scriptures, and the profane being ordered from the sanctum. The fumigation is performed in a circular motion around the room, representing the soul's downward procession away from the divine and its upwards reversion to its source. The theurgist holds the icon on his or her head and makes an invocation. The theurgist then rises, unwraps the icon, and places it on the altar where it will live. The Alleluia is sung and prayers of consecration are recited over the icon. This finished, the sign of the cross is made over the icon and it is given a sealing kiss of consecration. An announcement is made concerning the relationship between the icon and the theurgist and the rite is finished.

There are no *barbara onomata* in this ritual. Dionysius does not employ them as they are improper to the Christianity of his time. Instead, drawing on extant Neoplatonic theories of myth, and Proclus' theory of prayer, Dionysius develops an involved theory of sacred names drawn from scripture. This is primary content of his *Divine Names*. Instead of long strings of vowels and consonants, intelligible only to the gods, we use epitaphs from the *Hebrew Bible* and *New Testament*, as well as those drawn from the prayers of the Christian Neoplatonist Synesius. These names are, according to Dionysius, given directly by God and so are therefore appropriate for contemplation and invocation. Other invocations are drawn from the Syrian liturgy of St. Dionysius.

As with the ritual to ensoul the statue of Aphrodite, do not rush through this ritual. Practice it out loud and go through all the motions to make sure you can do them smoothly. Give yourself time to pray before and after the ritual. If this is being performed in the context of a sacramental group service, partaking of communion afterwards is appropriate. Also note that I have not included visualizations for this ritual. You should be able to determine appropriate visualizations and contemplations based on the previous ceremony.

Wrap the icon in silk. Dionysius describes this as being *"veiled under twelve sacred wings,"*[731] representing the twelve wings of two seraphim[732] covering the icon.

---

[730] Krulak, "Animated Statue," 263-4.
[731] EC IV.2.473A.
[732] *Ibid.* 480B-481B.

The wrapping should be in white or gold or alternating between the two colours. Place the icon on a side altar near the door to the room. Incense is on the main altar and lit before beginning. Frankincense is traditional.[733] While the ritual can be performed at any time, the day and hour of the sun is especially appropriate, as the visible sun has long been associated with the Son of God.

When you are ready, enter and approach the altar. Say:

Jesus Christ said:
I took my stand in the midst of the world, and outwardly I appear to them in the flesh.
I came to them and found them drunk, I did not find any of them thirsting,
and my soul felt pain for the sons of men, for they were blind to me in their minds, and they could not see
they had come to the world empty and they seek as well to leave the world empty.
But now they are drunk. When they cast off their wine, then they will repent.[734]

Take the incense from the altar and, going clockwise, fumigate the room until you return to where you began. Say the following:

Oh LORD,[735] *our Lord, how excellent is your name in all the earth! who sets your glory above the heavens.*
Out of the mouth of babes and sucklings you ordained strength because of your enemies, that you might still the enemy and the avenger.
When I consider your heavens, the work of your fingers, the moon and the stars, which your ordained;
What is man, that you are mindful of him? and the son of man, that you visit him?
For you made him a little lower than the angels, and crowned him with glory and honour.
You gave him dominion over the works of your hands; you put all things under his feet:
All sheep and oxen, and the beasts of the field;
The fowl of the air, and the fish of the sea, and whatsoever passes through the paths of the seas.

Oh LORD our Lord, how excellent is your name in all the earth!

Give thanks to the LORD,[736] *for he is good: for his mercy endures forever.*
Let the redeemed of the Lord say so, whom he redeemed from the hand of the enemy;
And gathered them out of the lands, from the east, and from the west, from the north, and from the south.

---

733 Frankincense and myrrh have long been used in Christian ceremonies. Dionysius, however, specifically describes the incense as sweet smelling, which suggests frankincense alone.
734 *Gospel of Thomas*, logion 28, translation by the author.
735 *Ps 8.*
736 *Ps 107.*

They wandered in the wilderness in a solitary way; they found no city in which to dwell.
Hungry and thirsty, their soul fainted in them.
Then they cried to the Lord in their trouble, and he delivered them out of their distresses.
And he led them by the right way, that they might go to a city of habitation.
Oh let them praise the Lord for his goodness, and for his wonderful works for humanity!

For he satisfies the longing soul, and fills the hungry soul with goodness.

Such as sit in darkness and in the shadow of death, being bound in affliction and iron;
Because they rebelled against the words of God, and contemned the counsel of the most High:
Therefore he brought down their heart with labor; they fell down, and there was none to help.
Then they cried to the Lord in their trouble, and he saved them out of their distresses.
He brought them out of darkness and the shadow of death, and broke their bands in sunder.
Oh let them praise the Lord for his goodness, and for his wonderful works for humanity!
For he broke the gates of brass, and cut the bars of iron in two.

Fools because of their transgression, and because of their iniquities, are afflicted.
Their soul abhors all manner of meat; and they draw near the gates of death.
Then they cry to the Lord in their trouble, and he saves them from their distresses.
He sent his word, and healed them, and delivered them from their destructions.
Oh let them praise the Lord for his goodness, and for his wonderful works for humanity!
And let them sacrifice the sacrifices of thanksgiving, and declare his works with joy.

They that go down to the sea in ships, that do business in great waters;
These see the works of the Lord, and his wonders in the deep.
For he commands, and raises the stormy wind, which lifts the waves.
They rise up to heaven, they go down again to the depths: their soul is melted because of trouble.
They reel back and forth, and stagger as though drunk, and are at their wit's end.
Then they cry to the Lord in their trouble, and he brings them out of their distresses.
He calms the storm, so that the waves are still.
Then are they glad; so he brings them to their desired haven.
Oh let them praise the Lord for his goodness, and for his wonderful works for humanity!
Let them exalt him also in the congregation of the people, and praise him in the assembly of the elders.

He turns rivers into a wilderness, and wells into dry ground;
A fruitful land into barrenness, for the evil of them that dwell there.
He turns the wilderness into a standing water, and dry ground into wells.
And there he makes the hungry to live, that they may prepare a city for habitation;
And sow the fields, and plant vineyards, which may yield fruits of increase.
He blesses them, so that they are made many; and does not suffer their cattle to decrease.

Again, they are diminished and brought low through oppression, affliction, and sorrow.
He pours contempt upon rulers, and causes them to wander in the wilderness, where there is no way.
Yet he sets the poor on high from affliction, and gives them families like a flock.
The righteous will see it, and rejoice: and all iniquity will stop her mouth.
Whoever is wise, and will observe these things, even they shall understand the loving kindness of the Lord.

In the beginning was the Word,[737]
and the Word was with God, and the Word was God.
The same was in the beginning with God.
All things were made by him; and without him was not
any thing made that was made.
In him was life; and the life was the light of humanity.
And the light shines in darkness; and the darkness comprehended it not.
And the Word was made flesh, and dwelt among us.

Turn to face towards the room's door and say:

I speak to those who lawfully may hear:
Depart all ye profane, and close the doors.

Moving clockwise, close the door and proceed to the covered icon. Kneeling on both knees, take the icon from the altar and hold it, fully covered, on top of your head. Say the following:

In the name of the Father +, the Son +, and the Holy Ghost +, Lord have mercy upon me, who seeks to bring forth an image of the Son of God. In the beginning you remained without image and beyond all Forms. With the incarnating Word, you, oh living God, took flesh and became an image manifest for those with eyes to see.

Holy and celestial crafter of Forms, pour out upon this sacred image your being, life, and mind that it is be filled with you essence, resounds with you power, and acts with your love and grace. Pantocrator, King of kings and God of gods, stand before your flock. You who are the Light from the fountain-head. Shine through this murky matter and enliven this image of your image.

Rise and take the icon directly to the altar upon which it will live. Unwrap the image, hold it on high, and sing:

Let all mortal flesh keep silence,
And with fear and trembling stand;
Ponder nothing earthly minded,

---

[737] *John 1.*

For with blessing in His hand,
Christ our God descends to earth
and is preceded by the six-winged seraphim
who cover their faces sing aloud:
Alleluia, Alleluia, Alleluia!

Place the icon on its altar. Raise your hands in invitation and pray:

Giver of Holiness,
And distributor of every good, Oh Lord,
Who sanctifies every rational creature
With holiness, which is from your;
Sanctify, through your Holy Spirit,
This image, that it may bring forth your mysteries;
Free all of your signs and tokens from the dross of matter
That it is worthy of your life.
Through the heavenly Pontiff, Jesus Christ Logos,
Your only-begotten Son,
Through Whom, and with Whom,
Your glory and honour is due.

Amen +

Kneel and pray:

Essentially existing, and from all ages;
Whose nature is incomprehensible, who is near and present to all, without any change of your sublimity;
Whose goodness every existing thing longs for and desires;
The intelligible indeed, and creatures endowed with intelligence, through intelligence;
Those endowed with sense, through their senses;
Who, although you are One essentially, nevertheless are present with us, and amongst us, in this hour, in which you called and led us to your holy mysteries;
And made us worthy to stand before the sublime throne of your majesty, and to handle this sacred vessel of your incarnation with our impure hands:
Take away from this heavenly image, Oh Lord, the cloak of matter in which it is garbed, as from Joshuah, the son of Josedech the High Priest, you took the filthy garments, and adorn it with justice and mercy, as you adorned him with a vestment of glory;
That it, clothed with you alone, as with a garment, and being like a temple crowned with glory, we may, through it, see you unveiled with a mind divinely illuminated.

Amen +

Remain kneeling and contemplate the eikon of the Pantocrator, awaiting a response. When you receive this rise and make the sign of the cross over the icon. Say:

O Christ Pantocrator +, the King of Glory, and Father of the Age to come;
Holy Sacrifice;
Heavenly Hierarch;
Lamb of God, Who removes the sin of the world, spare the sins of your people, and dismiss the foolishness of your flock.
Preserve us, through the communication of your divine activity, from every sin, whether committed by word, or thought, or deed;
And from whatever makes us far from the familiarity of your household, that our bodies may be guarded by your body, and our souls renewed through your holy actions.
And may your benediction, Oh Lord, be in our whole person, within and without;
And may you be glorified in us, and by us, and may your right hand rest upon us, and that of your blessed Father +, and of your most holy Spirit +.

Amen +

The rite is now finished. You may spend time in contemplation or prayer before the living Christ. When you leave the room, be sure to leave a light on so as not to rudely leave the eikon in darkness.

Divine Possession – If Someone Asks if You Are a God, You Say "Yes!"

Earlier, I suggested a connection between ensouled statues and human souls and their bodies. The main similarity is obvious: a human soul animates a physical body. However, that animation is not exactly as how a god ensouls their *eikon.* Gods do not identify themselves with their bodies. Gods not do dwell inside their statues but rule their bodies from without. What affects a god's body does not affect the god. The gods are immortal and perfect. None of this is true of the incarnate human soul except for the most pure. Still, the human body is the shrine of a divine being, even if of the least divine of divinities.

There is, however, another way in which the theurgist can act as an ensouled statue: divine possession. While the Athenian academy employs *agalmata empsychon* for anagogic purposes as well as divinatory ones, Iamblichus does not. No divinatory elements are found in his few tracts on the subject. Divine possession is another matter.

For Iamblichus, divine possession is the only true form of divination; everything else involves some element of human interpretation and is therefore fallible. Not so possessed divination. Rituals to establish the god in the theurgist may involve material tokens, but that is to be expected as only the visible and sub-lunar gods engage in this activity. The hypercosmic gods do not as they have no connection to the physical world through a pneumatic vehicle. That said, possession and what the god utters have nothing to do with the ritual itself. It has a great deal to do with the theurgist, and animated statues.

The descriptions of divine possession Iamblichus and the Athenian academy offers are similar to those of ensouled statues. This leads to the conclusion that the possessed theurgist is not only in effect, but in actuality, an ensouled *agalma* for the possessing god. *Agalma* means both statue and shrine, and this is precisely what the possessed theurgist becomes.[738]

The ensoulment of the god in the theurgist occurs by the same means as a statue. By associating him or herself with the tokens and symbols of a particular god, praying to that god, contemplating their divine image, eating sacred foods, and invocation the theurgist becomes a living amalgam of *synthemata* of the god. While the *synthemata* are not actual parts of the god, they participate the god's essence, as does the possessed theurgist. The difference is that the theurgist has a rational soul and participates the divine mind in a way inanimate objects and non-human animals cannot. This allows the theurgist to become a mouth for the god. Through this, true divination occurs. When the theurgist becomes a shrine to their leader god, initiation occurs.[739]

---

738 Uždavinys, *Theurgy*, 241.

739 C.f. Uždavinys, *Orpheus*, 82-4.

Chapter Nineteen

The Invocation of the Personal Daimon

This section, like the previous two, has seen a number of practical applications of Neoplatonic thought. Without these there is no living theurgy, no living philosophy, only facts and information. There is nothing wrong with facts and information, but if not put into use they become meaningless. It is not enough to know about moral virtues, you must practice them and live them. The same is true of theurgy.

I have said before it is necessary to fully engage in a philosophical life before performing theurgic rituals. The same may be said of a religious or spiritual life. Both of these build upon and support one another, and serve to purify and illuminate the soul, bringing it closer to the gods or God. From a late Neoplatonic perspective, this closeness is by no means complete or fully actualized only through philosophy and religion; it is only accomplished through *theourgia*. Even so, simply because you have successfully ensouled a divine *eikon* does not mean you are a master theurgist or have found your leader god. It is possible to participate essences with which our own essences are not aligned.

How can we know what is appropriate for us and our spiritual and theurgic development? Some modern occultists suggest reviewing our life by which we can see where we have been most successful and where things have gone horribly wrong. By doing so we can tell what kind of life is best for us, and through that recognize the nature of our essence. This works, provided you are a theurgic sage and perfected soul, always choosing a life appropriate to your nature. This does not describe the vast majority of us. There is no technical or psychological way of knowing if the life our soul projects is related to our essence and our leader god. What we need is our personal daimon or holy guardian angel.

The Personal Daimon . . . Again

Our daimon is assigned to us from before our incarnation, presumably from the moment we are sewn into the orbit of our leader. Being noetic, our daimon knows everything about us in every way imaginable, past, present and future. The daimon guides us through our lives, leads us to the heavens when we die, and back again when it is again time to incarnate. Through the daimon, we begin to truly remember who and what we are.

In many forms of modern ceremonial magic, contacting the "holy guardian angel," "higher self," or what-have-you, is seen as a top-tier activity. Everything else in one's occult education is geared towards this and when it is at hand the magician becomes an adept. The word "adept" means "completely skilled," and comes from the Latin *adeptus*, "having reached, attained." There might be higher "grades," depending on the esoteric system in question, such as a "magister," meaning "one who has authority," but these are founded on adepthood.

In Neoplatonic theurgy the practitioner who contacts their daimon is not an adept. They are a simply a theurgist, which is to say a philosopher and lover of both wisdom and the divine. Everything that has come before is something of an apprenticeship, preparing you to become a novice. Making contact with your daimon is in some ways your first real initiation as a theurgist.

This leads us to that most important of questions: how do we contact our daimon? In Book Three, chapter twenty-six, of the *Three Books of Occult Philosophy*, Henry Cornelius Agrippa, drawing on Hermetic thought, provides at least five different sets of instructions for discovering the "name of any genius,"[740] that is, any spirit or daimon. Each method involves the calculation of one's horoscope, and especially the "almuetz," or ruler of the horoscope. A name is fashioned by attributing letters to each degree, and finding the degree of the appropriate planets.

Unfortunately, this doesn't really work. Why? Are daimons physical beings? Are they ruled by Fate? Agrippa's methods might work for a daimon associated with a particular time and place, or those daimons whose vehicles have become mired in *hylē*, where there is some element connected to the realm of generation. Also, while Iamblichus says Fate is Providence, only seen from below, that does not change anything about discovering the daimon. If the daimon is viewing Providence from the same place as us, which it must if they are determined by our natal chart, then it cannot lead us upwards. Iamblichus has a very similar "conversation" with Porphyry on this very topic.

Porphyry complains about the near impossibility of discovering the almuetz, what he calls the "master of the house," *oikodespotis*, of our natal horoscope, which is somehow necessary for discovering one's personal daimon.[741] This, according to Iamblichus, makes no sense. If the daimon is connected to our horoscope, which pertains only to a particular incarnation, in what way can it lead us to transcend Fate and take us to the celestial gods and ultimately beyond? Any such daimon is mired in the same Fate as ourselves. If, on the other hand, we are somehow able to transcend Fate through our daimon, how can it be assigned to us on the basis

---

[740] Agrippa, *De occulta*, III.26, 547.
[741] DM IX.3, 329.

of our natal chart, which represents physical Fate?[742] The noetic daimon has nothing to do with technical astrology, how can it? Even if some sort of name is found from the natal chart, how does this comprehend the entirety of the soul? Iamblichus says the personal daimon is not from one part

> *only of the heavenly regions nor from any one element of the visible realm*[743] *. . . but from the whole cosmos and from the whole variety of life within it and from every sort of body, through all of which the soul descends into generation, there is apportioned to us an individual lot, assigned to each of the parts within us according to an individual authorizing principle. This daimon, then, is established in the Paradigm even before souls descend into generation. And when the soul selects him as its leader the daimon immediately attends to his task of fulfilling the lives of the soul, and he binds the soul to the body when it descends.*[744]

While this may suggest some connection between the daimon and the realm of generation, it is far greater than anything astrology imparts. The daimon is a "causal principle"[745] presiding over our lives, and is established in the Paradigm, that is, Aion. This is an ontological statement meaning daimons are prior to souls. As souls stem from the lowest part psychic realm, daimons must originate from some place higher. Even if that is the level of the World Soul it is still above generation and the physical world. And, of course, they come from above the psychic realm.

The above quotation leads to another question: how does a soul select its daimon? This doesn't make sense: ontologically posterior beings do not get to choose their superiors. Rather than select, it is more understandable for us to say acquiesces to. The soul can choose to live a life appropriate to its essence or it can not. If it chooses the latter, the daimon is invisible to us in our life. If the soul chooses the former the daimon is there, leading us. The daimon, of course, tries to lead us anyway, but in the first instance we blind ourselves to its promptings and lessons, in the second we do not.

However, this does not answer our question. We may know what won't work, but we still do not know what does. What works is the invocation of the "*single god who is their ruler, who from the beginning has apportioned a personal daemon to each individual, and who in the theurgic rites reveals, according to his good pleasure, their personal daemon to each.*"[746] This single god is the sub-lunar Demiurge.

---

[742] *Ibid.*, IX.3, 329-31.

[743] Later, the personal daimon is described as coming from *"all the regions of the universe"* (DM IX.7, 337).

[744]DM IX.6, modified from Shaw, *Theurgy*, 217.

[745] *Ibid.*, IX.9, 339.

[746] *Ibid.*, IX.9, 341.

One Ritual to Rule Them All

Iamblichus tells Porphyry, near the above quotation, that because personal daimons are ruled by a single god, there is a common invocation for them.[747] Again, this raises more questions than it solves. How, for instance, are all personal daimons commanded by a single god? Isn't each personal daimon under the domain of the series of its leader god? The answer is yes. At the same time, the visible gods, each existing in their own series, are also ruled by their Demiurge. The role of the sub-lunar Demiurge is to direct the realm of generation and all within it. That includes human souls fallen into generation and the daimons who's jobs it is to lead them upwards again.

Unfortunately, although there is a single ritual to invoke this god, we do not know what it is. At least, we do not know what the late Platonists used. There are, however, other extant rituals that may give us a clue. Specifically, we will look at the extended rite for invoking the holy guardian angel in the *Book of Abramelin*, the ritual of theurgic elevation described by Hans Lewy in the *Chaldean Oracles* and *Theurgy*,[748] and the various rituals for gaining a helper daimon in the *PGM*. None of these rituals are exactly what we are looking for, although the Abramelin working is clearly based on Jewish Neoplatonic lines and is likely close. However, they all contain elements relevant to the work at hand, possibly having informed, or have been informed by, the missing Neoplatonic ritual.

The *Book of Abramelin*, best known by the title of S.L. Macgregor Mathers' *The Book of the Sacred Magic of Abra-Melin the Mage*, is a 14th century book of Jewish theurgy. Written by Abraham of Worms, who is identified as Rabbi Jacob ben Moses ha Levi Möllin, the Maharil,[749] the *Book of Abramelin* is written by "Abraham" to his younger son Lamech, because as the second son he cannot be taught Kabbalah. The book contains advice, history, magical charms, and an eighteen month invocation of one's holy guardian angel, who then leads the theurgist on the proper spiritual life towards God.

There are two English-language translations of the *Book of Abramelin*. The oldest is by Samuel Liddell Mathers, one of the founders of the Order of the Golden Dawn. The Mathers translation comes from a French manuscript. Although Mathers does justice to the French, the manuscript is imperfect. Many of the talismans are incomplete or absent. The manuscript is missing an entire book, containing three rather than four sections. Twelve months of the ritual are also missing. The second is a translation from a complete German manuscript by Steven Guth. This edition, published in 2006, contains all the information absent

---

747 *Ibid.*

748 Some form of this ritual may have been employed by the later Neoplatonists to assimilate themselves to the celestial Demiurge once they had come into contact with their leader gods. Such a ritual is beyond the scope of this book.

749 Dehn, "Introduction," XXIII, in Abraham, *Abramelin.*

from the French manuscript, as well as Georg Dehn's research on the identity of "Abraham of Worms."

The most important parts of the *Sacred Magic* are the instructions concerning a proper life and the ritual itself. The former is not relevant to our work; it is covered in the first two sections of this book. The latter is surprisingly simple. In brief, the theurgist sets up a special prayer room, preferably in the wilderness. An altar is made and prayer clothing acquired. The theurgist prays to "Adonai"[750] at the altar twice a day for the next eighteen months. There are some lifestyle restrictions proscribed, but no specific prayers. At the end of the eighteen month the holy guardian angel is invoked through Adonai and, if successful, it appears and instructs the theurgist on how to contact it, how to control evil spirits, how to become closer to God, and so forth.

The ritual of theurgic elevation described by Lewy is somewhat more difficult. No complete version of the ritual exists. Instead, Lewy reconstructs a description of a ritual based on what he considers fragments preserved by various Neoplatonists. This ritual is somewhat farther afield than the Abramelin in that it seeks to unite the soul of the theurgic initiate with the celestial Demiurge. However, in doing this, the soul and its vehicle are cleansed and realigned with its series. Unlike the *Abramelin* ritual, the Chaldean ritual is deeply involved, including possibly an initiator and ecstatic trances wherein the initiate utters ineffable names known only to his or her soul. The underpinning of this ritual is not prayer as in *Abramelin*, but in the rites of purification. Without a purified soul and vehicle, the consummate theurgic act fails.

The *Papyri Graecae Magicae* contains at least four rituals or spells[751] for either acquiring an assistant daimon or the personal daimon. Of these, only two directly are related to our work. The first is *PGM VII.505-28*, entitled *"Meeting with your own daimon."* This spell is addressed to the goddess of Fate, Tyche. The spell invokes not only Tyche but Helios and the Egyptian scarab god Khepri, who is seen as the morning aspect of the sun god Re. The second spell, *PGM LVII.1-37*, is an untitled rite to acquire an assistant daimon. This invokes Adonai as well as Isis, whom the Hellenes often associate with Hekate, the Chaldean ruler of sub-lunar daimons. The magician promises to preserve the order of the universe and recites the many names of Isis, which she takes from Rê in order to resurrect Osiris.

The *PGM* treats the personal daimon, and daimons in general, as servants. This approach effectively treats them as ontologically inferior to the magician summoning them. Iamblichus, in *De mysteriis*, counters this ideology. The daimon is not ours to command but is the direct leader of our soul. At best, we might

---

750 In the German edition the term "Herr," which is used to refer to God, is translated as Adonai to best demonstrate the connotation of the term. You will recall this is the divine name we identified as the sub-lunar Demiurge.

751 See PGM I.1-42, PGM I.42-195, PGM VII.505-28, and PGM LVII.1-37. See also PGM VIII.1-63, "Love spell of Astrapsoukos," which invokes Hermes.

interpret the *PGM*'s attitude towards daimons as an extension of divine possession, where the magician, acting through the power of their leader god, is able to command an otherwise superior being. This attitude is suggested in some, but by no means all, of the *PGM* spells dealing with servant daimons.

The first ritual is explicitly for the personal daimon, rather than simply a daimonic assistant, and applies a solar theology to the working. This may seem inappropriate, looking towards Helios rather than Hades, but remember that although Helios is the noeric Demiurge, all the demiurges partake of a solar nature. There is also some evidence of a traditional association between Pluto and Helios in the form of Pluton Helios.[752] The spell also contains invocations of the place and time, which are also indicated in the Chaldean material. The second spell invokes the appropriate Demiurge, but has an element of command antithetical to theurgic thought. Both are relatively simple spells and neither appears to require any sort of substantive purification. Of these, even though it is for the gaining of an assistant daimon, rather than the personal daimon, the latter is closer to our cosmology and is of somewhat more use than the former.

What does all of this mean for our ritual? In the following ritual, elements of both the Abramelin and Chaldean rites, along with spells from the *PGM*,[753] are blended with our theories of Neoplatonic prayer and hieratic practice. We also incorporate elements of the *Chaldean Oracles* as well as themes from the *Phaedrus* and *Timaeus*. Why include elements from the *Oracles* and Plato? The reasoning behind the *Oracles* is fairly straightforward: they are the words of the gods and heavily influential on later Neoplatonism. As for Plato, we focus on the myth of the descent of the soul from the *Phadrus* and the creation of the soul in the *Timaeus*. While these may not be divine utterances, they reflect our cosmology and, as myths, represent a kind of theurgic symbol.

Our ritual of the daimon includes a period of ritualized preparation and prayer and a culminating rite where the sub-lunar Demiurge is invoked and the personal daimon revealed. This is as far as we can go in a static ritual. What happens once your daimon is revealed is between you and it and cannot be predicted beyond what Iamblichus writes: "*[W]hen the personal daimon comes to be with each person, then he reveals the mode of worship proper to him and his name, and imparts the particular manner in which he should be summoned.*"[754]

On the Invocation of the Personal Daimon

The invocation of the personal daimon is one of the most important theurgic rituals. In the *Republic*, Plato likens the relationship to the daimon with marriage.

---

752 Thompson, "ISmyrna 753," 111.
753 This includes those discussed above, as well as elements from others such as the solar-based "Mithras Liturgy" (PGM IV 475-829).
754 DM IX.9, 341.

As such, this ritual should not be performed until you have spent a considerable amount of time working with the first two sections of this book. How long is "a considerable amount of time"? I cannot answer that for you. Your work in philosophy and devotion is your guide.

The following rite is for the purpose of invoking the personal daimon. It is written in a style consonant with Hellenic pagan Neoplatonism. That said, it can be readily modified for non-Hellenic paganisms or for those engaged in esoteric forms of the Abrahamic religions. The ritual invokes the god Hades as the sub-lunar Demiurge, and Hermes as psychopomp. Hades commands the daimons, in the names of their leader gods, Hermes brings us to them.

The rite is divided into three phases. The first is a period of purification. This consists of religious devotion focusing on a solar theology, from Aion to Helios to Hades. Phase two includes a dedication to Hermes. The third phase is the invocation of the personal daimon through theurgic identification with Hermes and contains an element of divine possession. This is not exactly for oracular purposes in the common sense of the term[755] but so the god can directly present us with our daimon.

Phases one and two each take six months. The final operation can take less than an hour to perform. However, depending on how well you have transformed yourself into an *eikon* of the gods, it may need to be performed more than once. Once you have made contact with your daimon, it will instruct you on how to proceed.

Setting and Materials

Scholars are not certain where theurgic rituals of antiquity take place. It seems likely some occur at temples and some at personal homes, such as Proclus' devotions to Athena. Some possibly also happen in the wilderness. Given the public-good orientation of Neoplatonic political philosophy, retiring from public life to perform the operation is neither necessary nor desirable. Set aside a room in your home as your sacred precinct or *temenos*. Ideally, use the room only for the operation during the period of the work. A room already set aside for worship or devotion also works. This, of course, is not always possible, so using any room outside of a place where waste is disposed of, such as a bathroom or kitchen, is fine. If the room is used for mundane work it should be re-consecrated every time it is entered for the purposes of the invocation.

Ideally, your *temenos* has windows opening to the east and west, so the rising and setting sun is visible. If this is not possible, at least choose a room with some natural light. Place an altar in the middle of the *temenos* during the time of the

---

755 However, see Betz, "Delphic,"159-60, where the command to *"consult your personal daimon,"* as part of knowing thyself, has an oracular connotation.

ritual. If possible, leave the altar in place for the duration of the operation. If this is not possible, re-consecrate it every time it is used after it has been moved. Set nothing but the paraphernalia of the invocation on the altar during this time.

The altar is best made of wood, poplar or cypress is preferable. If possible, obtain or make an altar that opens and has a shelf or two to store the material of the invocation. Dress the altar with a golden cloth and place over this a somewhat smaller one of silver. On top of these is a white cloth, leaving a few inches of each layer of cloth visible. The borders the golden cloth can be decorated with the following divine Name of the celestial Demiurge:

ΑΘΗΖΟΦΩΜ ΖΑΔΗΑΓΗΩΒΗΦΙΑΘΕΑΑ ΑΜΒΡΑΜΙ ΑΒΡΑΑΜ
ΘΑΛΧΙΛΘΟΕ ΕΛΚΩΘΩΩΗΗ ΑΧΘΩΝΩΝ ΣΑ ΙΣΑΚ
ΧΩΗΙΟΥΡΘΑΣΙΩ ΙΩΣΙΑ ΙΧΗΜΕΩΩΩΩ ΑΩΑΕΙ

The silver altar cloth can bare the images of pomegranates, sacred to Hades as the fruit of the underworld. The white cloth is plain.

During the first phase of the work, light three olive oil burning lamps, representing demiurges, on the altar during devotion. Metal lamps are preferable to earthenware. Candles may also be used, but use either lamps or candles, not both. The candlesticks are simple, unadorned and of metal, preferably of golden hue, rather than wood or ceramics. If metal is not possible, paint the candlesticks gold or cover them with gold leaf. During the second phase a fourth light, for Hermes, is added. This candlestick or lamp is silver in tone. During the third phase a final light is added for the daimon. Use a glass candlestick or lamp rather than one of metal.

Besides the altar cloth and candles, have on hand plenty of incense. For the solar devotional phase of the invocation, make incense from this basic formula:

2 ½ t powdered frankincense

25 drops heliotrope oil

25 drops narcissus oil

2 ½ t sandalwood powder

1/8 t Tragacanth powder

2 ¼ t water

This is enough to make one hand rolled stick of incense approximately 6 ½ inches long and half an inch wide, which will burn for approximately an hour.[756] You will burn this two to three times a day, so make sure you have enough,

[756] For those unfamiliar with making incense, there are many books available on the subject, such as Steven R. Smith's *Wylundt's Book of Incense.*

making your supply on Saturday, preferable during the hour of the sun. During the second phase, storax resin is burnt on the days of Hermaic devotion.

For clothing, have a pure white robe. The robe should be long, coming at least to the calves, and have long sleeves. Wide, hanging sleeves are not recommended as they can get in the way when working over the altar, especially with open flames. Have a white belt to tie the robe close to the body. A shorter, open and sleeveless robe of golden yellow is worn over the white robe. This robe is something like a long vest and remains open and untied. The outer robe may be decorated with symbols sacred to Helios and Hades. For Helios this may include the chariot or horses, the aureole, a rooster or wolf. For Hades, a four-spoke wheel, keys, and owls are appropriate. Your own research will reveal other appropriate symbola. Signs of Helios are in gold, those of Hades in silver. All work within the ritual space is performed either barefoot or with sandals used only indoors. Ideally, such sandals are of simple, unadorned leather.

The anointing oil is made from one teaspoon of olive oil for every four drops of spikenard oil and four drops of narcissus oil. The oil is used to anoint yourself, your clothing, the altar, candles or lamps and the room. Lustral water is used for purifications as normal. Use whatever you normally use for this. If the room is used by people other than you, remove the altar from the working space to the side and store all of the ritual items, including clothing, inside, so as to avoid ritual pollution, *miasma*.

Consecrating the *Temenos*

The rite begins on either the summer or winter solstice. Ideally, you will consecrate the *temenos* the night before the first morning prayer session. As long as the *temenos* is used only for the invocation or other devotional work, it will be consecrated only at the summer and winter solstices, for a total of three consecrations. If, however, the room is used for other purposes, the *temenos* is re-consecrated before the next devotion. The consecration is neither complicated nor lengthy, so it is possible to perform it immediately before each session.

Place the altar in the centre of the space. Upon this are the three candles or lamps if for the first phase, the four during the second, and five during the last. Have the oil and incense on the altar. Fold the outer and inner robes and bind them both with the white belt. Place these on the altar. The lustral water is set on a nearby side altar. Have some water available outside the room as well. You may put whatever you use to light the lamps and incense on the side altar.

Dress in simple white clothing, over which you will wear your robes. Before entering the temple, purify yourself with lustral water. Enter the *temenos*, saying:

I speak to those who lawfully may hear:

Depart all ye profane, and close the doors.

Follow this with a loud clap of the hands and close the door to the room. Purify yourself with the lustral water, while saying:

So therefore first the Priest who governeth the works of Fire, must sprinkle with the Water of the loud-resounding Sea.

Light the incense and fumigate yourself. Do not let the incense go out during the consecration. As you feel the water on your skin and inhale the incense, see a heavy shell around your body. With each sprinkle and fumigation the shell cracks and pieces fall away. Once purified and fumigated, do the same to your ritual space and altar. See these actions as illuminating the room. When the room and altar have been purified and fumigated, set the water and incense aside. Stand before the altar, holding your arms up in a gesture of welcome, and say:

This is the hour for prayer to the gods. I invoke all the gods and Zeus-Helios, who reigns over them, with all my essence, and all my power, and all my activities.

Kneel on both knees, look up, and raise your hands, palms facing up, fingers away from your body. Say:

O gods, be propitious.

Lift one knee and touch the floor with your right hand. Say:

O gods, be propitious.

Remove your right hand from the floor and touch it with the left. Say:

O gods, be propitious.

Touch the floor with both hands and knees. Say:

O Zeus, be propitious. O Zeus, be propitious. O Zeus, be propitious.

Light the lamps. Hold the anointing oil up and say:

O holy Demiurgos, hear
my prayer. You who were born first
amongst the gods and who is the
second craftsman, who rehearsed
the gods in their movements. Hearken
intellect thinking himself,
image of the imageless, who
causes me to know myself.

O holy Craftsman, hear my prayer.
Master of daimons, you who
purifies souls, listen to my
cry. Saviour of the world, do
now touch this work with your hand and
perfect it so I may raise
myself to you. Shaper of wood,
whose craft always does amaze.

Bless and consecrate, o mighty
Craftsmen, this oil that your light
shines in all it anoints. Be here
through your logoi, cleanse, make bright,
and perfect this temenos and
all within it. Great Lords, I
consecrate this work to your
names, you who are always nigh.

Anoint your forehead and hands and then the collars of your robes and the four sides and top of the altar. Moving sun-wise around the *temenos*, anoint the window and door sills. Return to the altar and set aside the oil. Put on the robes. Spend some time in free prayer or quiet contemplation. When finished, extinguish the candles and incense and remove and fold your robes as before. The consecration is complete. You may either retire or begin the invocation's formal devotion.

Phase One: Devotional

The invocation's first phase is dedicated to Helios and Hades, or Pluton as he is usually called in late Antiquity. As Neoplatonic hierarchies are always invoked from the top down, it is essential to invoke Helios before Pluton. We also invoke Aion for this reason.

The first phase lasts six month, from summer solstice to winter solstice, or winter solstice to summer solstice. During this time you will enter the *temenos* to pray twice a day, once at sunrise and once at sunset during the week. Add a mid-day session on Sundays. If these times are impossible, at least make your prayers during the morning, midday, and evening before breakfast and lunch and after dinner.

If the *temenos* is dedicated to this work or worship in general it does not need to be re-consecrated every day. In this case, begin your daily devotional as below. If your devotions occur separately from the consecration of the *temenos*, and after the room has been used for some other purpose, begin each session in the same way as the consecration up to the point the whole room is sprinkled and fumigated and you stand before the altar. Put on your robes after you have purified and fumigated yourself, but before you proceed to the rest of the room. If the devotions occur concurrently to the consecration, begin them once you have returned to the altar from consecrating the room with oil, and skipping the opening section below.

Consecrate yourself with lustral water before entering the *temenos*. Enter the *temenos* saying:

I speak to those who lawfully may hear:
Depart all ye profane, and close the doors.

Follow this with a loud clap of the hands. Close the door to the room. Go to the altar and sprinkle and fumigate yourself. Standing before the altar, hold your arms up in a gesture of welcome, and say:

This is the hour for the morning (or the evening) prayer to the gods. I invoke all the gods and Demiurges, who reign over them, with all my essence, and all my power, and all my activities.

Kneel on both knees, look up, and raise your hands, palms facing up, fingers away from your body. Say:

O gods, be propitious.

Lift one knee and touch the floor with your right hand. Say:

O gods, be propitious.

Remove your right hand from the floor and touch it with the left. Say:

O gods, be propitious.

Touch the floor with both hands and knees. Say:

O Aion, be propitious. O Helios, be propitious. O Pluton, be propitious.

If the lamps are not already lit from the consecration, sprinkle and fumigate them, then light each one after a brief prayer. If the lamps are already lit, say the following prayers over them:

Hail to you, invisible sun,
holy Aion. I invoke
you by your hidden and holy
names. Be present without cloak:
AChBA IEOYĒOĒ IAĒAIĒŌĒYOEI

Envision this lamp emitting the brilliant, blinding nothing of the eternal and invisible sun. Breathe deeply of the lamp's pre-essential light.

Light the second lamp, saying:

Hail to you, mighty Helios,
Great lord of noeric flames,
I invoke you by these holy
word, come to your calling Names:
AChEBYKRŌM ANAG BIAThIARBAR BERBI SChILATOYR BOYPhROMTRŌM

Envision this lamp emitting the brilliant, blinding light of the noeric sun and breathe in its solar rays.

Light the third lamp, saying:

Hail to you, chthonic Pluton,
Lord of daimons, I invoke
you by these hidden and holy

Names, by which my soul awoke:
YESEMMIGADŌN MAARChAMA

Envision the lamp emitting the dark light of the sun at midnight, breathing in the sub-lunar rays. Next, kneel on both knees, raising both hands into the air. Say:

Hail,[757] *King, I call to you God of*
Gods, mighty, boundless and pure,
beyond description, established,
great Aion who does endure.

PhŌGALŌA ERDĒNEY MEREMŌGGA

Never leave me, O lord Aion,
Be inseparable, Lord,
From now until to the end of my
days. Make me always your ward.

Remain kneeling, touch your right hand to the floor. Say:

Hail,[758] *fire's dispenser, the world's*
all-seeing king, O great lord
Helios, with noble steeds, the
eye of Zeus, guarding with sword
in hand the earth, far-seeing one,
who travels high paths, divine
gleam, who moves through the heavens, bright,
blinding, with aureole fine.

Wearer of the fiery disk and
Gleaming armour, chariot
driving glory, skirting round
your course without variate,
watching, encircling, hearing all
the earth. For your flames give birth
to Êôs, and past midheaven the
Hesperides trail your dearth.

---

[757] Derived from *PGM* I.160-165 and *PGM* IV.1115-1120.
[758] Derived from *PGM* II.64-183.

Nyx flees the heavens when she hears
the cracking of your whip so
close to your four horses' strong flanks
AAAAAAA EEEEEEE ĒĒĒĒĒĒĒ IIIIII OOOOOOO *YYYYYYY*
ŌŌŌŌŌŌŌ
O sceptre-wielding leader of
the Muses, giver of life,
come forth to your temple, golden
haired, to the sound of your fife.

Fire's friend and flaming guard I call
O *ARARAChChARA*
ĒPHTh*I*SIKĒRE, *and hail, three*
Moirai: Klotho spins the law
Lakhesis who allots the time
and Atropos at the end.
Fate abater, I call you, who
are great in heaven. Descend,
ruler of God's endless dream.

Still kneeling, lift your right hand and touch the floor with your left. Say:

Hail,[759] *Lord, who beneath the earth makes*
his dwelling in thick-shaded
Tartaros' meadow. Earthly
god of a realm vast faded,
sceptre-bearer, accept this prayer,
Pluton, keeper of the keys
to the entire Earth. Its gates
are yours to open or freeze.

To humanity you give fruit
in abundance, and your lot
fell to the third realm, earth, queen of
all, basis of gods, and plot
upon which mortal live. Your throne
lies in a shadowy realm,

---

759 Based *on Orphic Hymn* XVII and *PGM* IV. 885-895.

endless Hades and Acheron,
and life you do overwhelm.

Cloaked in gloom, you took Kore as
your bride, taking her away
from her meadow home. Your deathly
steeds brought her to Hades gray
gates. You alone judge obscure deeds
and conspicuous. Frenzied
god, come with favor to the devout.
OSIR-PhRE who is gloried.

Pluton-Helios, I speak your
names, which thrice-grand Hermes wrote
in Heliopolis in the
sacred script, from this I quote:

ARBAKŌRIPh MĒNIAM ŌBAŌB ABNIŌB MĒRIM BAIAX ChENŌR PhĒNIM ŌRA ŌRĒSIOY OYSIRI PNIAMOYSIRI PhRĒOYSIRI HŌRIOYSIRI NAEIŌROYSIRI MĒNIMOYSIRI MNĒKOYSIRI PhLĒKOYSIRI PĒLĒMYSIRI ŌNIŌ RABKOYSIRI ANIŌBOYSIRI AMĒAOYSIRI ANŌROYSIRI AMĒNĒPhBOYSIRI I AMĒNIOYSIRI XŌNIŌR ĒOYROYSIRI

Be present, O great Hades, you
great image maker, that I
may receive your blessings and your
communion before I die.

The session is complete. Extinguish the lamps and disrobe, folding and tying the robes as before and placing them on or in the altar. If the room is used for other purposes, store everything in the altar and place it to the side, otherwise you may now leave the *temenos*.

Phase Two: Devotional

Phase two is nearly identical to phase one. On the evening before the winter or summer solstice, re-consecrate the *temenos* using the same rite as before. The daily prayer sessions remain the same, with two sessions during weekdays and three on Sundays. The only addition is a midday session on Wednesday dedicated to Hermes Khthonios. On these days the fourth lamp is added to the altar below the first three. This hymn is said after those to the Demiurges while keeling on one knee and touching the floor with you left hand.

Hail,[760] *Zeus' son and messenger,*
eye of Helios, basis
of speech. Send forth your oracles,
show me my god's great faces.
Child of the divine mind, sacred
herald and divine voice, hear
my hymn, arise on winged feet
and to me do you appear.

Son of Maia, child no longer,
dweller on the road most dire. Guide
of daimons and mortal souls both
upon death's long path both sides
you tread. You frequent Kore's home
leading necessity's souls
to Pluton's dire judgment hall
which none but Hades controls.

ThŌOYTh PhŌKENTAZEPSEY AERChThAThOYMI SONKTAI KALBANAChAMBRĒ

Sacred wand in hand, O Hermes,
lead me to my soul's high chain.
Travelling through Hades dark halls,
I call you, guide of the slain.

760 Derived from *Orphic Hymn* 57 and *PGM* V.400-22.

Phase Three: The Invocation of the Daimon

Phase three begins six months after the start of phase two, on the solstice. The first year of devotional work serves to liken yourself to the powers governing the leader gods and their daimons. While the first two phases are ritualized, what follows is a more complex and involved ritual practice.

The invocation may be performed up to three times, depending both on your success or failure to receive knowledge of your daimon and the day on which the solstice falls. The year of devotion, combined with the invocation, for numerous reasons, may not have elevated your soul to the degree necessary for contact with either Hermes or the daimon. However, it is possible a repetition of the invocation will bring about the necessary contact.[761] The invocation proper may be performed on the solstice as well as the following Sunday and Wednesday. If the solstice falls on a Sunday or Wednesday, the days associated with the sun and Hermes, it may be performed on the following appropriate day. If two or three repetitions of the invocation fail to bring about communion with the daimon wait until the following solstice and begin again with phase one, taking the time in between to further purify yourself with the philosophical life.

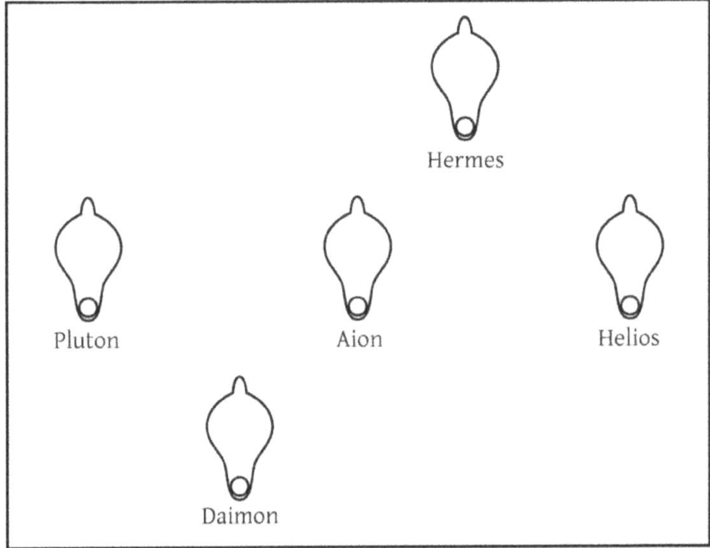

Altar Diagram

Set up the *temenos* as before, adding a banner bearing a triangle within a rectangle, or some other symbol representing Mercury and Hermes. Place this in the part of the *temenos* closest to the planet's position at the time of the ritual.

[761] Repetition of ritual is not uncommon in the *PGM*.

Place all five lamps on the altar as in the diagram above. The lamps are placed in the shape of the letter Chi, representing the World Soul. The line representing the circle of sameness is occupied by the lamps for Demiurges, the circle of difference holds Hermes and the daimon. The folded and tied robes, anointing oil, and incense can be placed in the spaces to the top and bottom of the lamps. During this phase it is unnecessary to consecrate the *temenos* before as it is consecrated with each performance of the invocation.

Take a shower, bath or otherwise clean yourself thoroughly before entering the temple to begin. Dress in simple white clothing, over which you will wear your robes. Before entering the temple, purify yourself with lustral water. Enter the *temenos*, saying:

> *I speak to those who lawfully may hear:*
> *Depart all ye profane, and close the doors*

. Follow this with a loud clap of the hands. Close the door to the room. Purify yourself with the lustral water while saying:

> *So therefore first the Priest who governeth the works of Fire, must sprinkle with the Water of the loud-resounding Sea.*

Light the incense and fumigate yourself. Add more incense as necessary and do not let it go out during the consecration. As you feel the water on your skin and inhale the incense, see a heavy shell around your body. With each sprinkle and fumigation the shell cracks and pieces fall away. Once purified and fumigated, do the same to your ritual space and altar. See these actions illuminating the room. When the room and altar have been purified and fumigated, set the water and incense aside. Stand before the altar, holding your arms up in a gesture of welcome, and say:

> *This is the hour for prayer to the gods. I invoke all the gods and Zeus-Helios, who reigns over them, with all my essence, and all my power, and all my activities.*

Kneel on both knees, look up, and raise your hands, palms facing up, fingers away from your body. Say:

> *O gods, be propitious.*

Lift one knee and touch the floor with your right hand. Say:

> *O gods, be propitious.*

Remove your right hand from the floor and touch it with the left. Say:

> *O gods, be propitious.*

Touch the floor with both hands and knees. Say:

> *O Aion, be propitious. O Helios, be propitious. O Pluton, be propitious.*

Sprinkle and fumigate each lamp and then light each one after a brief prayer:

> *Hail to you, invisible sun,*
> *holy Aion. I invoke*
> *you by your hidden and holy*
> *names. Be present without cloak:*

AChBA IEOYĒOĒ IAĒAIĒŌĒYOEI

Envision this lamp emitting the brilliant, blinding nothing of the eternal and invisible sun. Breathe deeply of the lamp's pre-essential light. Light the second lamp, saying:

Hail to you, mighty Helios,
Great lord of noeric flames,
I invoke you by these holy
word, come to your calling Names:
AChEBYKRŌM ANAG BIAThIARBAR BERBI
SChILATOYR BOYPhROMTRŌM

Envision this lamp emitting the brilliant, blinding light of the noeric sun and breathe in its solar rays. Light the third lamp, saying:

Hail to you, chthonic Pluton,
Lord of daimons, I invoke
you by these hidden and holy
Names, by which my soul awoke:
YESEMMIGADŌN MAARChAMA

Envision the lamp emitting the dark light of the sun at midnight, breathing in the sub-lunar rays.

Anoint your forehead and hands and then the collars of your robes. Next, anoint the four sides of the altar. Moving clockwise around the *temenos*, anoint the window and door sills. Return to the altar and set aside the oil. Put on the robes. Kneel on both knees, placing the palms of your hands on the floor. Looking up to the heavens, say:

Hail, King, I call to you God of
Gods, mighty, boundless and pure,
beyond description, established,
great Aion who does endure.

PhŌGALŌA ERDĒNEY MEREMŌGGA

Never leave me, O lord Aion,
Be inseparable, Lord,
From now until to the end of my
days. Make me always your ward.

If there is an east facing window in the *temenos*, kneel before it and touch the floor with your right hand. If there is no window, face the east and do the same. Look up to the heavens and pray:

Hail, fire's dispenser, the world's
all-seeing king, O great lord
Helios, with noble steeds, the
eye of Zeus, guarding with sword
in hand the earth, far-seeing one,
who travels high paths, divine
gleam, who moves through the heavens, bright,
blinding, with aureole fine.

Wearer of the fiery disk and
Gleaming armour, chariot
driving glory, skirting round
your course without variate,
watching, encircling, hearing all
the earth. For your flames give birth
to Êôs, and past midheaven the
Hesperides trail your dearth.

Nyx flees the heavens when she hears
the cracking of your whip so
close to your four horses' strong flanks
AAAAAAA EEEEEEE ĒĒĒĒĒĒĒ
IIIIIII OOOOOOO YYYYYYY ŌŌŌŌŌŌŌ
O sceptre-wielding leader of
the Muses, giver of life,
come forth to your temple, golden
haired, to the sound of your fife.

Fire's friend and flaming guard I call
O *ARARAChChARA*
ĒPhThISIKĒRE, and hail, three
Moirai: Klotho spins the law
Lakhesis who allots the time
and Atropos at the end.
Fate abater, I call you, who
are great in heaven. Descend,
ruler of God's endless dream.

If there is a west facing window, stand and move kneel before it on one knee, touching the floor with your left hand. If there is no window, turn to face the west and kneel in the same manner. Look up to the heavens and pray:

Hail, Lord, who beneath the earth makes
his dwelling in thick-shaded
Tartaros' meadow. Earthly
god of a realm vast faded,
sceptre-bearer, accept this prayer,
Pluton, keeper of the keys
to the entire Earth. Its gates
are yours to open or freeze.

To humanity you give fruit
in abundance, and your lot
fell to the third realm, earth, queen of
all, basis of gods, and plot
upon which mortal live. Your throne
lies in a shadowy realm,
endless Hades and Acheron,
and life you do overwhelm.

Cloaked in gloom, you took Kore as
your bride, taking her away
from her meadow home. Your deathly
steeds brought her to Hades gray
gates. You alone judge obscure deeds
and conspicuous. Frenzied
god, come with favor to the devout.
OSIR-PhRE who is gloried.

Pluton-Helios, I speak your
names, which thrice-grand Hermes wrote
in Heliopolis in the
sacred script, from this I quote:

ARBAKŌRIPh MĒNIAM ŌBAŌB ABNIŌB MĒRIM BALAX ChENŌR PhĒNIM ŌRA ŌRĒSIOY OYSIRI PNIAMOYSIRI PhRĒOYSIRI HŌRIOYSIRI NAEIŌROYSIRI MĒNIMOYSIRI MNĒKOYSIRI PhLĒKOYSIRI P ĒLĒMYSIRI ŌNIŌ RABKOYSIRI ANIŌBOYSIRI

AMĒAOYSIRI ANŌROYSIRI AMĒNĒPhBOYSIRI I AMĒNIOYSIRI XŌNIŌR ĒOYROYSIRI

Be present, O great Hades, you
great image maker, that I
may receive your blessings and your
communion before I die.

Stand and move to the banner of Hermes. Kneel on one knee, touching the floor with your left hand. Pray:

Hail, Zeus' son and messenger,
eye of Helios, basis
of speech. Send forth your oracles,
show me my god's great faces.
Child of the divine mind, sacred
herald and divine voice, hear
my hymn, arise on winged feet
and to me do you appear.

Son of Maia, child no longer,
dweller on the road most dire. Guide
of daimons and mortal souls both
upon death's long path both sides
you tread. You frequent Kore's home
leading necessity's souls
to Pluton's dire judgment hall
which none but Hades controls.

ThOŌYTh PhŌKENTAZEPSEY AERChThAThOYMI SONKTAI KALBANAChAMBRĒ

Sacred wand in hand, O Hermes,
lead me to my soul's high chain.
Travelling through Hades dark halls,
I call you, guide of the slain.

Return to the altar. Add incense and say:

Hail and be gracious to me, oh Pronoia and Psychê, as I offer this incense in your honour. Hail, you, the daimon of this place, and the present hour, and the present day-

and every day. Hail, Psychê Kosmou. Hail, Helios, who has established himself as invisible light over the holy firmament ORKORĒThARA.

First origin of my origin, AEĒIOYŌ. *Fire of my soul given by the god of the mixing bowl, craftsman of the fiery cosmos, to my mixture of the mixtures in me,* AAAAAAA EEEEEEE ĒĒĒĒĒĒĒ IIIIII OOOOOOO YYYYYYY ŌŌŌŌŌŌŌ. *O lord of nocturnal and implacable thunder, chthonic Zeus* OSIR-PhRE, *who shaped my body from the four elements* ĒY ĒIA EĒ, MMM, ŌŌŌ AAA EEE, YĒ YŌĒ. *I, [your name], whose mother is [name], have stood in your presence and sacrifice to you. Now, if it is your will,* OSIR-PhRE *give me immortal birth from your holy realm. Seat me upon my fully winged chariot that I may know my underlying nature. So that after the pressure of Necessity recedes I may gaze upon the immortal realm, that I may be born again in thought,* PEPh ThA PhŌ ZA PhNEB ENN OY NI, *and know the eternal daimon set over my by the hand of the god who holds me.*

Today I will behold with immortal eyes – I, born mortal from mortal womb but transformed by the tremendous power of holy Aion, master of the fiery diadems, ZARAChThŌ *– I, sanctified through holy consecrations – while there subsists in me from the beginning the might of my soul, once fallen, now set towards reversion, which I will behold once Necessity is past and Pronoia reigns over me. I, [name], whose mother is [name], stand before you, O Pluton, O image maker, according to the immutable word of god,* EYĒ YIA EĒI AŌ EAIY IYA IEŌ. *I set aside my mortal nature, perishable and impermanent, to incline towards the immortal heavens and my true and eternal essence. Lift me, raise me, reveal to me, lord of the immortal brilliance,* ŌĒY AEŌ ĒYA EŌĒ ŌYAE . *For I am the son* PsYChŌN DEMOY PROChŌ PRŌA, *I am* MARChARPhON MOY PRŌPSYChŌN PRŌE!

See divine rays flooding the *temenos*. Breathe them in three times, filling yourself with as much of the divine glory as you are able. Look upwards and see the ceiling above you torn away, revealing the sky and the planets and all the stars of the heavens, the bodies of the visible gods. Behold the gods above you, even as they behold you below. Watch as they ride their chariots in their orbits around the heavens. The gods are followed by a myriad of beings, shining like stars. One of these, still as yet indistinct, flashes in your eyes. The words of the gods are a glory of inaudible, immortal roar. Immediately place your finger against your mouth and say:

Silence! Silence! Silence! Symbol of the eternal Demiurgos, guard me, O Silence, NEChThEIR ThANMELOY! PROPROPhEGGĒ MORIOS PROPhYR PROPhEGGĒ NEMEThIRE ARPSENTEN PITĒTMI MEŌY ENARTh PhYRKEChŌ PsYRIDARIŌ TYRĒ PhILBA.

See the heavenly gods still in their chariots, voices quiet, their gaze upon you one of eternal benevolence. Once all is calm in the heavens, say:

Holy Pluton-Helios, OSIR-PhRE IAŌ PhŌGALŌA ERDĒNEY MEREMŌGGA, *send me your messenger, he who walks between the worlds as no other may tread. He who circles the four corners of heaven. Come, Lord Hermes, by your manifold names,* LAMPhThEN OYŌThI OYASThEN OYŌThI OAMENŌTh ENThOMOYCH. *Come, Lord Hermes, serve well, benefactor of the world. Hear me and make me agreeable to my holy daimon, whose name is known to*

> *you. Come, PhARNAThAR BARAChĒL ChThA, for I am a star shining forth from the deep, OXY XERThEYTh!*

See a rising star, brilliant and flashing. As the star approaches inhale its rays. Do this three times, inhaling as fully as possible.

> *I know you, Lord Hermes, and you know me. I am you and you are me. And so do everything for me as I do so for myself, and may you turn within me and lead from the realm of Pluton-Hades my daimon. For the daimon and I are one: mixed in the same holy vessel, sewn into the orbit of one god, linked by adamantine chains. Let me know that holy Child, born upon the shoulder of the celestial, fiery steed, clothed with gold, armed with light. PYThORON PhThIONĒ ThŌYTh, act immediately, quickly, with the haste of a winged sandal. IAŌ SABAŌ ADŌNAIE ABLANAThANALBA AKRAMMAChAMAREI, give the keys to your kingdom to your servant and messenger that I may know the bond of my soul, who guides me the days of my life. For I have put on the armour of resounding Light, and I am fortified with the triple-barbed strength that empowers the soul and mind. I am filled with your symbols, O lord, and would walk with you upon empyrean ways.*

The earth will crack and the heavens rush downwards until they meet before you. From the darkened skies the rising star glows brilliantly, a brilliant chain running from it to your soul. Say:

> *O holy daimon, my soul's guide and companion, come to me, be known to me, give me your knowledge and guidance that I may revert to my true nature and know the god which reigns over my soul. By the names IAŌ SABAŌ BARBARE ThIŌTh LAILAMPS OSORNŌPhRI EMPhERA, the god of heaven and daimons, come unto me and reveal your name!*

The daimon will approach you and take a form meaningful to you, but not of your choosing. Repeat this final prayer until the daimon reveals its name, and how it should be contacted, and what offerings are appropriate to it and its god. Ask that it reveal your leader god and the nature of your soul. The daimon will reveal what is necessary and then depart, though it will always be with you, guiding you, rewarding you, and submitting you to the will of the god.

If you have successfully gained knowledge of your daimon, it is now time for prayer and thanksgiving. When you are finished, you may extinguish the lamps and leave the *temenos*, allowing the incense to burn completely. If you have not succeeded, you may try again as outlined above. This ends the invocation of the personal daimon.

Appendices

Appendix A

An Apophatic Theoria

Pseudo-Dionysius is largely silent on the subject of worship outside of the liturgical framework of the *Celestial Hierarchy*. However, his apophatic work in *The Mystical Theology*, when combined with the positive theology of *The Divine Names*, provides a framework for what we may call "worship in silence."

Concerning apophatic statements about God, Dionysius writes:

> *"...it being our duty both to attribute and affirm all the attributes of things existing to It, as Cause of all, and more properly to deny them all to It, as being above all, and not to consider the negations to be in opposition to the affirmations, but far rather that It, which is above every abstraction and definition, is above the privations."*[762]

Taking this into consideration, what follows is an apathetic *theoria*. Unlike previous contemplations in this book, this *theoria* takes the form of a poem. The poem begins by affirming many divine names as found throughout *The Divine Names*. Following this, those qualities impossibly connected to God are denied, as are the previously affirmed qualities. To leave behind everything that is understandable and not understandable, the negation is finally also negated, so that nothing discursive is left to grasp, allowing Nous flood the practitioner's consciousness.

Unspeakable are you, the One
above every speech and thought.
Perfect are you who is One, whose
Divine perfection is sought.

Great are you, Holy of Holies.
Lord of Lords who is above
all things, I worship you. God of
Gods whom all below do love.

---

[762] MT I.2.1000B

Magnificent is your great Peace,
which originates Being-
and Life- and Power- itself.
From you no one is fleeing.

Divine are you, the source of
all life from Eternal Life.
Praise is yours who distributes
forever lives free from strife.

Blessed are you, Omnipotent
and holy. All is within
your grasp, oh Ancient of Days, lift
me above the worldly din.

Glorious is your Power and
Righteousness. Your Salvation
brings forth the Redemption of all
people without cessation.

Sacred is the Wisdom of your
Mind, which thinks eternal Word
from which Truth flows. Sacred is the
holy Faith with which I'm gird.

Holy are you that is the Good,
whose Light illumines with Love
yourself as the source of Being
and Beauty like a white dove.

Nothing that partakes of you lacks
existence. Evil's grasp will
not hold, though the accident of
non-being leaves all life chill.

No ignorance rests in you, the
noetic source of hidden
truth. Falsehood finds no place in you
and no faith is forbidden.

Nowhere is inequality
found in your justice. You save
without discrimination lives
where slavery does lave.

Beyond the temporal cosmos
lies your vast eternity.
No time exists within you, no
space marks your fraternity.

Above mortality is your
eternitude. Not deathless
for life is posterior to
you who does leave me breathless.

Dependent upon nothing, you
are beyond all needs. Giving
all, never used, nothing lost, no
change but in earthly living.

None are before you, princes and
messengers kneel before you.
Secondary to nothing, you
all who thought they knew.

Without imperfection are you,
who lies beyond manifold
existence. Without the walls
of many is no foothold.

Words without end give meaningless
titles. You are and are not.
There is you and no you. Not One
nor more. I know I know naught.

Appendix B

Guide to Pronouncing Hieratic Names

A: Alpha = ah as in *father*

B: Beta = b

G: Gamma = g as in *game*, but n as in *ink* before K, X, Kh or another G

D: Delta = d

E: Epsilon = e as in *met*

Z: Zeta = sd as in *wisdom*

Ē: Eta = ai as in *air*

Th: Theta = th as in *thing*

I: Iota = e as in *need*

K: Kappa = k

L: Lambda = l

M: Mu = m

N: Nu = n

X: Xi = x as in *axe*

O: Omicron = o as in *lot*

P: Pi = p

R: Rho = r

S: Sigma = s as in *sign*

T: Tau = t

Y: Upsilon = u as in *you*

Ph: Phi = ph

Kh: Chi = ch as in the Scottish *loch*

Ps: Psi = ps

Ō: Omega = oa as in *broad*

Dipthongs:

AI = ai as in *aisle*

OI = oi as in *oil*

AY = ow as in *cow*

OY – oo as in *cool*

EI = ei as in *rein*

YI = we

EY/ ĒY = eu as in *feud*

Appendix 3

Glossary

agalma (ἄγαλμα), statue, shrine

agalma empsychon (ἄγαλμα ἔμψυχον), ensouled statue or shrine

agape (αγάπη), love

Aion (Aἰών), Eternity, the pre-essential Demiurgos

aletheia (ἀλήθεια), truth, the substance of the noetic and/or psychic realms, the primary virtue of the celestial Demiurge

alitheias prostatis kai sofias (ἀληθείας προστάτης και σοφιας), master or protector of truth and wisdom, title of Amoun and the celestial Demiurge

anamnesis (ανάμνησης), recollection, the true form of learning according to Platonic thought

agalma, pl. *agalmata* (αγαλμα, pl. αγαλματα), statue, image, shrine. A composite thing made holy, such as a talisman or ensouled statue.

ametheketos (ἀμέθεκτοσ), the first, unparticipated moment of Eternal Time. The hypostasis as it is in itself.

andreias (ἀνδρείας) bravery, courage

apophatiki theologia (αποφατική θεολογία): Apophatic theology

archon, pl. *archontes* (ἀρχων, pl. ἀρχοντες), governors, one of Iamblichus' terms for the visible and hylic gods

aretin edoke pan toian (Gk: ἀρετὴν ἔδωκε παντοαν), saviour of the whole world, title of Asklepios and the sub-lunar Demiurge.

autarchis (αὐτάρχης,), principle of himself, title of the pre-essential Demiurge

autopater (αὐτοράτωρ), father of himself, title of the pre-essential Demiurge

barbara onomata (βάρβαρη ονόματα), "foreign names," theurgic divine names that only have meaning to the gods

cherniptomi (χερνίπτομαι), Be purified! An exclamation proclaimed in the east during rites of fumigation in Hellenic tradition

Demiurgos (Δημιουργός), Craftsman, public worker

dimiourgikos nou (δημιουργικὸς νοῦς), "demiurgic intellect," or "creative mind," a title of Amoun and the celestial Demiurge.

dikaiosinis (διχαιοσύνης), justice.

dunamis (δύναμης), power, the entirety of the soul's potential activities

eidolon (εἰδωλον), A reflected image, ontologically posterior to an *eikon.*

eidos (εἶδος), Form, universal archetype. Also rendered as idea.

eidolopoietike techne (εἰδωλοιητικὴ τέχη), non-theurgic "image making"

eidolopoios (εἰδωλοποιὸς), image-maker, title of the sub-lunar Demiurge.

eikon (εικών), image, ontologically superior to an *eidolon.*

Eimarmei (Εἱμαρμέη), Fate.

energeia (ενέργεια), activity, what the soul does.

enyla eida (ἔνυλα εἴδη), forms in matter.

epekeina tou nou (ἐπέκεινα ιου νου), Supra-intelligible, beyond the mind, a title of Aion and the pre-essential Demiurge.

epistrophê (επιστροφή), reversion, circularly returning to the monad of the soul.

epouranion theon igoumenon (ἐπουρανίων θεῶν ἡγούμενον), leader of the celestial gods, a title of Kmeph and the celestial Demiurge.

eros (ἐρως), love, a daimon, god, and/or substance of the noetic realm and virtue connected to Aion.

hamartia (ἁμαρτία), sin, to miss the mark, doing something for the good that ends up bad

harmonia (αρμονία), harmony, concordance, unity, joining.

hieratike (ιερατικη), liturgy, another name for theurgy.

hieratike technê (ιερατικη τεχνη), sacred art, another name for theurgy.

hierougia (ιερουργια), sacred rites, another name for theurgy. Used by Dionysius as a correlate to the pagan Neoplatonists' use of "theurgy."

Henad, henas (ἑνας) unities. Pre-essential gods in Proclus' system, the hypercosmic gods in Iamblichus', within which all being are unified.

henosis (ἑνωσης) divine union, unity with the divine.

ho haplos hen (ὁ ἁπλῶς ἕν), simply One, the One after the ineffable One.

hylē (ὕλη), wood, matter or the "stuff of matter."

hypodochai (υποδοχέα), receptacle [for the gods].

idea (ιδέα), Form, universal archetype. Also rendered as *eidos.*

idean ton onton (ἰδέαν των ὄντων) Idea of Being, title of Aion and the pre-essential Demiurge.

kalon (καλλονή), beauty.

*kata methexin (*κατὰ μέθεξιν), in participation. The final moment of Eternal Time. the hypostasis as it is reflected in those lower being.

katharsis (κάθαρσης), purification, the first of the divine hierarchy's functions.

kathartis psychon (καθαρτὴς ψυχῶν), purifier of souls, title of the sub-lunar Demiurge.

kosmos (κόσμος) world, realm, universe.

kreittonon genon (κρεηττόνων γδνῶν), "greater kinds" or "superior class of beings," the entities superior to human souls.

logos, pl, *logoi* (λόγος, , λόγοι), word, argument, reason, proportion, intelligence reason-principle, divine ratio.

megistos daimon (μέγιστος δαίμων), master daimon, title of the sub-lunar Demiurge.

metachomenos (μετεχόμενος), participated, the second moment of Eternal Time. The hypostasis as viewed by ontologically posterior beings.

metalipsis (μετάηψις), Participation. The engagement of ontologically inferior beings with their ontological superiors.

miasma (Μίασμα), ritual pollution.

mimesis (μίμησις), imitation.

monas ek tou enos (μονὰς ἐκ τοῦ ἑνός), monad from the One, title of the pre-essential Demiurge.

mone (μονή), remaining, staying with one's divine principle, the monad of the soul.

monoeide (μονοειδῆ), uniform, the single essential nature of the gods.

mustagogia (μυσταγωγια), initiated mysteries, another term for theurgy.

noesis (νοήσις), intellection.

noetarchis prosagoreoetai (νομτάρχης προσαγορεύεται), principle of intellection, title of the pre-essential Demiurge.

noun einai aton eaton noounta (νοῦν εἶναι αὐτὸν ἑαυτὸν νοοῦντα,), intellect thinking himself, title of Kmeph and the celestial Demiurge

nous (νοῦς) mind. Capitalized as Nous, the divine Mind and lowest part of the Noeric realm.

ochema-pneuma (ὄχημα-πνεῦμα), pneumatic vehicle.

oikeios daimon (οἰκειος δαίμων), the personal daimon.

oikodespotis (οικοδεσπότης), master of the house, the almuetz, the planetary ruler of a horoscope.

on (ὂν), Being.

ontos (ὄντος), "that which is," the root of the word "ontology."

ousia (ουσία), essence.

ousiopator (οὐσιοπάτωρ), father of essence, title of the pre-essential Demiurge.

pantelos arrheton (παντελῶς ἄρρητον), entirely ineffable, title of the transcendent One.

Pantocrator (παντοκράτωρ), Ruler of All, a title of Christ as the noeric Demiurge.

patros ton demiourgon (πατρὸς τῶν δημιουργῶν), Father of the Demiurges, title of the pre-essential Demiurge.

phantasia (φαντασία), imagination.

pharmaka (φαρμακα), medicines, poisons, anesthetic or stimulants, kinds of drug, used in both medicine and theurgic practices.

philosophia (φιλοσοφία) philosophy, lit. Love of Wisdom. A philosopher is one who seeks after the object of their love; Wisdom..

philia (φιλία) love, given the connotation of "brotherly," as opposed to sexual, love in later Christianity.

photismos (φωτισμός), illumination, the second of the divine hierarchy's functions.

phroniseos (φρονήσεως) practical deliberation, prudence.

pistis (πιστις), faith, the substance of the sub-lunar realm, the primary virtue from the sub-lunar Demiurge.

pneuma (πνεῦμα), spirit, anima.

polis (πόλις), city, city-state, citizenship in a city-state.

prohödos (πρόοδος), procession, moving away, circularly or lineally, from the monad of the soul

Pronoia (Πρόνοια), Providence, lit. Foresight

proousios (προούσιος), pre-essential

pro tos duados (πρὸ τῆς δυάδος), that which is before duality, a title of the simply One.

psyche (ψυχή), the soul.

psychopompos (ψυχοπομπός), guide of the soul.

sema, pl. *semeia* (σῆμα pl. σημεία), signs, divine signs made manifest in generation.

sophrosýnis (σωφροσύνης) literally "sound-mindedness." Temperance, moderation, self-control, the lower form of the virtue of wisdom.

sophia (σοφία), theoretical wisdom, the higher form of the virtue of wisdom.

symbolon, pl. *symbola* (σύμβολον, pl. σύμβολα), divine symbols made manifest in generation.

synthema, pl. *synthemata* (συνθεμα, pl. συνθεματα) signatures or tokens, divine tokens made manifest in generation.

technê (τεχνε) art or technical skill, human-originated crafts and techniques.

teleiosis (τελείωσις), perfection, to achieve the goal, the third of the divine hierarchy's functions.

telestike technê (τελεστική τέχνη), telestic art. There is no adequate translation of this term, but it includes talismancy, statue animation and other forms of theurgy.

telos (τέλος) end, goal, ultimate purpose.

temenos (τέμενος), a sacred precinct from the size of a shrine to an entire city-state.

theoria (θεωρία), contemplation.

theosis (θέωσις), divinization.

theosophia (θεοσοφια), divine wisdom, another name for theurgy.

theos theon (θεὸς θεῶν), god of gods, title of the pre-essential Demiurge.

theourgos, a practitioner of theurgy, a theurgist.

theourgia (θεουργια), theurgy, lit. "divine activity." Ritual activity in imitation of the gods or God. Used by Dionysius to indicate Christ's divine work, not ritual enactments of that work.

to hen on (τὸ ἓν ὄν), One-Being or One-Existent, the final moment of the One, the source of being..

tou agathon (του αγαθον), the Good, a form of the One.

tou agathou idean (του αγαθού ιδέαν), the Idea of the Good.

vasilea ton olon (βασιλέα των ὅλων), king of all, title of Helios and the celestial Demiurge

zoe (ζωή), life.

Bibliography

Primary Sources:

Abraham of Worms, *The Book of Abramelin.* Translated by Steven Guth. Lake Worth, FL: Ibis Press, 2006.

—. *The Book of the Sacred Magic of Abra-Melin the Mage.* Translated by S. L. MacGregor Mathers. Wellingborough, UK: Aquarian Press, 1976.

Agrippa, Henry Cornelius. *The Three Books of Occult Philosophy.* Edited by Donald Tyson. St. Paul, MN: Llewellyn Publications, 2000.

Anonymous. *The Picatrix: Liber Rubeus Edition.* Translated by John Michael Greer and Christopher Warnock. Adocentyn Press, 2011.

Aristotle. *The Basic Works of Aristotle.* edited by Richard McKeon. NY: Random House, 1941.

—. *Nichomachean Ethics,* translated by Martin Ostwald. NY: The Bobbs-Merrill Company, Inc., 1962.

Betz, Hans Dieter, editor. *The PGM in Translation.* Chicago: University of Chicago Press, 1986.

Copenhaver, Brian P., translator. *Hermetica.* Cambridge, UK: Cambridge University Press, 1992.

Ficino, Marsilio. *De Amore: Commentary on Plato's* Symposium *on Love.* Translated by Sears Jayne. Dallas, TX: Spring Publications, Inc., 1985.

—. *Three Books on Life: A Critical Edition and Translation with Introduction and Notes.* Translated by Carol V. Kaske and John R. Clark. Tempe, AZ: Medieval & Renaissance Texts & Studies, 1998.

Iamblichus. *De Anima: Text, Translation, and Commentary.* Translated by John F. Finamore and John M. Dillon. Atlanta: Society of Biblical Literature, 2002.

—. *De Mysteriis.* Translated by Emma C. Clarke, John M. Dillon and Jackson P. Hershbell. Atlanta. GA: Society of Biblical Literature, 2003.

— *In Platonis Dialogos Commentariorum Fragmenta.* Translated by Dillon, John M. Wiltshire, UK: Prometheus Trust, 2009.

— *The Exhortation to Philosophy.* Translated by Thomas M. Johnson. Grand Rapids, MI: Phanes Press, 1988.

— *The Letters.* Translated by John M. Dillon and Wolfgang Polleichtner. Atlanta, GA: Society of Biblical Literature, 2009.

—. *On the Pythagorean Way of Life.* Translated by John Dillon and Jackson Hershbell. Atlanta, GA: Scholars Press, 1991.

— *The Theology of Arithmetic.* Translated by Robin Waterfield. Grand Rapids, MI: Phanes Press, 1988.

Ibn Qurra, Thabit. *Astral High Magic: De Imaginibus of Thabit Ibn Qurra.* Translated by John Michael Greer. Renaissance Astrology, 2011.

Josephus, Flavius. *Antiquities of the Jews.* Translated by William Whston. Project Gutenberg. Viewed 21 December, 2012. http://www.gutenberg.org/files/2848/2848-h/2848-h.htm.

Julian. *The Works of the Emperor Julian: Volume I.* Translated by Wilmer C. Wright, 352-441. Cambridge, MA: Harvard University Press, 1913.

—. *The Works of the Emperor Julian: Volume II.* Translated by Wilmer C. Wright, 352-441. Cambridge, MA: Harvard University Press, 1913.

Julianus the Theurgist. *The Chaldean Oracles: Text, Translation, and Commentary.* Translated by Majercik, Ruth Dorothy. Leiden, The Netherlands: Brill, 1989.

—. *The Chaldean Oracles of Zoroaster.* Edited by William Wynn Westcott. Northamptonshire, UK: Aquarian Press, 1983.

Kant, Immanuel. *Grounding for the Metaphysics of Morals.* Translated by James W. Ellington. Indianapolis, IN: Hacket, 1993.

Pearson, Birger A., trans. "Marsanes." In *The Nag Hammadi Library*, ed. James M. Robinson, 417-426. San Francisco: Harper & Row, 1977.

Plato. *Collected Dialogues.* edited by Edith Hamilton and Huntington Cairns. Princeton: Princeton University Press, 1980.

Plotinus. *The Enneads.* Translated by Stephan MacKenna. London: Penguin Books, 1991.

Porphyry. *De Abstinentia.* Translated by Thomas Taylor. Viewed October 25, 2012. http://www.ccel.org/ccel/pearse/morefathers/files/index.htm#Porphyry_Abstinence.

—. "Letter to Anebo." Translated by Thomas Taylor. Viewed October 25, 2012. http://www.ccel.org/ccel/pearse/morefathers/files/porphyry_anebo_02_text.htm.

—. "On the Life of Plotinus and the Arrangement of His Work." In *The Enneads.* Translated by Stephen MacKenna, cii-xxxv. London: Penguin Books, 1991.

Proclus. *Elements of Theology.* Translated by E. R. Dodds. Oxford: Clarendon Press, 1963.

—. *Hymns: Essays, Translations, Commentary.* Translated by Van Den Berg, R. M. Leiden, The Netherlands: Brill, 2001.

—. *On the Existence of Evils.* Translated by Jan Opsomer and Carlos Steel. Ithaca, NY: Cornell University Press, 2003.

Pseudo-Agrippa. *Of Occult Philosophy or Of Magical Ceremonies: The Fourth Book.* Edited by Robert Turner. PDF version compiled by Benjamine Rowe, 2000.

Pseudo-Dionysius. *The Complete Works.* Translated by Colm Luibheid. NY: Paulist Press, 1987.

—. *The Works of Dionysius the Areopagite.* Translated by John Parker. Veritatis Splendor Publications, 2013.

Pseudo-Dionysius. "Liturgy of St. Dionysius, Bishop of the Athenians: *Liturgiarum Orien. Collectio E. Renaudoti. T. ii. p. 201*, translated by Rev. John Parker. Viewed 10 January, 2013. http://www.voskrese.info/spl/dionysius-lit.html.

Sallustius. *Concerning the Gods and the Universe.* Translated by Arthur Darby Nock. Chicago: Ares Publishers, Inc., 1926.

Smoley, Richard, translator. "The Emerald Tablet of Hermes." In *Gnosis: Journal of the Western Inner Tradition* 40 (1996):17-19.

Synesius. *The Ten Hymns of Synesius, Bishop of Cyrene.* Translated by Alan Stevenson. Printed for private circulation, 1865.

Taylor, Thomas. *The Hymns of Orpheus.* London, UK: printed for the author, 1792.

Westernick, L.G., translator. *Anonymous Prolegomena to Platonic Philosophy.* Amsterdam: North-Holland Publishing Company, 1962.

Wise, Frederik, trans. "The Apocryphon of John." In *The Nag Hammadi Library*, ed. James M. Robinson, 98-116. San Francisco: Harper & Row, 1977.

Secondary Sources:

Alexandrakis, Aphrodite. "Neoplatonic Influences on Eastern Iconography: A Greek-rooted Tradition." In *Neoplatonism and Western Aesthetics*, edited by Aphrodite Alexandrakis and Nicholas J. Moutafakis, 75-88. Albany, NY: SUNY Press, 2002.

Ambrosi, Gerhard Michael. "Social Justice: Aristotle versus Pythagoreans – and Implications for Modern Debates." Lecture manuscript for the 13th Summer Institute for the History of Economic Thought, Jepson School of Leadership Studies, University of Richmond, VA, June 29-July 2, 2012. http://jepson.richmond.edu/conferences/adam-smith/paper12ambrosi.pdf.

Anastos, Milton V. "Pletho's Calendar and Liturgy." *Dumbarton Oaks Papers* 4 (1948): 183-305.

Benedict XVI. "General Audience: Pseudo-Dionysius the Areopagite." Viewed 6 February, 2012.

http://www.vatican.va/holy_father/benedict_xvi/audiences/2008/documents/hf_ben-xvi_aud_20080514_en.html.

Betts, Gavin and Henry, Alan. *Teach Yourself Ancient Greek: A Complete Course.* Chicago: Contemporary Publishing, 1993.

Betz, Hans Dieter. "The Delphic Maxim 'Know Yourself' in the PGM." *History of Religions* 2.2 (1981): 156-171.

Bradbury, Scott. "Julian's Pagan Revival and the Decline of Blood Sacrifice." *Phoenix* 49.4 (1995): 331-356.

Burns, Dylan. "Proclus and the Theurgic Liturgy of Pseudo-Dionysius." *Dionysius* XXII (2004): 111-132.

Butler, Edward P. "Offering to the Gods: A Neoplatonic Perspective." *Magic, Ritual, and Witchcraft* 2.1 (2007): 1-20.

Chlup, Radek. "Proclus' Theory of Evil: An Ethical Perspective." *The International Journal of the Platonic Tradition* 3 (2009): 26-57.

Clark, Dennis C. "Iamblichus' Egyptian Neoplatonic Theology in *De Mysteriis*." *The International Journal of the Platonic Tradition* 2 (2008): 164-205.

—. "The Gods as Henads in Iamblichus." *The International Journal of the Platonic Tradition* 4 (2010): 54-74.

Copenhaver, Brian P. "Hermes Trismegistus, Proclus, and the Question of a Philosophy of Magic in the Renaissance." In *Hermeticism and the Renaissance*, edited by Ingrid Merkel and Allen G. Debus,79-110. Washington, D.C.: Folger Books, 1988.

Corey, Isaac Preston. *Ancient fragments of the Phoenician, Chaldaean, Egyptian, Tyrian, Carthaginian, Indian, Persian and Other Writers*. London: William Pickering, 1832.

Darrow, F. S. "Studies in Orphism, VII: Concluding Study." In *The Theosophical Path*, vol IV. Edited by Katherine Tingley, 200-208. Point Loma, CA: New Century Corporation, 1913.

Devereux, James. A., S.J. "The Textual History of Ficino's *De Amore*." *Renaissance Quarterly* 28.2 (1975): 173-182.

Dillon, John. "Iamblichus and Henads Again." In *The Divine Iamblichus: Philosopher and Man of Gods*. Edited by H.J. Blumenthal and Gillian Clark, 48-54. London: Bristol Classical Press, 1993.

—. "Porphyry and Iamblichus in Proclus' *Commentary on the Paremenides*." In *The Great Tradition*. Edited by John M. Dillon, 21-48. Aldershot, Hampshire, UK: Ashgate Publishing Limited, 1997.

—. "The Theology of Julian's Hymn to King Helios." *Ítaca: Quaderns Catalans de Cultura Clàssica* 14-15 (1999): 103-115.

Dodds, E. R. *The Greeks and the Irrational*. Berkeley, CA: University of California Press, 1973.

Ewing, Katherine P. "Dreams from a Saint: Anthropological Atheism and the Temptation to Believe." *American Anthropologist* 96 (1994): 571-583.

Finamore, John F. *Iamblichus and the Theory of the Vehicle of the Soul*. Chico, CA: Scholars Press, 1985.

—. "Iamblichus' Interpretation of the *Parmenides*' Third Hypothesis." In *Plato's* Parmenides *and Its Heritage: History and Interpretation From the Old Academy*, vol. 2. Edited. by John D. Turner and Kevin Corrigan, 119-132. Atlanta: Society of Biblical Literature, 2010.

Gandz, Solomon. "The Calendar-Reform of Pletho (c. 1355 – c. 1450): Its Significance and Its Place in the History of the Calendar." *Osiris* 9 (1950): 199-210.

Hadot, Pierre. *Philosophy as a Way of Life*. Translated by Michael Chase. Malden, MA: Blackwell Publishing, 1995.

Hanegraaff, Wouter J. "The Platonic Frenzies in Marsilio Ficino." In *Myths, Martyrs and Modernity: Studies in the History of Religions in Honour of Jan N. Bremmer*, edited by Jitse Dijkstra, Justin Kroesen and Yme Kuiper, 553-567. Leiden, The Netherlands: Brill, 2010.

Hardon, John A., S.J. *Modern Catholic Dictionary*. Garden City, NY: Doubleday & Company, Inc., 1980.

Hellenismo, "On purifications- some details . . ." Viewed 2 January, 2013. http://hellenismo.wordpress.com/2012/09/01/on-purifications-some-details/.

Hines, Brian. *Return to the One: Plotinus's Guide to God-Realization*. Salem, OR: Adrasteia Publishing, 2004.

Hoeller, Stephan A. "The Gnostic Catechism." Viewed 9 March, 2012. http://www.gnosis.org/ecclesia/catechism.htm

Idel, Moshe. *Studies in Ecstatic Kabbalah*. Albany, NY: State University of New York Press, 1988.

Johnston, Sarah Iles. "Animating Statues: A Case Study in Ritual." *Arethusa* 41.3 (2008): 445-477.

Kieckhefer, Richard. *Magic in the Middle Ages*. NY: Cambridge University Press, 1989.

Krulak, Todd. "The Animated Statue and the Ascension of the Soul: Ritual and the Divine Image in Late Platonism." PhD diss., University of Pennsylvania, 2009.

Kupperman, Jeffrey S. "Eros and Agape in Dionysius the Areopagite." *The Journal of the Western Mystery Tradition 25* (2013): http://jwmt.org/v3n25/kupperman.html.

—. "Marsilio Ficino and the Neoplatonic Roots of Modern Hermeticism." *The Gnostic* 5 (2012): 151-159.

—. "Hitbodedut, Theurgia and the Modern Magus." *The Journal of the Western Mystery Tradition* 22 (2011): http://www.jwmt.org/v2n20/hitbodedut.html.

Lankila, Tuomo. "The Corpus Areopagiticum as a Crypto-Pagan Project." *Journal for Late Antique Religion and Culture* 5 (2011): 14-40.

Levy, Donald. "The Definition of Love in Plato's Symposium." *Journal of the History of Ideas* 40.2 (1979): 285-291.

Lewy, Hans. "A Latin Hymn to the Creator Ascribed to Plato." *The Harvard Theological Review*, 39(4), 1946: 243-258.

Lloyd, David R. "Symmetry and Beauty in Plato." *Symmetry* 2 (2010): 455-465.

Majercik, Ruth. "The Existence-Life-Intellect Triad in Gnosticism and Neoplatonism." *Classical Quarterly* 42(ii), (1992): 475-488.

Mazur, Zeke. "Plotinus' Philosophical Opposition to Gnosticism and the Implicit Axiom of Continuous Hierarchy." In *History of Platonism*, edited by Robert Berchman and John Finamore, 95-112. University Press of the South, 2005.

Mead, G.R.S. *Echoes from the Gnosis*. Wheaton, IL: Quest Books, 2006.

Merlan, Philip. "Plotinus and Magic." *The History of Science Society* 44.4 (1953): 341-3.

Needleman, Jacob. *The Heart of Philosophy*. San Francisco: Harper, 1986.

O'Meara, Dominic J. "Patterns of Perfection in Damascius' *Life of Isidore*." *Phronesis* 51.1 (2006): 74-90.

— *Platonopolis: Platonic Political Philosophy in Late Antiquity*. Oxford: Clarendon Press, 2003.

— "Plato's *Republic* in the School of Iamblichus." In *La Repubblica di Platone Nella Tradizione Antica*, ed. by Mario Vegetti and Michele Abbate. 193-205. Naples, Italy: Bibliopolis, 1999.

— *Pythagoras Revised: Mathematics and Philosophy in Late Antiquity*. NY: Oxford University Press, 1990.

Pappas, Nickolas. "Plato's Aesthetics." In The Stanford Encyclopedia of Philosophy (Summer 2012 Edition), Edward N. Zalta (ed.), Viewed 12 September, 2012. http://plato.stanford.edu/archives/sum2012/entries/plato-aesthetics/.

Perl, Eric D. Theophany: The Neoplatonic Philosophy of Dionysius the Areopagite. Albany, NY: SUNY Press, 2008.

Pike, Kenneth L. "Emic and Etic Standpoints for the Description of Behavior." *The Insider/Outsider Problem in the Study of Religion: A Reader*, ed. by Russell T. McCutcheon, 29-36. NY: Cassell, 1999.

Plaisance, Christopher. "Of Cosmocrators and Cosmic Gods: The Place of the Archons in *De Mysteriis.*" In *Daimonic Imagination: Uncanny Intelligence*, edited by Angela Voss and William Rowlandson, 64-85. Newcastle upon Tyne, UK: Cambridge Scholars Publishing, 2013.

Printery House. "Christ Pantocrator." Viewed 7 January, 2013. http://www.printeryhouse.org/icons/C07.asp.

Richardson, Cyril C. "Love: Greek and Christian." *The Journal of Religion* 23.3 (1943): 173-185.

Rist, John M. "A Note on Eros and Agape in Pseudo-Dionysius." *Vigiliae Christianae* 20.4 (1966): 235-243.

Salomonsen, Jone. "Methods of Compassion Or Pretension? the Challenges of Conducting Fieldwork in Modern Magical Communities." In *Researching Paganisms*, edited by Jenny Blain, Douglas Ezzy & Graham Harvey, 43-58. Walnut Creek, CA: AltaMira Press, 2004.

Shaw, Gregory. "The Geometry of Grace: A Pythagorean Approach to Theurgy." In *The Divine Iamblichus: Philosopher and Man of Gods*, edited by H.J. Blumenthal and E.G. Clark, 117-137. London: Bristol classical Press, 1993.

—. "Neoplatonic Theurgy and Dionysius the Areopagite." *Journal of Early Christian Studies* 7.4 (1999): 573-599.

—. "Theurgy as Demiurgy: Iamblichus' Solution to the Problem of Embodiment." *Dionysius* XII (1988): 37-59.

—. *Theurgy and the Soul: The Neoplatonism of Iamblichus.* University Park, PA: Pennsylvania State University Press, 1995.

Sheppard, Anne. "Iamblichus on Inspiration: *De Mysteriis* 3.4-8." In *The Divine Iamblichus: Philosopher and Man of Gods*, edited by H.J. Blumenthal and E.G. Clark, 138-143. London: Bristol Classical Press, 1993.

Sider, David. "Plato's Early Aesthetics: The Hippias Major." *The Journal of Aesthetics and Art Criticism* 35, 4 (1977): 465-470.

Siorvanes, Lucas. "Neo-Platonic personification," in *Personification in the Greek World: From Antiquity to Byzantium*, edited by Emma Stafford and Judith Herrin, 77-98. Aldershot, Hampshire, UK: Ashgate Publishing Limited, 2005

Smith, Steven R. *Wylundt's Book of Incense.* York Beach, ME: Samuel Weiser, Inc., 1989.

Sorabji, Richard, *The Philosophy of the Commentators, 200 – 600AD, A Sourcebook, Volume 1: Psychology (with Ethics and Religion).* Ithica, NY: Cornell University Press, 2005.

Stern-Gillet, Suzanne. "Neoplatonist Aesthetics." In *A Companion to Art Theory*, ed. Paul Smith and Carolyn Wilde, 40-48. Oxford: Blackwell Publishers, Ltd, 2002.

Terezis, Christos and Polychronopoulou, Kalomoira. "The Sense of Beauty (κάλλος) in Proclus the Neoplatonist." In *Neoplatonism and Western Aesthetics*, edited by Aphrodite Alexandrakis and Nicholas J. Moutafakis, 53-608. Albany, NY: SUNY Press, 2002.

Thompson, Leonard L., "ISmyrna 753: Gods and the One God," in *Reading Religions in the Ancient World: Essays Presented to Robert McQueen Grant on His 90th Birthday.* Leiden, Netherlands: Brill, 2007.

Turner, John D. "The Gnostic Threefold Path to Enlightenment: The Ascent of Mind and the Descent of Wisdom." *Novum Testamentum* XXII, 4 (1980): 324-351.

Uždavinys, Algis. *Orpheus and the Roots of Platonism.* London, UK: The Matheson Trust, 2011.

—. *Philosophy & Theurgy in Late Antiquity.* San Rafael, CA: Sophia Perennis, 2010.

—. *Philosophy as a Rite of Rebirth.* Wiltshire, UK: The Prometheus Trust, 2008.

Ward, Keith. *God: A Guide for the Perplexed.* Oxford: Oneworld Publications, 2002.

Wear, Sarah Klitenic and Dillon, John. *Dionysius the Areopagite and the Neoplatonist Tradition: Despoiling the Hellenes.* Hampshire, England: Ashgate, 2007.

Index

A

Abulafia, Abraham........................119
Adonai.................................119, 232
Against the Christians...............19, 119
Against the Galileans........................19
Against the Gnostics....................11, 19
agalma...189, 191, 206, 207, 209, 210, 212, 213, 214, 220, 227, 259
agalma empsychon....................206, 212
agalmata empsychon.........................226
agape...................................78, 81, 259
Agathon..78
Agrippa...65
Agrippa, Henry Cornelius...187, 194, 197, 229
Ain...15, 113
Aion......93, 94, 96, 99, 100, 103, 104, 109, 112, 113, 114, 119, 134, 148, 165, 182, 230, 234, 238, 239, 240, 245, 246, 250, 259, 261
Alcibiades..............................37, 80, 93
Al-Kindi..186
ametheketos................................94, 260
Ammonius Saccas..............................20
Amoun..........114, 115, 116, 259, 260
Anatolius..............................8, 21, 50
andreias..45
angels16, 25, 39, 54, 56, 58, 109, 123, 124, 126, 127, 131, 133, 136, 137, 138, 139, 140, 165, 168, 173, 208, 209, 222
Anonymous Prolegomena to Platonic Philosophy.......................................36
Anubis..202
Aphrodite....80, 81, 83, 84, 129, 152, 161, 162, 163, 164, 209, 210, 212, 213, 214, 215, 216, 217, 218, 219, 220, 221
Apollo....83, 117, 128, 129, 133, 152, 210
archangels 25, 54, 127, 131, 136, 137, 138, 139, 140, 154
Ares..............129, 152, 164, 217, 268
Aries..............................188, 196, 198
Aristotle .8, 11, 14, 22, 23, 31, 36, 42, 49, 50, 51, 55, 63, 93, 105, 122
Arte...49
Asklepios.....117, 118, 119, 134, 152, 260
Asphalius.....................................8, 43
Athena......43, 84, 115, 128, 129, 134, 161, 162, 163, 167, 177, 234
Attis..156
Atum-Re.......................112, 114, 115
Augustus, Emperor................19, 110
Aurelius, Marcus............60, 174, 175
autarchis..................................111, 260
Autogenes Christos..............113, 116
autopater..................................111, 260

B

barbara onomata.....158, 160, 161, 177, 212, 221, 260
Barbelo..................................109, 113
Benedict XVI, Pope.........................24
Bible...............................211, 212, 221
Book of Revelation...........................198

C

Castricius, Firmus.........................155

catharsis 147, 180
Celestial Hierarchy 8, 116, 126, 130, 255
Ceres 196
Chaldean Oracles .. 8, 11, 22, 24, 35, 37, 79, 94, 96, 145, 160, 175, 176, 182, 209, 214, 231, 233
Christ.. 24, 27, 76, 109, 119, 162, 163, 183, 208, 209, 210, 211, 212, 213, 222, 225, 226, 263, 264
Christianity 11, 14, 15, 18, 19, 21, 24, 25, 80, 109, 110, 123, 143, 159, 168, 183, 208, 212, 221, 263
Coffin Texts 112, 114
Constantine, Emperor 64
Corpus Hermetica 26, 35, 185
Corpus Pythagoras 36
Corybantes 128
Cratylus 9, 37, 62, 80, 177
cultus 17, 154, 155, 157, 161, 168

D

daimon ... 3, 17, 35, 56, 58, 59, 62, 78, 82, 102, 117, 119, 121, 122, 123, 127, 128, 133, 136, 137, 139, 140, 141, 142, 143, 149, 150, 151, 153, 173, 178, 179, 193, 202, 203, 204, 205, 207, 209, 212, 228, 229, 230, 231, 232, 233, 234, 235, 237, 239, 243, 244, 245, 246, 249, 250, 251, 261, 262
Damascius ... 24, 51, 52, 95, 124, 130, 175
De Amore 8, 82, 85
De Anima 8, 22, 37
De Caelo 37
De Imaginibus 75, 187, 189
De Interpretatione 37
De Mysteriis. 8, 12, 14, 26, 53, 81, 110, 111, 112, 114, 116, 117, 118, 121, 124, 128, 130, 136, 137, 140, 144, 153, 156, 175, 186, 191, 205
De Radiis Stellicis 186
De vita libri tres 8, 26, 184, 186, 195
Demeter 129, 196, 198
Demiurge 7, 16, 23, 27, 34, 54, 55, 56, 63, 64, 71, 73, 79, 96, 103, 105, 106, 107, 108, 109, 110, 111, 112, 113, 114, 115, 116, 117, 118, 119, 120, 121, 124, 128, 129, 133, 134, 135, 136, 137, 139, 140, 146, 148, 149, 150, 153, 157, 176, 177, 179, 182, 183, 189, 191, 192, 193, 196, 198, 202, 207, 208, 211, 230, 231, 232, 233, 234, 235, 239, 243, 245, 259, 260, 261, 262, 263, 264, 265
dikaiosinis 49, 260
dimiourgikos nous 114
Dionysos 83, 115, 117, 118, 119, 134, 177, 182
Diotima 72, 78
Divine Names 8, 221
Djehuti 3, 112
Dodds, Professor E.R. 12, 31, 83, 94
dunamis 91, 163, 260
dyad 92, 95, 103
Dyscolius 8, 64, 65

E

Ecclesiastical Hierarchy 8, 159, 221
Eheieh 113
eidolon 207, 208, 260
eidôlopoiêtikê technê 205
eidolopoios 118, 260
eikon 206, 207, 208, 209, 216, 225, 226, 228, 234, 260
Eimarmei 106, 149, 260
Elements of Theology 9, 97
Emerald Tablet of Hermes 177, 189
energeia 91, 260
Enneads ... 9, 11, 19, 20, 41, 51, 52, 67, 188
enyla eida 76, 260
epekeina tou nou 111, 261
epistrophê 180, 261
ergon 175
eros 76, 78, 79, 81, 84, 261

Eros...78, 79, 80, 81, 84, 98, 217, 219
Eucharist 159
Eunapius.............................. 21, 22, 31
Eustathius... 64
Exhortation to Philosophy....... 33, 36, 42
Exodus 113, 211

F

Ficino, Marsilio.. 8, 12, 13, 14, 23, 24, 25, 26, 38, 78, 82, 83, 84, 85, 99, 105, 124, 133, 152, 179, 184, 185, 186, 187, 188, 189, 191, 195, 196, 197, 198, 209, 210, 214
Fourth Book of Occult Philosophy 181

G

Gallienus, Emperor 65
Ghayat al-Hakim........... 75, *See Picatrix*
Golden Verses............................ 33, 174
Gorgias 9, 37
Greater Hippias........... 9, 69, 71, 72, 73

H

Hades ... 117, 118, 182, 202, 216, 233, 234, 235, 236, 238, 242, 243, 248, 249, 251
hamartia 59, 261
harmonia.............................71, 214, 261
Heikton......... 112, 113, 114, 115, 116
Heka 112, 114, 116
Hekate........... 128, 161, 182, 209, 232
Helios.42, 43, 97, 108, 112, 114, 115, 116, 117, 118, 119, 128, 129, 134, 146, 148, 163, 167, 168, 232, 233, 234, 236, 237, 238, 239, 240, 242, 243, 245, 246, 247, 248, 249, 250, 265
henad 112, 113
henosis...20, 21, 98, 131, 135, 161, 261
Hephaistos 117, 129, 217
Hera.. 129
Heraclitus 118, 149
Heraiscus 53
Hermes...3, 8, 12, 112, 117, 129, 152, 177, 189, 191, 195, 202, 209, 232, 234, 235, 242, 243, 244, 248, 249, 250, 251
heroes ... 123, 125, 127, 136, 137, 142, 143
Hestia 129, 196, 197, 198
hieratike 175, 261
hieratike techne 175
Hierocles 64, 65
Hippias Major ... 69, *See Greater Hippias*
ho haplos hen 94, 261
hylē.............55, 56, 106, 148, 229, 261
Hymn to Aphrodite........................... 162
Hymn to King Helios .. 43, 85, 110, 114, 119, 133
Hymn to the Creator......................... 162
Hymn to the Mother of the Gods 156

I

Iamblichus ... 8, 11, 12, 14, 15, 16, 21, 22, 23, 24, 25, 26, 31, 32, 33, 34, 36, 37, 38, 41, 42, 43, 46, 47, 49, 50, 51, 52, 53, 54, 55, 56, 58, 59, 60, 64, 65, 67, 72, 74, 75, 79, 80, 81, 83, 84, 91, 92, 93, 95, 96, 98, 99, 101, 103, 104, 105, 106, 107, 110, 111, 112,됬113, 114, 115, 116, 117, 118, 119, 121, 123, 124, 125, 126, 127, 128, 129, 130, 133, 134, 136, 137, 139, 140, 143, 144, 145, 146, 149, 151, 152, 153, 154, 156, 157, 158, 160, 161, 169, 174, 175, 176, 177, 179, 180, 183, 185, 186, 190, 191, 192, 193, 195, 198, 204, 205, 207, 214, 226, 227, 229, 231, 232, 233, 260, 261
Ibn Sina 50
icon 76, 208, 209, 210, 211, 212, 221, 224, 225
idean ton onton 111, 261
Ikton 112

incense...86, 159, 160, 165, 181, 191, 203, 213, 214, 215, 222, 235, 236, 237, 238, 245, 249, 251
Isidore........52
Isis........232
Islam.....113, 155, 159, 160, 168, 194, 208, 212

J

Jesus......116, 119, 208, 211, 222, 225
Judaism.155, 159, 168, 194, 208, 212
Julian, Emperor.....14, 43, 84, 85, 99, 110, 111, 112, 114, 115, 116, 117, 118, 119, 129, 133, 134, 146, 156, 159, 160, 175, 206
Julian, the Chaldean........175
Jupiter...152, 185, 186, 191, 196, 202

K

Kabbalah.....113, 116, 159, 182, 192, 198, 231
Kalliope........12
kalon........69, 76, 261
Kant, Immanuel........40, 50
kata methexin........94, 261
kathartis psychon........118, 261
Kematef........115
Keter........113
Khepri........232
Kmeph..112, 114, 115, 116, 261, 262
Kore........128, 242, 243, 248, 249
kosmocratores........124
kosmos........71, 262
Kronos...62, 105, 120, 124, 129, 152, 177

L

Laws...37, 38, 45, 62, 63, 65, 155, 169
lectio divina...34, 35, 43, 47, 49, 50, 60
Letter to Anebo........20, 21, 22, 156
Letter to Macedonius on Fate........149
logoi........55, 71, 75, 76, 106, 118, 189, 213, 215, 238, 262
Luna........152, 189, 196

M

Macrobius........66, 163
Maia........202, 243, 249
Malkhut........119
Marinus........23
Marsanes........113
Mercury152, 185, 189, 191, 195, 196, 202, 203, 244
metachomenos........94, 262
Metaphysics........37
Mikhael........208
Mill, John Stuart........40
monad42, 68, 91, 92, 96, 98, 99, 103, 111, 112, 113, 180, 261, 262, 263
monas ek tou enos........111, 262
monê........180
monoeide........133, 134, 262
mustagogia........175, 262

N

New Testament........59, 81, 221
Nicomachean Ethics........42, 49, 63
Nicomachus........49, 75
noeric realm.....84, 93, 100, 101, 103, 105, 111, 114, 115, 151, 176, 177, 207
noetarchis prosagoreoetai........111, 262
noetic realm...70, 93, 96, 97, 98, 100, 101, 103, 105, 108, 109, 111, 112, 113, 114, 119, 122, 128, 131, 145, 182, 196, 261
Nous.......23, 31, 42, 43, 63, 102, 103, 104, 114, 119, 124, 142, 146, 147, 151, 174, 176, 180, 189, 194, 195, 215, 255, 262
Numenius........54, 75

O

O'Meara, Dominic J. .. 18, 31, 33, 36, 37, 41, 42, 45, 51, 52, 53, 62, 63, 64, 67, 72
oikodespotis........229, 262
Olympiodorus........23, 181, 207
Olympius........9, 20, 46, 47

on 91
On Arithmetic in Ethical Matters........42
On General Mathematical Science......190
On Nichomachus' Introduction to Arithmetic.......................................36
On Obtaining Life from the Heavens.184, 186, 187
On Providence......................................64
On Statues...207
On the Existence of Evil.........56, 58, 60
On the General Theory of Mathematics 36
On the Gods..........................25, 37, 110
On the Good, or the One......................20
On the Life of Plotinus and the Arrangement of His Work.............19
On the Virtues.............................. 51, 55
On True Happiness.............................67
Origen Adamantius 34
Orpheus.................................214, 227
Orphic Hymns....................26, 160, 181
Osiris......................114, 117, 118, 232
Ouranos...62
ousia...................................91, 100, 263
ousiopator................................111, 263

P

Papyri Graecae Magicae.8, 115, 232, *See* PGM
Parmenides...........9, 37, 91, 92, 95, 136
Penia..78
Peri Theon...37, 110, 111, 114, *See* On the Gods
Persephone 118, 128
PGM.8, 115, 161, 163, 179, 198, 200, 204, 231, 232, 233, 240, 241, 243, 244
Phaedo.37, 39, 54, 106, 108, 110, 146, 147, 148, 153
Phaedrus 9, 37, 54, 60, 82, 83, 85, 146, 147, 148, 150, 151, 154, 182, 233
Philebus............................9, 37, 70, 82
philosophia................32, 187, 197, 263
Philostratus 75
Phorcys 105
phroníseos..42
Picatrix......................75, 186, 189, 194
Plato 9, 11, 13, 14, 15, 18, 19, 22, 26, 27, 31, 32, 41, 44, 46, 47, 50, 60, 62, 64, 65, 66, 68, 69, 70, 72, 73, 74, 75, 78, 79, 80, 82, 83, 84, 91, 92, 95, 96, 97, 100, 110, 115, 116, 118, 122, 145, 146, 153, 155, 162, 169, 178, 185, 189, 206, 233
Platonic Theology.......................... 14, 26
Plethon, Gemistus........ 163, 168, 169
Plotinus..9, 11, 13, 14, 15, 18, 19, 20, 21, 22, 23, 24, 26, 32, 36, 41, 51, 52, 54, 55, 56, 59, 62, 65, 67, 75, 92, 93, 99, 109, 111, 115, 145, 146, 155, 174, 185, 188, 191, 192
Pluto 118, 128, 233
pneuma....163, 192, 206, 216, 262, 263
Poros 78
Porphyry 9, 14, 19, 20, 21, 22, 23, 26, 51, 65, 93, 109, 118, 121, 133, 136, 153, 155, 156, 157, 158, 174, 175, 192, 205, 229, 231
Poseidon 128, 129
Prior Analytics.....................................37
pro tos duados.............................94, 263
Proclus ...9, 12, 14, 15, 19, 22, 23, 24, 25, 26, 38, 53, 56, 57, 58, 59, 60, 71, 80, 81, 82, 83, 84, 93, 94, 96, 97, 99, 111, 112, 118, 119, 122, 124, 128, 129, 130, 143, 145, 152, 157, 158, 161, 162, 163, 169, 180, 181, 183, 185, 189, 191, 192, 208, 209, 221, 234,됫261
prohödos..................................180, 263
Pronoia..........113, 149, 249, 250, 263
Psellus, Michael 37, 51
pseudo-Agrippa 181
Pseudo-Dionysius .14, 16, 23, 24, 38, 58, 78, 81, 116, 159, 221, 255
pseudo-Pythagoras....................... 174
Psyche 22, 104, 145, 151, 153, 215
Ptah 114, 117, 200
pure soul...............122, 143, 152, 193

purification 38, 52, 83, 124, 125, 126, 140, 148, 149, 151, 156, 168, 180, 181, 184, 193, 198, 205, 232, 233, 234, 261
Pythagoras. 22, 32, 33, 36, 37, 42, 45, 72, 155

Q

Qur'an 155

R

Re 114, 115, 232
Republic ... 9, 37, 38, 41, 42, 43, 44, 50, 62, 63, 64, 65, 72, 73, 74, 85, 96, 98, 101, 153, 155, 206, 233
Rhea 105, 124, 161

S

Sacred Magic of Abramelin 141, 204, 231
Saint Augustine 41, 50
Saint Paul 24
Sallustius 9, 25, 80, 111, 117, 128, 129, 181
Selene 129, 152
semeia 176, 264
Seneca the Younger 60
Sethian Gnosticism 11, 20
Severus of Antioch 24
Shahab al-Din Suhrawardi 113
Shahrivar 113
Shaw, Gregory 25, 63, 79, 80, 103, 124, 130, 145, 150, 157, 158, 180, 190, 191, 194, 230
Shekhinah 119, 198
Socrates 11, 12, 32, 35, 38, 39, 47, 62, 63, 69, 70, 71, 72, 78, 82, 97, 146, 147, 148, 155
Sol 191, 196, 198
Sopater 9, 41, 64
sophia 32, 42, 264
Sophia 32, 108, 110, 198
Sophist 9, 32, 34, 37, 75, 112, 118
sophrosýnis 47, 264
Statesman 37
statue 76, 164, 189, 191, 194, 205, 206, 207, 208, 209, 210, 213, 214, 215, 216, 217, 218, 219, 221, 226, 227, 259, 264
Sufism 113, 159
symbola ... 176, 177, 178, 182, 186, 189, 191, 206, 208, 236, 264
Symposium 9, 37, 64, 69, 70, 72, 78, 79, 80, 82
Synesius 159, 161, 162, 163, 221
synthemata 176, 177, 178, 182, 185, 186, 189, 191, 206, 227, 264

T

talisman 179, 187, 189, 191, 192, 194, 195, 197, 198, 202, 203, 204, 206, 259
technê 185, 190, 191, 261, 264
telestikē 221
telestikê technê 187, 205
temenos ... 234, 236, 238, 242, 243, 244, 245, 246, 250, 251, 264
Thabit Ibn Qurra 75, 186, 187, 214
The Apocryphon of John 8, 108, 109, 110, 113, 141, 269
The Divine Names 58, 81, 255
The Theology of Numbers 190
Theaetetus 9, 37, 63, 173
Theologia Platonica 26, 37
theoria . 20, 21, 44, 145, 174, 175, 180, 255, 264
theos 111, 175, 264
theos theon 111, 264
theosis 98, 131, 135, 178, 264
theosophia 175, 264
theourgia .. 154, 161, 175, 182, 228, 264
Thoth .... 112, *See* Djehuti
Three Books of Occult Philosophy 187, 198, 229
Tiferet 182
Timaeus 9, 22, 27, 37, 55, 64, 73, 79, 93, 94, 103, 106, 108, 109, 110, 115, 116, 122, 137, 146, 147, 148,

149, 151, 188, 189, 192, 194, 207, 233
to prepon 71
Torah 155, 194, 208
tou agathon 96, 264
triad ..17, 25, 93, 95, 96, 99, 100, 113, 122, 125, 126, 136, 137, 138, 139, 142, 182, 214

V

Venus 80, 83, 152, 187, 189, 196, 202, 209, 212, 214, 215
Vesta 196
Virgin Mary 76, 166, 208, 210
Virgo 189
Vita Pythagoras 32

W

World Soul 57, 71, 103, 110, 115, 116, 127, 145, 146, 188, 189, 195, 196, 198, 199, 207, 213, 215, 230, 245

Y

Yaldabaoth . 108, 113, *See* Yaltabaoth
Yaltabaoth 108, 109, 110

Z

Zeus. 43, 62, 112, 114, 115, 116, 117, 124, 128, 129, 134, 148, 152, 161, 164, 167, 169, 185, 186, 202, 210, 216, 217, 219, 237, 240, 243, 245, 247, 249, 250

Published by Avalonia
www.avaloniabooks.co.uk

Milton Keynes UK
Ingram Content Group UK Ltd.
UKHW051350141223
434366UK00023BA/1009